BOOKS BY T. H. BREEN

The Character of the Good Ruler: A Study of Puritan
Political Ideas in New England, 1630–1730

Shaping Southern Society: The Colonial Experience
(Editor)

"Myne Owne Ground": Race and Freedom on Virginia's
Eastern Shore
(with Stephen Innes)

Puritans and Adventurers: Change and Persistence
in Early America

America: Past and Present
(with Robert A. Divine, George M. Fredrickson,
and R. Hal Williams)

Tobacco Culture: The Mentality of the Great Tidewater
Planters on the Eve of Revolution

Imagining the Past

Imagining the Past

EAST HAMPTON HISTORIES

BY T.H. BREEN

Photographs by Tony Kelly

ADDISON-WESLEY PUBLISHING COMPANY, INC.

Reading, Massachusetts   Menlo Park, California   New York
Don Mills, Ontario   Wokingham, England   Amsterdam   Bonn
Sydney   Singapore   Tokyo   Madrid   San Juan

Library of Congress Cataloging-in-Publication Data

Breen, T. H.
   Imagining the past : East Hampton histories / T.H. Breen.
     p.   cm.
   Bibliography: p.
   Includes index.
   ISBN 0-201-06749-8
   ISBN 0-201-52338-8 (pbk.)
   1. East Hampton (N.Y.)—Historiography. I. Title.
F129.E13B74 1989
974.7′25—dc19   88-31578
                                  CIP

Cover design by Marianne Perlak
Cover photograph by Milt Price
Text design by Janis Capone
Set in 11-point Bembo by NK Graphics, Keene, NH

ABCDEFGHIJ-MW-943210
First printing, April 1989
First paperback printing, March 1990

This book is dedicated to the members of a wonderful family, all of whom, one way or another, seem to love the study of history: Susan, Sarah, Bant, Mary and George

Contents

Preface   xi

INTRODUCTION
Meanings in Time   1

CHAPTER ONE
Guardians of Tradition   17

CHAPTER TWO
Inventing a Community   75

CHAPTER THREE
The Whale Design   141

CHAPTER FOUR
Bank Where the Whale Was Tried   207

EPILOGUE
The Worlds of Samuel Mulford   277

Sources   297

Index   301

Preface

Marco resumed saying, enumerating names and customs and wares of a great number of lands. His repertory could be called inexhaustible, but now he was the one who had to give in. Dawn had broken when he said, "Sire, now I have told you about all the cities I know."

"There is still one of which you never speak."

Marco Polo bowed his head.

"Venice," the Khan said.

Marco smiled. "What else do you believe I have been talking to you about?"

Italo Calvino, *Invisible Cities*

Imagining the Past began as a question. I wondered what history would become if it self-consciously explored the process of interpretation. Historians like myself tell stories about the past, but we seldom pause to consider just how we came to know a particular "fact." In these matters, people working in other disciplines seem far in advance of the historians. Although the literature of textual criticism and critical theory is often unnecessarily obscure, it has forced me in recent years to confront issues that I once ignored or took for granted. Quite simply, I wanted to discover how bundles of meanings—what I have called in a phrase borrowed from the anthropologists "stories about ourselves"—are generated and sustained, contested and modified, embedded in the texts that I had been trained to read as objective reports.

This book is not about critical theory. We have had enough pronouncements about how other people might go about transforming theory into practice. Rather, this is a historical ethnography dealing with a "real" community. As I go about the business of interpreting its past—or of finding out how other people have interpreted that past before I came along—I maintain a running conversation with the reader. I try to explain how so-called objective accounts are actually no more than partial truths, incomplete insights that we continually interpret and reinterpret and in the process inevitably alter by adding something of ourselves to the narrative.

There is nothing objectionable about this fundamentally human effort to organize what we discover about the past into comprehensible patterns, to translate the experiences of others into a language that the members of our own culture might readily understand. That is what Marco Polo seemed to be telling the Khan. What must be avoided is the specious claim that the teller of the story is not himself or herself a part of that story, an inventor of meanings.

This is not, therefore, another history of East Hampton; it is a history of interpretation in East Hampton, or, even more precisely, an exploration of how the members of a community come to imagine themselves in the flow of time. I set out to learn something about—in the marvelous phrase of a modern historian of the Middle East—the "subjective presence of the past in the minds of contemporary" Americans. We shall be talking about East Hampton, but, as we do so, I trust that the reader will be thinking about other imagined communities.

Seen from this perspective, the project required that the "I" telling the story come forward and announce his active participation in the making of a history. Some people may prefer what appears to be a more objective analytic language, a traditional voice of the third person. For such readers my speculations, doubts, reactions, disapprovals—at times, just plain foolishness—may seem "unprofessional." Such is the nature of experiments. In these pages I explore the possibilities of an unusual literary form for historians and confront difficult narrative problems that seem to be peculiar to the form itself. I have tried to move gracefully back and forth from past to present, changing temporal registers, weaving an interpretation as I go along. But this is also a book that addresses the future. Our dreams of things to come are built upon the interpretation of past experience. We are what we were even when we most passionately reject our own history. In that sense, *Imagining the Past* might be seen as a parable.

Many people I want to thank appear in the pages of the text. They are, in fact, the co-authors. They shared their perceptions of East Hampton's past—and in the process, of its future—with a stranger. They helped me discover something not only about their community, but also about myself. I have attempted to present their views exactly as I heard them expressed in their homes and offices, and if I have inadvertently misrepresented their opinions, I apologize.

Without the generous and continuing support of David Swickard, Jay Graybeal, and Ralph Carpentier, I would never have completed this experiment. Along the way, I received valuable assistance from Leonard Barkan, Ricardo Elia, Todd Lee Savitt, Dorothy King, James Walsh, John Shelton Reed, Timothy Hall, James Horn, Nigel Thompson, James Truex, Edwin and Averill Geus, Frank Dayton, Kent Lightfoot, Ted Carpenter, and Adelaide de Menil. I am especially grateful to Janice Harper for preparing the map of Northwest Harbor. Martha Moutray is the kind of imaginitive editor that authors hope to find, but in fact, seldom encounter. She helped me discover the dimensions of my own story.

Tony Kelly's contribution to this enterprise is evident in the many photographs illustrating the text. Working with him involved a creative partnership, for he possessed an uncanny ability to capture on film something more than specific images. He photographed an interpretation. We shared a historic vision. Several colleagues at Northwestern University provided timely suggestions: James Oakes, Josef Barton, and Harold Perkin. Northwestern University and Christ Church, Oxford University, arranged a splendid research position for me during the academic year 1987–1988. Three Christ Church colleagues were particularly helpful during my stay at Oxford: William Thomas, A. K. Bowman, and M. Vaughan-Lee. During this period I held the Fowler Hamilton Senior Research Fellowship. I received research support from the Illinois chapter of the Society of Colonial Wars. Funds for the "Resident Humanist" program came from the New York Institute for the Humanities.

Readers should be aware that all dates are given in new style, with the new year beginning on January 1. The spelling in quotations has generally been modernized. Moreover, abbreviations have been expanded and punctuation added where necessary.

T. H. B.
Christ Church, Oxford
July 24, 1988

INTRODUCTION

Meanings in Time

Tell ye your children of it, and let your children tell their
children, and their children another generation.

Joel I:3

$\mathcal{J}$t is true that I am a historian. Or an ethnographer. Or perhaps a little of each. Distinctions of this sort do not much matter. More to the point, I had never given the slightest thought to writing about the history of East Hampton. That event occurred quite by chance. In fact, if it had not been for the hard winters of northern Illinois, I would probably not have found myself in East Hampton at all. But because the weather in Chicago in March is often painfully cold, I refused one morning to leave the comfort of my house. That turned out to be a crucial decision, for as I was browsing through the normally unrewarding pages of an academic journal, an unusual advertisement caught my attention; wanted:

> A social historian with a background in New England colonial history and a familiarity with the content and methodology of New England town studies . . . to work with the Mulford Farm Planning Task Force of the East Hampton Historical Society.

Although I knew almost nothing about the community, the announcement sparked my curiosity. The position seemed to have been designed with me in mind; I had written about the development of early American societies, and fancied that I knew something about agriculture. Without further reflection, I dispatched a letter of application. Only after many weeks had passed—indeed, only after I had been selected for the job—did I fully come to appreciate that I had been hired to interpret the early history of a community famous for many things, but most certainly not for its colonial agriculture.

East Hampton is not an easy place to reach. The highway leading from New York City to the eastern end of Long Island cuts across what I regard as some of the duller stretches of contemporary America. The road is lined with fast-food restaurants, gas stations, shopping malls. A depressing sameness

3

rules until at some point well out on the Island the landscape abruptly changes. Nondescript buildings give way to scruffy evergreens, to patches of sandy soil. There is more open space, cleaner air.

Eventually the highway crosses the Shinnecock Canal, sometimes grandly described as the gateway to the Hamptons. It would be an easy landmark to miss. I follow Route 27 as it snakes its way eastward toward Montauk Point. Although this is the central artery of the South Fork, it was obviously not designed to handle the continuous stream of cars and trucks that use it today. Even on a weekday morning it's slow going as vehicles back up at the stoplights. Approaching the Hamptons, signs of affluence appear more regularly: a few antique shops, a distributor of luxury cars, specialty food stores, a celebration of American boutique. The road skirts Southampton, goes by a large windmill at Bridgehampton, and passes many vegetable stands and great potato fields smelling this day faintly of insecticide.

At the junction of Town Line Road, the highway enters East Hampton. As I drive into the town, my reaction is a mixture of disappointment and puzzlement. I had fully expected to encounter weather-beaten old houses encircling a picturesque green. Instead, Route 27 yields to more potato fields and vegetable stands.

What I had received, although I did not then appreciate it, was my first lesson in local history. There are actually two East Hamptons. The Town of East Hampton was laid out in colonial times and encompasses much of Long Island's South Fork. Over time what must have originally been no more than scattered clusters of farms became distinct villages, each with its own government and each evolving its own personality. Amagansett and Wainscott are today affluent communities, offering magnificent ocean beaches. The Springs is still considered an artist colony, though not many young artists can afford to live there today. Montauk draws sport fishermen and weekend visitors. At the center of all this is the Village of East Hampton. Confusion is compounded because the larger unit, the Town of East

Hampton, exercises considerable authority over people living within the separate villages. Both levels of government—town and village—maintain police departments, planning commissions, and recreation boards. There are even competing historical societies.

The highway eventually makes its way to the Village and, turning abruptly north at a stoplight, it briefly becomes Main Street. It is here that a colonial past has been lovingly preserved. For a mile or so East Hampton has been transformed into a living museum, a sort of drive-thru history. The visitor's eye sweeps up across a small pond to the Old South End Cemetery, where the founders of East Hampton lie buried. The lichen-covered markers are arranged in neat rows. Only the stone for Thomas James, the town's first minister, stands apart. It is reported that when he died in 1696, James insisted on having his grave face those of the members of his congregation. On the Day of Judgment, he reasoned, they would arise and be greeted immediately by the man who had cared for their souls.

The Reverend Mr. James and his neighbors now rest on a gentle, well-manicured slope. On the crest of the small hill, just above the old burying ground, two seemingly identical colonial saltboxes have survived, the Mulford Farm and the "Home, Sweet Home" house, so called because one of its owners, John Howard Payne, wrote a popular song by that name in 1823. A huge windmill towers above the "Home, Sweet Home" house. It too has taken on a warm, weather-beaten quality. A colorful flower garden located in front of the Mulford Farm completes a postcard scene that is all that most passing drivers ever know about life in seventeenth-century East Hampton.

The historic district continues up Main Street for another half mile. Across the road from Mulford Farm stands a curious half-timber and stucco building that turns out to be the local library. It is a replica—or so I have been told—of a structure located in Maidstone, Kent, the English town from which so many of East Hampton's earliest settlers emigrated. Just beyond the library Main Street becomes broad and straight. It was once lined with great elms.

On Main Street time seems to have stopped around the time of the Civil War. The offices of the town newspaper, the *East Hampton Star,* could pass for a nineteenth-century dry-goods store. Immediately to the north stands Clinton Academy, an impressive building constructed in 1784 of brick and clapboard. It is now a museum. And a few paces beyond the academy and almost invisible behind the shrubbery is the Town House, a small wooden structure that served during the eighteenth century as the local school and meeting place for the town trustees.

Most of Main Street, however, remains residential. The houses date from various periods over four centuries. Some proudly display historic markers. Others, obviously of more modern construction, blend with reasonable success with the earlier architectural styles. The Reverend Lyman Beecher, the famous nineteenth-century revivalist and father of several remarkable children who were even more gifted than he, lived briefly in one of the older homes. It now stands empty, the object of a fierce controversy between a local realtor who wants to transform the structure into an office and a village committee that insists he should leave Beecher's house exactly as it is.

I

The Reverend Mr. Beecher was also a historian of East Hampton. Others before and after him have recounted the story of this town more fully, more dramatically, and with greater sensitivity than did Beecher. But of the various people who have interpreted East Hampton's long development—that is, until quite recently—Beecher stands alone as an outsider, as a person who was, as it were, passing through this community on his way to greater accomplishments and who paused briefly to consider just how it got to be the way he found it during the first decade of the nineteenth century.

Beecher was not a member of one of East Hampton's founding clans. Had the local Presbyterian church not invited him to serve as its pastor in 1799, it seems unlikely that he would ever have even visited the place. But as a recent Yale College graduate, Beecher needed a steady income, and the church offered him an annual salary of $400, a sum just barely adequate to cover his household expenses. As the Beecher family grew, this modest compensation no longer sufficed, and he was forced repeatedly to beg local officials to reward his good work with more money. His requests for a raise were to no avail, however, and in 1810 Beecher transferred his ministry to Litchfield, Connecticut, becoming in time the nation's most renowned evangelical preacher.

Before he departed from East Hampton, Beecher made a genuine attempt to become a part of this community. Indeed, he seems to have been quite popular with many parishioners. Local traditions apparently aroused his curiosity and, a few years after his arrival, he focused his considerable intellectual energies on the history of the town. Beecher did not rely upon the memories of his neighbors, but turned instead to the manuscript records of the town, a remarkable chronicle running unbroken from the first settlement, in 1648, to the present day. Beecher's friend and the local lord of the manor, John Lyon Gardiner, assisted in the research, helping the minister to decipher difficult seventeenth-century documents.

The fruits of these labors appeared in a lengthy sermon that Beecher delivered on New Year's Day, 1806. In published form the work carried an honest, if uninspiring, title: *A Sermon, Containing a General History of the Town of East-Hampton from Its First Settlement to the Present Time.* Beecher began with a quotation from Joel, surely the most obscure book of the Old Testament. Speaking before a congregation composed of people who bore many of the same surnames as the founders of East Hampton, the minister linked even minor events in the community's past to an all-encompassing interpretation of human history. He made the facts speak a language that he and presumably his parishioners could understand. Beecher was too well read, of course, not to recognize that one could derive purely academic gratification "from being able to look back

7

upon the transactions of the past." But this was not the stuff of *true* history. Scholasticism of this sort provided no moral instruction.

What Beecher extracted from the records, in fact, was irrefutable evidence of God's special concern for East Hampton. Here for Beecher was the key that explained not only the history of this particular community, but, even more important, that community's place in the great struggle between Good and Evil. God, the minister declared, intended "this town . . . as a theatre, on which to make memorable displays of his mercy thro' Jesus Christ. He therefore took care to plant it with the choicest vine." The original settlers had been temperate, pious, compassionate individuals—model Christians. The meaning of local history was clear: East Hampton had prospered not because its inhabitants had been especially clever or diligent, but because they had feared God.

It was a classic theological formula upon which New England divines had relied for more than a century. Beecher played this familiar theme masterfully. Had your fathers, the preacher observed, "been men of learning, of enterprise and ambition, but destitute of religion and regardless of morals—had they neglected the support of the gospel, the education and government of their children, and the morals of society, you would have experienced to this day the bitter fruits of their conduct."

This was a forward-looking history. It provided a blueprint for present and future conduct; if the people sitting before Beecher that New Year's Day behaved as their fathers had in the past, they could be virtually certain of pleasing God.

It was no easy task. The world was full of temptations, and Beecher suspected that some people had already fallen away from the old standards. Religious education was not what it once had been. Observance of the Sabbath seemed a little lax. The local minister had spotted what he regarded as an unhealthy interest in "the innovations of modern luxury." And although he did not list his own request for a higher salary among these provoking sins, Beecher did point out that the original settlers had "made liberal provision" for the support of their minister.

"They gave him fifty, and afterwards sixty pounds per annum—exempted his property from taxation—gave him the use of the parsonage land and several other privileges, which rendered his salary probably better than any that has since been given by the town."

Other historians since Beecher have accepted the challenge of interpreting East Hampton's past. Although they have organized their stories around different themes—the rise of democracy, for example—the general problem confronting them has remained basically the same as it was for Beecher in 1806. Like him, they returned to the original town records, selecting bits and pieces of evidence and weaving these materials into coherent interpretations that spoke to contemporary concerns. And paradoxically, though they called themselves historians, their attention seemed to be focused on East Hampton's future. For them the past provided inspiration; it was capable of shaping events to come. It spoke of marvelous potential. Even the least self-conscious of them seemed dimly aware that as the keepers of the past, as the creators as well as interpreters of historical meanings, they possessed a privileged voice in determining East Hampton's future. After all, these were the people who recorded how a community imagined itself in the flow of time.

Like Lyman Beecher, I too am an outsider. Although I am a trained historian, my participation in the continuing search for meanings in the history of East Hampton was entirely adventitious, the result of my appointment by the local historical society as the town's "Resident Humanist." And, like Beecher, I was immediately attracted to the early records of East Hampton. Only after I had had an opportunity to reflect upon what I had found in these remarkable documents did it occur to me to inquire about contemporary perceptions of the town's history. How exactly do men and women who currently live in East Hampton and who profess to care deeply about its future view the past? How do they imagine themselves in time?

Although the specific answers varied, I soon became aware of a commonly accepted mythic history, a broadly shared sense of how East Hampton got to be the way it is, that bears only problematical relation to what I encountered in the records. The people with whom I came into contact seemed to be telling themselves stories about a corporate past that, if not actually false, struck me as peculiarly irrelevant for a society composed for the most part of relatively recent arrivals. These migrants could not credibly claim a direct or intimate connection to the lost world of the "founding fathers." In other words, social change had overtaken an older mythic view of the past, and though it was tempting to correct misperceptions, I was not ultimately interested in preparing another history of East Hampton. Rather, I found myself writing a book about history *in* East Hampton, a topic of much greater complexity—even intrigue—than I had anticipated.

The events that have called an older historiography into question really amount to a full-scale social crisis. East Hampton is today obsessed with change. The community has in recent years experienced a dramatic, often wrenching, transformation. For many people a familiar world seems to be coming apart. A failure to address the problems of development, they argue, threatens to leave East Hampton looking pretty much like any other American town. At stake is a distinctive historical identity.

It soon became apparent, however, that no one is quite sure just what having an historical identity means. For some the love of local traditions amounts to little more than an appreciation for picturesque old houses. For others the commitments run deeper, and many people greet proposals for change with hyperbolic pronouncements about East Hampton's "last stand." It was in the context of this explosive debate between past and future that I returned to the early town records in search of a set of "meanings" that might speak to the current generation.

There are those who in the specific case of East Hampton argue that the past, however fascinating it may have been, bears no special relation to the unprecedented problems of the present. But this is surely mistaken. The very notion of such a break in the continuity of time tends to obscure enduring human processes and structures. Indeed, if the past is truly a "foreign country," then it seems unlikely that it can speak coherently to the present, let alone to the future.

I prefer to stress continuities. From time out of mind, East Hampton has contained men and women intent on maximizing their own welfare and willing to exploit the environment and their neighbors to achieve that end. This does not mean that cooperation never occurred. Of course, it did, in the 1680s as well as the 1980s. But for me what leaps out of the early town records is a story of competitive economic behavior that has repeated itself through the centuries and continues today.

Two examples immediately come to mind. As Peter Matthiessen has shown in *Men's Lives,* a wonderfully evocative depiction of East Hampton's modern commercial fishermen, the abuse of an ecological system has essentially destroyed a living resource, the striped bass. This disaster has been traced to industrial pollution, bureaucratic confusion, and private greed. But in the early eighteenth century, offshore whales disappeared just as mysteriously as have the striped bass. The environment simply could not sustain the economic demands that the townsmen made upon it, and their response to this particular crisis is not without significance for more modern times. And as the Bonackers—as the members of East Hampton's oldest and often poorest families are called—now find themselves driven off the land by rising real estate prices, so too were the Montauk Indians once pushed aside by colonial entrepreneurs who bore the same surnames as the surviving twentieth-century Bonackers. The point is simply that a process, a bundle of values, a set of relations between human beings and the environment have powerfully bound past and future in this town.

But contemporary observers of East Hampton who profess to hear the trumpet of doom cannot be so easily dismissed. A crisis of unprecedented magnitude does confront East Hampton, and whatever the structural links beween past and present, it is possible that they may not long survive what has come to be termed "instantaneous development." If people in this community are genuinely concerned about preserving East Hampton's historical identity, and if there is anything in fact to be learned from the long discourse between human beings and the environment, then now is the time to act. My own sense of emergency animated this project and is responsible for the double entendre in the title of this introduction. On one level, I describe a general search for meanings in time, a reflective, interpretive process. On another, however, I am concerned with meanings *just* in time or in the *nick* of time, meanings revealed before it is too late.

II

Over a period of four years this enterprise took several bizarre and unexpected turns. Quite early in my investigation I concluded that a warehouse constructed in the late seventeenth century by Samuel Mulford might hold a vital key to a radical reinterpretation of East Hampton's past. This structure symbolized for me a complex, but largely forgotten, past. It certainly did not fit comfortably into a familiar local history that had awarded high marks to the town founders for self-sufficiency. As an outsider, I seized upon the warehouse as a vehicle for opening up to reinterpretation the history of early East Hampton. One way or another, the business conducted in this building had touched the lives of everyone in this community, African-Americans and Indians as surely as Europeans. Through Mulford's warehouse had flowed the harvests of land and sea on their way to distant markets. Returning vessels carried a flood of consumer goods. In short, the warehouse became emblematic of a process linking a people and their ecological environment to an expanding commercial economy.

This ancient building, however, proved frustratingly elusive. Just when I was certain that I had discovered its exact location, the warehouse slipped away, mocking the attempt to reclaim whatever artifacts it might still hold. The search became its own reward. My detective work introduced me to an im-

Schooner off Northwest Harbor

pressive group of local people, some who supported my work, a few who doubted my good sense, and still others who regarded my activities as a threat to their own financial interests. Whenever appropriate to the narrative I allow these people to speak for themselves. Whatever their opinions about the location of the warehouse, they inevitably had a great deal to say about the meaning of history in contemporary East Hampton.

Imagining the Past is not a traditional history. I make no attempt in this book to present myself as a neutral observer. To have done so would have been doubly disingenuous. For one thing, I played a small role in the events that I describe. And as an actor in the story I found that I cared, often very deeply, about the rest of the cast. I wanted desperately to find what remained of the warehouse. I worried about the future of the scallops of Northwest Harbor. I was appalled by the face of unrestrained development. I attempt, therefore, to be candid about my reactions to the people whom I encountered in the seventeenth as well as the twentieth century. I observe myself going about the business of interpreting the past out of a concern to let the reader know where I stand.

The pretense of neutrality would have been intellectually dishonest for a second reason. I do not see myself as a social scientist, as someone in search of positivist truths. There are, in fact, no "truths" of this sort out there waiting to be discovered. Even the most elaborate, quantitative explanations of past behavior are really only plausible reconstructions based on the analysis of selected bits of surviving evidence. A hermeneutical history of the kind that I have written explores the creation of truths. It is fundamentally an interpretive exercise, a sorting out of conflicting perceptions and an appreciation of the narratives that humans have always invented to make sense out of their lives.

But for the interpreter, what survives? In the case of East Hampton, not as much as one would like. To be sure, we possess a full run of official town records, a chronicling of tax assessments, local regulations, and land allotments. They provide an account of the affairs of government. But since most of the church records have been lost, we are doomed from the start to an unbalanced view of the past. We know more about the material culture of the early inhabitants than about their spiritual values. Personal letters and diaries for the early colonial period are virtually nonexistent. These people surely loved and hated, knew frustration, shared their private joys, found their children disappointing or a source of pride, experienced a host of emotions associated with the human condition. All of this has been irretrievably lost. Moreover, to complicate matters further, historical "facts" that once seemed solid melt under close scrutiny. As we shall discover, the sources become ambiguous. Certainties are transformed into probabilities, and authoritative political and legal documents turn out to have been the voice of special pleading, the testimony of partisans in which winners always speak louder than losers.

These problems do not, of course, warrant despair. The interpretive process must go forward with whatever materials are at hand. I would argue, however, that historians have a responsibility to converse openly with their readers. Together they should examine the sources, exposing hidden assumptions and special purposes that lurk within the texts. They should also pay close attention to the awkward silences that punctuate so many official documents and that demand an explanation. We are ultimately dealing in East Hampton—as in the history of other American communities—with contending perceptions of reality. And that is why in *Imagining the Past* I can claim no more than to have presented a personal reading of how various people have thought about East Hampton's past. It aspires to be consistent, honest, and plausible.

East Hampton is hardly a typical American community. It is an extraordinarily wealthy town, the summer home of celebrities who settle here in part to be seen by others who also claim celebrity status. Indeed, inhabitants regularly draw attention to the town's highly unusual character. One resident, for example, stated with startling assurance that everyone in East Hampton was either actively writing a book or intended to write one soon. This turned out not to be as great an exaggeration as I first thought. Even quite ordinary men and women seem to possess a heightened awareness of social relations, as if they are consciously entertaining the possibility of incorporating bits of everyday conversation into their next novel.

But this is mere surface static. The residents of East Hampton may sometimes seem bigger than life, but the problems they confront do not. Like the "regular" folk who inhabit so many other imagined communities throughout modern America, they articulate concerns that perplex us all. We sense that there is a past worth preserving, but we are not certain just what it is. We grow increasingly skeptical of progress but know that in some form it will occur whether we like it or not. We are not quite sure what it means to live with our own history. During a period not so long ago when Americans dreamed of a Great Society, we often ignored these questions and allowed ourselves to be beguiled by the vision of planners who transformed our cities and towns and neighborhoods in ways that paid not the slightest attention to the historic context of our lives. These are the issues in East Hampton. And at this moment, it is not clear how they will be resolved.

CHAPTER ONE

Guardians of Tradition

The town of East-Hampton is bounded South-easterly by the Atlantic Ocean, the shore on this side is a sand beach, free from rocks; the sea gains on the shore & it has been said by aged people that in some places the Sea now washes the shore where Indian corn had been planted by their fathers. The sand near the Sea shore is blown into hills on which nothing grows but a grass called the beach grass & a shrub bearing the beach Plumb.

John Lyon Gardiner,
*"Notes and Observations
on the Town of East Hampton"* (1798)

*A*bout one thing Tony Kelly is insistent. "You can't publish a book about East Hampton if it doesn't contain a picture of a fisherman. Before we leave Long Island, we've got to photograph one of these guys."

I could tell by the dogged tone of Kelly's voice that he already knew what sort of photograph he wanted to take. It would most certainly not be a picture of a wealthy weekend enthusiast, nor of a charter boat loaded down with recreational fishermen hoping to make the big catch. Kelly wanted to photograph someone who actually lived off the sea, an honest-to-God workingman. But the problem we confront in East Hampton is finding a commercial fisherman. In recent years the number of fishermen has dwindled and, like members of an endangered species whose habitat has been profoundly disturbed, they have withdrawn into secret places to escape the people who have transformed their world. A local person who once crewed for a Bayman—that is what commercial fishermen are called in this part of Long Island—points us in the right direction, and armed with an unwieldly map of the town, we set out early one morning to find our Bayman.

"Turn here," Kelly shouts, as I drive down a narrow, winding country highway near Three Mile Harbor. I am not at all sure that the little road he has spotted will actually take us to the place that we are looking for, but Kelly is right. This is in fact the location where our friend assured us we would find some of East Hampton's last commercial fishermen. The place is depressing, deserted and a bit overgrown. An old boat has been pulled from the water. A homemade "For Sale" sign carries a telephone number. Both boat and sign look as though they have been here for a long time.

Kelly is not discouraged. He gets out of the car and, following the sound of voices, comes upon two boats on which men actually seem to be working. He approaches a vessel and begins fiddling with his camera. A middle-aged man, his face prematurely wrinkled from long hours in the sun, eyes Kelly closely. No words are exchanged. More technical adjustments. A lens change. The fisherman smokes a cigarette.

"Mind if I take a picture?" Kelly asks him.

"Rather you wouldn't."

The laconic response comes as a surprise. For a moment Kelly does not know what to say. Seconds pass.

"What good will it do?" the Bayman asks angrily. "Just cause a lot of trouble."

It is clear after this outburst that for the Bayman at least the conversation is over. Kelly does not press the issue. Nearby we find another boat in which two younger men are preparing to set out. Their motor chugs loudly as they untie various ropes. Despite all this activity, something about their movements suggests that they are in no great hurry to get wherever it is that they are going.

"Can I take your picture?" Kelly asks.

They seem amused.

"What's it for?" a husky man yells over the sound of the engine.

"It's for a book. My friend is a historian." Kelly motions in my direction with is thumb.

"Sure, take the picture." They return to the business of casting off. Within a minute or two they are twenty feet or more offshore. Suddenly, one of them calls out to Kelly.

"You've come to the right place. This is all going to be history real soon."

I

I am standing in the offices of the East Hampton Historical Society. The scene is utter chaos as volunteers rush from desk to desk. They are engaged in arranging thousands of little cards in little file boxes. The telephone rings constantly. People are paged by shouting. Through walls. Up the stairs. "Where's Jay?" "Has anyone seen Ralph?" The confusion is amplified because the rooms of this eighteenth-century house are so small. The people just do not seem to fit into the space allotted for them. Objects like typewriters and copying machines take on gigantic proportions.

David Swickard, the man who invited me to come to East Hampton, greets me. He is director of development, but in this organization job descriptions do not mean much. Everyone is on call to do almost anything, move furniture, make coffee, drive a truck, write grant proposals, and, perhaps most important, cheer on the volunteer workers, the ones who are sorting out the little cards. Indeed, there is a constant air of crisis about the Historical Society, as if the staff believe that some unanswered telephone call could instantly bring the whole organization to its knees.

David is a pleasant, extremely articulate young man. His tiny office is lined with books, most of which deal with contemporary European politics. A football on the floor next to his desk looks as if it has had a lot of use. David explains that these are relics from his days as a graduate student at Harvard. He holds a degree in political science and has written, among other things, a thesis on political parties in modern Sweden. David did not pursue an academic career, however, and after a brief stint as the director of a small foundation in New York City, he migrated to East Hampton. In part, he came here to escape the pressures of urban life. He also hoped to find the time to write poetry, and perhaps even a novel. For the moment, however, he prepares grant proposals for the Historical Society, which is perpetually in need of revenue.

We meet in David's office to discuss exactly what a "Resident Humanist" is supposed to do in East Hampton. That is really my title: Resident Humanist. It possesses a Gilbert and Sullivan quality. As David introduces me to the members of the staff as the new Resident Humanist, I find myself trying to act the way a Resident Humanist is supposed to act. Of course, it is impossible. No one—least of all me—has the slightest idea what such a position might involve. I might as well be called the grand vizier of local history.

David and I make little progress. There are too many interruptions. In any case, as he suddenly announces, we are late for a meeting with Ralph Carpentier, the director of the Historical Society. I am assured that over lunch my duties will be more fully explained. We find Ralph at the Marine Museum, located several miles from the central historic district. He is an intense, although good-humored, middle-aged man. Like David, he moved to East Hampton to escape a job that he could not stand. Over the years he has worked as a house painter and as a commercial fisherman. It was Ralph, in fact, who told Kelly and me where we might take a photograph of the last of the East Hampton Baymen.

With Ralph at the wheel of his aging car, we return to the village. We drive down Main Street. Pedestrians scatter before us, one of them catching Ralph's attention.

"Did you see that guy?" he asks David. "Wasn't he that folksinger? You remember his name?"

David did not notice. I have just missed my first opportunity to observe a genuine East Hampton celebrity.

Over lunch in a local restaurant called O'Malley's I receive a crash course on the workings of the Historical Society. By the director's own admission, the organization, which was founded in 1921, currently lacks focus. It tries to do too much. It runs a tiny boat shop, for example, devoted entirely to reproducing nonmotorized vessels associated with East Hampton's past. By comparison, the Marine Museum at Amagansett—the place where we picked up Ralph—is much more substantial. It draws more visitors than do all the other units of the Historical Society combined. The explanation for its success is not difficult to discern. Children love to climb over the old ships located in the yard. And once inside the museum, everyone seems to enjoy the exhibits, which trace three centuries of Long Island whaling. In addition to the boat house and the Marine Museum, the society administers the Osborn-Jackson House (c. 1740), the Town House (1731), Clinton Academy (1784), and Mulford Farm (c. 1680), a group of buildings that frankly do not have much in common with each other.

Our conversation turns to the duties of the Resident Humanist. David explains that my stay in East Hampton has been made possible through a grant from the New York Institute for the Humanities. The Institute has recently launched a program called "Humanists in Museums," and David shows me an Institute announcement describing its goal as well as his own successful application for funds. His appeal opened with a general statement of purpose: "The Society has organized its program . . . to illuminate the history of a town settled by emigrants from Massachusetts and Connecticut and founded by a closed corporation, religiously homogeneous and nearly self-sufficient from its farms and fishing—a town which ironically has become a fashionable resort." Why "ironically," I wonder. Lots of farm towns throughout New England have become fashionable resorts—although admittedly not so fashionable as East Hampton.

David and Ralph planned to have the Resident Humanist focus entirely upon Mulford Farm, a group of buildings that David refers to rather distressingly as the "Mulford complex." It sounds like a nervous disorder. As he explained in his proposal to the Institute, "The history of the house is the history of the family living in it, which in turn is the history of the community 'writ small.' " Simply put, David and Ralph want me to poke around in the early records of this town and discover just how the people who had once owned this farm organized their lives. What crops did they grow in that self-sufficient society? What sorts of animals did they raise? How exactly had they structured their household economy?

As we talked I found my enthusiasm for the project growing. Ralph and David were entrusting me—or so I thought at the time—with a major interpretive responsibility. The Historical Society was asking me to relate a past—an historic culture generally associated with East Hampton's formative decades—to a present that seemed the very antithesis of early American agrarian life. I was being hired, in fact, to serve as a kind of historical anthropologist, who would attempt as best he could to translate past values and experiences into meanings that twentieth-century Long Islanders might readily comprehend. Even during this preliminary conversation, I sensed an opportunity to make Mulford Farm come alive, to liberate, as it were, these seventeenth-century buildings from the picturesque but essentially sterile world that they presently occupied.

I did not pause to consider whether Ralph and David shared my perceptions. They obviously subscribed to the view that early East Hampton had been a self-sufficient, homogeneous, religious community—in other words, a classic New England town that just happened to have been established in New York. But about such matters they seemed remarkably flexible. After all, as David reminded me more than once, I was a "professional" historian. It was a description that had always made me a little uneasy. It seemed to suggest that I possessed special insights into the past and that my training had somehow prepared me to get the story of this town's early development "right," to establish the "truth." To have protested at that particular moment that I did not believe that any "truth" was out there waiting for me to discover would probably have struck both men as singularly unprofessional.

II

To comprehend the peculiarity—perhaps, I should say in retrospect, the absurdity—of my appointment as Resident Humanist, one needs to understand something about contemporary East Hampton or, more accurately, my perceptions of it. Put bluntly, it is one of the strangest communities that I have ever visited. The town itself strikes me as a kind of Historical

Society writ large. It seems a little out of control. There are too many people trying to do too many things in a space not quite large enough. My perception, of course, says as much about my own background as it does about the culture of the Hamptons.

But whatever personal assumptions I may have brought to this place, there is no mystery about why East Hampton has become one of America's most celebrated resorts. It is the place to be. This is where the action is. From its beaches to its exclusive clubs, East Hampton holds special attractions for the rich and the glamorous, especially during the summer months. In June, the population explodes, rising quickly from a year-round population of 15,000 people to almost 80,000 people. These summer people come from many different backgrounds. Some of them have inherited great wealth; others have earned it. There are people who own property and others who rent cottages. There are doctors and lawyers and chief executive officers, writers and publishers and agents. There are many who come here to watch the show, to be near the action. There are others who come here to escape the action in the city, although finding peace in East Hampton is harder and harder. In August, according to one New York City newspaper, an extraordinary number of psychiatrists take up residence in this community.

This is not a cultural environment in which one would expect to find much interest in history of any sort. Many people seem obsessed by the desire to get all they can out of their stay in the Hamptons. They are firmly committed to the present. But I suspect that the more reflective among them, even as they speed along Main Street, sense that their summer paradise is really quite fragile. As in so many other modern American communities, this knowledge has precipitated a painful debate over East Hampton's future. Even visitors just passing through note an air of crisis that pervades the community. It is present in idle conversation, and in stories in the local newspaper. Sections of East Hampton are obscenely overbuilt. The supply of drinking water may be running out. Open land is growing scarce. Daily traffic is more than the local roads can handle. The ocean itself contains garbage, some of it potentially hazardous.

Even East Hampton's architecture, for long a source of local pride, has become in recent years an embarrassment. Hard-edged abstract structures have sprung up in the middle of potato fields, above the beaches, and along the wooded lanes. Some are tastefully executed, but many of the new constructions clash violently with the physical setting, creating a "belligerent" landscape. Paul Goldberger, a critic for the *New York Times,* described this as "an architecture of shrill egotism," adding that "its arrogance says as much about its owners' aesthetic tastes as about the extent of their responsibility to the land on which they have settled." As the very rich compete in building grander and grander monuments to themselves, they drive up land prices, making it virtually impossible for the children of older, but less affluent, families to remain in the community of their birth.

Although anxiety about East Hampton's future increasingly sparks sharp public exchanges, the battle lines do not yet appear to have hardened into irreconcilable factions. Rather, public response to these issues is still a bit unfocused, the product of fluid associations that change as the issues themselves shift. No doubt, for many occasional visitors the future character of East Hampton is not a pressing concern. Even so, it would be fair to state that one side of this debate enlists what might in Europe be labeled the "greens," ecologists of various degrees of militancy. They are often supported by the Baymen and other people who happen to have moved to East Hampton when it could still credibly claim to be a rural community. On the other side of the debate are the developers and the real estate interests—in other words, almost anyone who stands to profit from East Hampton's continued growth.

Even the suggestion of new construction can spark angry debate in East Hampton. Many people whom I encounter have a story to tell about some unnamed developer who is threatening to destroy a historic building or who plans to bulldoze what is

New Buildings on the Road to Montauk

allegedly a Native American grave site. The whole discussion has acquired a dark, conspiratorial tone. Even in private conversation people are reluctant to name names, as if the enemy had planted listening devices everywhere. The developers, I am assured, are powerful figures capable of all sorts of mischief if they encounter obstructions. One has to be careful.

How much of this loose talk is true is impossible for me to gauge. I do know that the *East Hampton Star* regularly reports new real estate developments as if they were forms of terrorism: an attack at Wainscott, a defeat at Hither Woods, a desecration at Montauk. The developers fight back, frequently suing town officials who attempt to stop them or slow them down. They argue most fiercely over zoning regulations, knowing full well that the larger lots that their opponents advocate mean fewer new homes and decreased profits. The time for compromise may have passed. "All of us have seen areas around the country and the world spoiled by over-development," announced East Hampton Councilman Randall T. Parsons in 1985. "We are going to make a stand here and protect this town for the future."

In this uneasy atmosphere it is not surprising that some people have begun to think more seriously about East Hampton's past, about the historic cost of progress, about the meaning of local tradition. I first observed this turn of mind during an acrimonious debate over the future of the striped bass. Within this troubled community a fish has acquired almost totemic qualities, as if its fate were somehow symbolic of East Hampton's struggle to survive further development. The bass has long played an important role in the town's economy. It brings a good price on the market, and the commercial fishermen of East Hampton have traditionally kept New York City restaurants supplied with bass. Every year thousands of sportsmen flock to the area in hope of catching one of these exceptionally strong swimmers. One man confided to me that although he could not stand the taste of the striped bass, he loved the fight and would endure the discomfort of standing for long hours on a cold beach just for the opportunity to battle a large fish.

During the 1980s the striped bass began to disappear. Since declines in the harvest had been known in the past, no one at first seemed worried when large numbers of migrating fish failed to reappear off the Atlantic shore. Such things occurred in cycles. This time, however, the bass did not rebound, and everyone had a theory about what had gone wrong. The sportsmen claimed that by overfishing these waters the Baymen had depleted the breeding stock. The commercial fishermen, who are also known locally as Bonackers, dismissed these charges as self-serving nonsense. They had harvested these waters for generations. Their fathers had taught them the habits of the striped bass, and in this crisis, the Bonackers were not about to be pushed around by a bunch of noisy weekenders. But pushed they were. East Hampton's commercial fishermen were forced to organize a group, called the Baymen's Association, to lobby in the state capital against the efforts of the sportsmen to restrict their fishing.

Still, the bass declined. Only slowly did people come to appreciate what was happening. The Baymen were not in fact to blame. Nor were the sportsmen. Pollution appears to have poisoned the shallow waters of Chesapeake Bay where the striped bass spawn, and unless the governments of Virginia and Maryland act swiftly, it seems unlikely that the great harvests of the past will ever occur again. Even more disturbing, at least for state inspectors, those adult fish that still manage to make it to the coast of East Hampton have been found to contain unacceptable levels of PCBs. After an unusually bitter debate, the state legislature placed a moratorium in 1986 on all bass fishing.

For the Baymen of East Hampton this was a disaster. They were disconsolate. To be sure, the governor offered state funds for retraining programs, but the Bonackers wanted neither pity nor welfare. As one of them, Daniel King, explained, "I'd be out catching bass if I could. That's what I want to do. That's what I know how to do."

The dispute over the striped bass struck a responsive chord within the larger community. Villagers who might once have regarded the Baymen as no more than a nuisance—I heard more than one complaint about their unsightly pickup trucks—took up the cause. Even relative newcomers were suddenly transformed into Bonackers. The striped bass, facing possible extinction, became emblematic of a whole range of local conservation issues. At risk were the clams and scallops, the birds and wild flowers. Pollutants were killing them too, but in this case, the source of the destruction seemed to be the overdevelopment of East Hampton itself. The rhetoric became shrill, even militant. One automobile bumper sticker summoned citizens to prepare for the "Last Stand."

The crusade against the developers required considerable

optimism, if not naïveté. As anyone could see, construction was continuing at record pace, even though a rising chorus of criticism was becoming audible in political debate. There is too much money tied up in real estate; there are too many deals to be made. Those last remaining acres of open space are too tempting.

During the summer of 1985, as the level of public acrimony became more intense, the "brown tide" appeared in East Hampton for the first time. This algae, whose bloom literally turns the water brown, chokes out the phytoplankton on which the scallops feed. No one knows for certain what initially brought the tide. People assured me that it was a temporary phenomenon caused by a period of abnormally hot and dry weather. They were wrong. The next year the "brown tide" reappeared. It seemed somehow connected with overdevelopment. It was another sign that the end was near.

Something more was at stake in the controversy over the Baymen than the protection of the scallops and striped bass. It involved the community's basic sense of its own historical identity. What was imperiled by these ecological disasters was a way of life, a set of local traditions that many townsmen had taken for granted and that now seemed doomed. As Peter Matthiessen argued, even those people who have been most critical of the Baymen "must acknowledge a gritty spirit that was once more highly valued in this country than it is today. Because their children can no longer afford to live where their families have harvested the sea and land for three hundred years, these South Fork baymen—old-time Americans who still speak with the Kentish and Dorset inflections of Elizabethan England—may soon become rare relics from the past, like the Atlantic right whales."

Matthiessen has become something of a modern Jeremiah, a contemporary Lyman Beecher calling the people of East Hampton back to the simplicity and decency of a former way of life. The Bonackers themselves are now an endangered species. And confronted with the possibility of their imminent extermination—with this judgment lodged against the com-

The Bonacker II

munity—many local people seem to have persuaded themselves that if only the old fishing families can be spared, just this once, then surely East Hampton will reform itself. It will somehow preserve a traditional culture, one that they are not quite able to define but that they nevertheless believe will keep East Hampton from becoming just another Long Island town.

Matthiessen was not the only person to voice such concerns. As Judith Hope, the town supervisor of East Hampton, explained in the *New York Times* in 1986, "The fishermen are very important to us. They are a very unique breed of characters who have managed to make a living in perhaps one of the most difficult enterprises remaining. They are part of the whole history and social fabric of this 300-year old community." Arnold Leo, secretary of the Baymen's Association, agreed. "The social fabric of this very old community is starting to break up," he observed. "Some of these families have been fishing for many generations, and suddenly the younger generation is confronted with the fact that they cannot do what their fathers have done."

At stake is the town's identity. No one to whom I spoke gave the Baymen much chance. Like the Montauk Indians of an earlier era, the Bonackers' time has apparently come to be pushed aside in the name of progress. Already oral historians are busy gathering interviews from old Baymen, a sure sign that the days of commercial fishing in East Hampton are numbered. One man with close ties to these families told me that the wife of a fisherman he knew had had a dream. She dreamt of an apocalypse, a ritual cleansing of a society that seemed to have lost its way. In her dream a great hurricane, the biggest ever recorded, blew in from the open Atlantic. In its fury, the storm swept the beaches of the summer cottages and destroyed the alien culture that they represent.

The Baymen have dramatically focused public attention on the fragile traditions of East Hampton. But they are by no means the only people in this community who have expressed concern about preserving a way of life that now seems threatened. I discovered, for example, that the members of the Ladies Village Improvement Society have worked for years to maintain at least the externalities of an earlier, less commercial, culture. This volunteer organization was formed in 1895 by what one pamphlet proudly described as a "handful of determined women." Today, the society's more than four hundred members, like the members of the Baymen's Association, profess great concern about explosive development in East Hampton. Society members are pledged to uphold "East Hampton's reputation for being one of the loveliest villages in the United States."

Unlike the commercial fishermen, the members of this organization offer a critique of development that is more aesthetic than economic or ecological. "The L.V.I.S. Constitution," as an official handout states, "is a continuing commitment to the community, implemented each year by programs that assure that East Hampton's storied charms will not be disturbed by the pressures of contemporary growth and development." The society provides generous funds for planting trees and for the upkeep of village greens. During the 1940s, it was instrumental in saving Mulford Farm, and, during these more difficult times, it fights every attempt to alter the historic face of Main Street.

Both the Baymen and the members of the L.V.I.S. are participating in a process that Benedict Anderson has brilliantly termed "imagining" a community. Anderson, a political scientist, means that people regularly make assumptions about the values and beliefs of other persons, even of those whom they may in fact never see. We imagine ourselves to be Americans, and although we are often hard pressed to explain why we exclude Canadians or Germans from our "imagined community," we nevertheless are certain that they do not belong. On a very large scale, of course, this communication among strangers is the basis of nationalism. But the field need not be so broad. "In fact," Anderson writes, "all communities larger than primordial villages of face-to-face contact (and perhaps even these) are imagined. Communities are to be distinguished not by their falsity/genuineness, but by the style in which they are imagined."

In East Hampton, as in many other American communities,

a sense of the past, however amorphous it may be, shapes how people perceive a common future. Everywhere in this community men and women talk about tradition. It is manifest in debates over the striped bass, the fate of the Baymen, and the need to save elm trees along Main Street. And the pressing need to define local tradition echoes through the pages of a perceptive, though clumsily written, report published in 1976 under the title *Historical and Cultural Features of the Town of East Hampton, New York*. The committee that prepared this document declared that "communities with strong historic and cultural ties are less likely to be willfully downgraded in comparison to those which have little or no such unifying identity." In the context of East Hampton's fast-growing society, it is hard to understand the meaning of that statement. Does the preservation of "identity" involve more than planting trees on Main Street or contributing money to the Baymen's Association? Indeed, we must ask what is the connection between history and identity, between style and imagination?

III

*M*ulford Farm seemed an appropriate place to begin looking for answers to these questions. When I undertook my assignment, I did not know much about the plight of the striped bass, or about the development controversy. It was immediately apparent, however, that Mulford Farm had acquired special symbolic significance within the community. Whatever stories local people now tell themselves about the historic character of East Hampton are projected onto this weathered saltbox. These collective fictions are in turn told to newcomers, who assume that the stories they hear from the locals are facts rather than interpretations. Mulford Farm is really a kind of text that the passing generations have read and will continue to read in an ongoing effort to understand who they are.

Mulford Farm passed through many hands over three centuries. The house was apparently constructed around 1680 by

Josiah Hobart, but we do not know a great deal either about the man or his residence. Sometime around the turn of the eighteenth century, Hobart sold the property to Samuel Mulford, then the town's most prominent citizen, and except for several short periods during the nineteenth century, it has been in the possession of Mulfords ever since. The last of this long line were two widowers, a father and his son, who died at about the same time during the Second World War.

When the Mulford Farm came on the market, it immediately attracted the attention of the Brooklyn Museum. The curators were eager to acquire the interior woodwork, particularly the exposed beams, of a room that they thought might date from as early as 1656. However accurate their estimate may have been, they did not in the end obtain the house. The threat to Mulford Farm spurred the people of East Hampton into action, and they raised sufficient money to purchase the landmark. Responsibility for its upkeep—a major chore, since the last Mulfords had not paid much attention to routine maintenance—fell to the Historical Society.

At the time of the sale the house looked almost nothing as it had during the seventeenth century. A prominent architectural historian examined the structure from attic to cellar and concluded that the saltbox had begun its life as a large (at least for the 1680s), rectangular, two-and-one-half-story, sharply gabled Tudor building. Daniel Hopping produced a masterful piece of detective work. Anachronistic framing members, an empty mortice, differences in paint chronologies of adjacent woodwork provided him with the kinds of clues he needed to document fully the transformation of Mulford House to its present saltbox form. Each generation, he discovered, had altered the house. Two major changes apparently took place during the early to mid-eighteenth century. Around 1720 a natural disaster, most likely a fall hurricane, severely damaged the house. The east, or seaward, end was reduced by a story and a half. The Mulfords compensated for their loss by adding a lean-to kitchen on the rear. Thirty years later, almost certainly in anticipation of the marriage of their eldest son, the Mulfords rebuilt the east

Mulford Farm and the Eighteenth-Century Addition (circa 1750)

end to a full two and one-half stories. Later came a curious addition, which was once a freestanding structure. All this remodeling gave the structure the softer, sloping lines that we see today.

Recent analysis conducted at Columbia University for the staff of the Historical Society has revealed that the colonial inhabitants of Mulford House preferred bright, even gaudy, colors. Buried under layers of old paint and wallpaper, researchers found blues and oranges, demonstrating that the Calvinists of East Hampton were not the dour colorless folk that some may have imagined.

Tracing the physical metamorphoses of Mulford Farm was

one thing; understanding exactly how it fit into the early history of East Hampton quite another. Like the architectural historian, I was a detective asking questions about the world of Samuel Mulford, about the structure of a society and the character of its economy. I was curious about the lives of the men and women who had actually occupied these rooms, but the evidence refused to cooperate. On several occasions the Resident Humanist would have been pleased to come across something so revealing as a paint chip.

To be sure, the Mulford name appeared regularly on official lists. I could follow the members of this family as they went about their business, but they always kept me at a distance. They were like persons who greet you without fail on the street with a cordial smile but who never become intimate friends. To my knowledge the early Mulfords left no personal letters, no diaries, no portraits, no sustained commentary about their emotional lives. The only personal items that have survived from the colonial period are a cryptic account book that Samuel kept during the early years of the eighteenth century, scattered documents concerned mainly with the transfer of property, and several speeches that Samuel delivered before the assembly of colonial New York. The women of the family are silent. We do not even know the maiden name of Samuel's first wife. There is nothing about raising children or disciplining slaves. Although the Mulfords belonged to the local church, none of them bothered to record his or her thoughts on religion.

Confronted with such patchy evidence, I did what other historians had done before me. I turned to the town records. Almost everything that people claim to know about the early development of the community comes from this remarkable source. It is amazing that the records have survived at all. A courthouse fire, hungry worms, a leaky roof, human error— any of these things could easily have destroyed the early records of East Hampton. Today, in printed form, they possess a formal character. Town leaders seem to have started making entries around 1650, almost immediately after the first settlers arrived in East Hampton, and the records continue unbroken to the present day. Like most government files from the colonial period, these include a range of judicial as well as administrative actions. One finds, for example, lists of officeholders, some wills and contracts, a few depositions, and long accounts of the allocation of land and the laying out of roads.

But herein lay a trap. Previous experience had taught me that official records are often less solid than they at first appear. It seemed prudent, therefore, to consider just what the source might tell me about whom. What type of window onto East Hampton's colonial past did it in fact provide? The answer, I am afraid, is that we can see through this particular glass only darkly. The town records contain perceptions about life in early East Hampton, one layered upon another, so that when I actually read the documents in the local library, I found myself at three removes, at least, from the world of Samuel Mulford.

The interpretive process commenced the moment that local officials decided to discuss some occurrence—theft of a horse or the breaking down of a fence, for example—and though the village magistrates may not themselves have actually witnessed the event, they gave it meaning. After all, it was the local justices, not the original horse thieves or fence breakers, who determined that one aspect of the testimony was more significant than another. They translated the human experiences that ordinary people described in everyday language into a more formal legal discourse. We see horse stealing and fence breaking, illicit lovemaking and contests over status, through a veil of legal procedure that for obvious reasons serves to distort our access to events that took place outside the village court. We do not even possess the litigants' actual words. The local Indians or the black slaves do not speak directly to us, nor for the most part do the town leaders such as Mulford. A clerk who himself may have been a little bored with the proceedings determined what actually went into the official records. In other words, he interpreted an interpretation. And if we read a historical account based on these records—this one included—we find yet another interpreter—or layer—between us and the past.

Penetrating these layered perceptions is difficult, perhaps

virtually impossible from the distance of several centuries. Nevertheless, it is useful at the start of this interpretive journey to remember that people like ourselves have ultimately decided what will or will not be treated as a historical "fact." It is important also to realize that most of them have been quite accomplished at disguising their biases and assumptions, even from themselves. This was true in the seventeenth century. It is true today. It is true for me. My point is simply that under scrutiny, these records unravel, transforming themselves into little more than loose threads of competing fictions. They are products of an interpretive process that at the very best can generate only partial truths.

IV

*W*e all tell ourselves stories about ourselves: about the Founding Fathers, about the frontier, about the rise of American democracy. In early East Hampton the process probably involved a kind of informal oral history. People shared remembered traditions. They recounted genealogies. At some point local historians began to put the stories into written form, and, as they did so, they often organized the facts in new ways. They projected new meanings onto the records. Over time interpretations—fictions absorbed into new fictions—were amalgamated into a popular understanding of the communal past, and it eventually became impossible to distinguish the actual past from stories that local historians had written about the past. And slowly, almost imperceptibly, the accretion of interpretation gave birth to mythology.

Print, of course, closes off interpretive possibilities. Oral traditions are by their very nature open, fluid, easily revised to reflect the perceptions and purposes of whoever happens to be telling the story. Published history is another matter; it cannot be so conveniently modified. A published past becomes a shared text, an unchanging reference, a recognized standard of memory to which others—even revisionists of the late twentieth century—must refer. In East Hampton the transition from oral tradition to print culture began during the last years of the eighteenth century.

John Lyon Gardiner was the town's first and arguably its ablest historian. As the quotation at the beginning of this chapter suggests, Gardiner's prose still has a vital, even lyrical, quality. I am not certain why in 1798, at the age of twenty-eight, he was moved to write a highly personal account of the local society, entitled *"Notes and Observations on the Town of East Hampton."* He seems to have fancied himself as an intellectual—albeit one who found himself cut off from regular contact with polite company. As a historian, Gardiner seems to have been a careful scholar. He had mastered the town records, but he also drew upon his rich personal knowledge of the local culture. Members of his family had lived in this area a decade before the English settled in East Hampton. Stories about the early years had been handed down from one generation to another, and when Gardiner used an anecdote in his history, he attributed it quite genuinely to "tradition."

Although a warm friend of Lyman Beecher, Gardiner developed an interpretation of East Hampton's past strikingly different from that of his minister. To Beecher the records had revealed the hand of Providence. This was God's special settlement, a diligent, pious, temperate community. By contrast, Gardiner was much more a child of the Enlightenment. One imagines him as being more comfortable in the company of Benjamin Franklin than of George Whitefield or Jonathan Edwards. However skeptical Gardiner may have been of revealed religion, his radicalism did not extend to politics. He was not a man of the people. Throughout his history, his tone is slightly patronizing, as if he were the lord of the local manor amusing himself by recording the curious habits of an American peasantry.

Gardiner tells a story of unassuming men and women who left the Old World in the mid-seventeenth century in search of a better life. They were driven as much by economic as religious concerns. Gardiner seems to have imagined East Hampton as a fragment of a larger, more cultured world that had somehow been cut adrift, and, in its isolation from other communities, had turned in on itself. The early townsmen did not develop meaningful ties even with Southampton only a few miles away. As Gardiner asserts,

> An E:H: man may be known from a Southampton man as well as a native of Kent in England may be distinguished from a Yorkshire man. The original settlers of these towns probably came from different parts of England. Besides the names that prevail in one town are not met with in the other. The names Pierson, Halsey, Howell, Toppin, Sandford, Cooper, White, Post, &c. are common in Southampton and confined there as are the names Mulford, Osborn, Conkling, Baker, Parsons, Miller, Gardiner, Dayton, &c. to East Hampton.

He assures us that "very little intercourse took place between the two towns before the Revolutionary War." Separated from other communities in New England as well as New York, seventeenth-century East Hampton developed social institutions that struck Gardiner as anomalous. The town government, for example, was pure "Republican." By this Gardiner apparently meant that the early village assemblies were noisy and contentious, a little too democratic for his liking. "Their town meetings," he declared, "were frequent & became burdensome on the people, but being their own law makers they made a multiplicity of them." The church structure was more obscure. "Very little is to be found on the records relative to Ecclesiastical affairs," Gardiner admitted. "The Original settlers of the town were what were then called Puritans. In their religious principles & Discipline [they] answer'd nearly to the present independents or more rigid Congregationalists." Although the founders of East Hampton encouraged commercial whaling, nothing much had come of it. The villagers had developed a largely self-sufficient agricultural economy.

The people of East Hampton were so removed from the flow of commerce, in fact, that they were reputed not even to know how to use tea, surely the major consumer product of the eighteenth century. A "Mrs. Miller," a seventy-eight-year-old woman, told Gardiner that she remembered "when they first began to drink tea on the east end of Long Island." None of the local farmers apparently had the slightest notion how to brew the dry leaves. "One family boiled it in a pot and ate it like samp-porridge," the old woman explained. "Another [man] spread tea leaves on his bread and butter, and bragged of his having ate half a pound at a meal, to his neighbor, who was informing him how long a time a pound of tea lasted him." According to Mrs. Miller—and this interview may have been one of the earliest American examples of oral history—the arrival of the first teakettle was a particularly memorable day in East Hampton. "It came ashore at Montauk in a ship, (the *Captain Bell*). The farmers came down there on business with their cattle, and could not find out how to use the tea-kettle, which was then brought up to the old 'Governor Hedges.' Some said it was for one thing, and some said it was for another. At length one, the more knowing than his neighbors, affirmed it to be the ship's lamp, to which they all assented." Mrs. Miller may have been pulling Gardiner's leg, or for that matter, he ours, but whatever the truth of her tale, she depicts a sleepy, backwater community, out of the path of consumer fashion.

Only the Indians disturbed the pastoral world of Gardiner's imagination. To be sure, he regarded the local whites as a bit oafish, as fitting objects for a gentleman's wit, but the Native Americans were contemptible. Some miles from the village center, on the eastern tip of Long Island, a remnant of the Montauk tribe lived in squalor. They had no one but themselves to blame for their degenerate condition. After all, they were allowed to use the "lands of the White people that are proprietors of Montock [sic]." Moreover, the Indians had shown considerable talent as "whalemen." Yet, despite these resources, the Montauks had fallen into desperate poverty. Gardiner thought he knew why. "Their idle disposition and savage manners," he wrote, "prevent the most of them from living comfortable altho' the soil is easily tilled & good. Rum has reduced them from a very powerful tribe to a few persons; they are continually disappearing. As they say, the pure old Indian blood does not run in their veins; it is corrupted by the black and white men." The Montauks had further offended Gardiner by their alleged support of the British during the American Revolution, behavior that he simply could not comprehend.

In *"Notes and Observations,"* one can discern elements of a local mythology already falling into place. Gardiner focuses attention upon the evolution of a white society. Indeed, the central figures in this narrative are families named "Mulford, Osborn, Conkling, Baker, Parsons, Miller, Gardiner, Dayton, &c." For Gardiner, the fact that this was a triracial community holds no particular significance. From his perspective, early East Hampton was a beautifully situated, although isolated, largely self-sufficient, Puritan village that had developed extremely democratic forms of local government. Gardiner provided East Hampton with a plausible interpretation of its own past, one based on town records and local tradition, and it is perhaps not surprising that for the descendants of the first families, this reading of East Hampton history acquired the characteristics of an origin myth.

For Lyman Beecher the history of East Hampton possessed an Edenic character. It was the story of a community working out its destiny with God's assistance within a breathtakingly beautiful environment. He liked to imagine how this region must have appeared to the first settlers. "They found an interminable beach of snowy sand," he rhapsodized, "on which the ocean never ceased to beat in sparkling foam; dark forests, overgrown with tangled vines; wild-fowl in countless flocks; throngs of admiring and astonished savages."

Embedded within this poetic description are the seeds of two new mythic themes, both of which in later years came to figure prominently in how the people of East Hampton saw themselves. First, there was the physical environment. In Beecher's account, the original settlers—no doubt trusting in Providence—had selected a site of extraordinary beauty. This unusual setting became a central element in the story East

Hampton told itself about itself. Nature not only provided for these people, but also tested them. It shaped their sense of self. "It is now but 168 years," Beecher declared in 1806, "since this town was one great forest, swarming with wild beasts and savage men. Our harbors, bays and creeks, were lined with wigwams, as is testified by those masses of mouldering shells, which still whiten their shores.—A numerous and warlike people possessed the soil."

Second, there was the matter of the historical Indian. Beecher recognized that the Montauks had fallen on hard times during recent years. Only a "remnant" of the tribe survived into the early years of the nineteenth century. A "savage" race of hunters and warriors had become basket weavers. A sensitive white person, Beecher suggested, might look upon these pitiful creatures and wonder whether the founding fathers of East Hampton had wantonly destroyed the Montauk people. Was there a dark side to the community's history? Had the original settlers mistreated the Indians? Did the past have the capacity to embarrass the current generation?

The questions were largely rhetorical. Beecher assured his parishioners that the town records exonerated the founders. Their hands were clean. The white settlers not only had brought Christianity to the heathen, but also had preserved them from the ravages of alcohol. Your fathers, he told the members of his flock, "manifested a benevolent concern for the welfare of the Indians; and to prevent abuse among them by the use of strong drink, ordained [as stated in the town records] 'that no man carry any of the aforesaid article to them.' " Here was unimpeachable evidence of deep human concern. Such paternalism struck Beecher as almost sublime. "What care—what benevolence," he observed.

The Reverend Timothy Dwight, another of Gardiner's contemporaries, was not a historian. If this man held a position in an American university today, he would probably find himself in a department of sociology. While serving as president of Yale College, Dwight traveled throughout New York and New England recording local customs. These reflections were published in a multivolume set that blends elements of a private diary with a scientific report. During the first decade of the nineteenth century, Dwight journeyed to the eastern end of Long Island, and, if nothing else, his jottings show a refreshing capacity for astonishment.

Time seemed to have stopped in Jeffersonian East Hampton. It was a virtual museum. In all his travels, Dwight had seen nothing quite like it. The town itself was not all that impressive. The houses, he thought, needed fresh coats of paint. But as Dwight discovered, none of the local residents cared about such things. The people whom Gardiner had depicted as clownish peasants struck Dwight as simple rustics. "The passion for appearance," he observed, "so far at least as building is concerned, seems, hitherto, to have fastened very little on the inhabitants of East Hampton. A general air of equality, simplicity, and quiet is visible here in a degree perhaps singular."

For Dwight, this notable self-denial demanded explanation. There were several possibilities. One, of course, was Beecher's providential framework. From that perspective, the town's unworldliness could be seen as a divine favor. The community's spiritual values had preserved it from the corrupting influence of consumer luxury. But even though he was a Congregational minister, Dwight adopted a more secular approach to the problem. Quite simply, the people of East Hampton had missed out on the great commercial revolution of the eighteenth century. Their "social character," Dwight reasoned,

is regulated rather by the long-continued customs of this single spot, than by the mutable fashions of a great city, or the powerful influence of an extensive country intimately connected in all its parts, and controlling by the general opinion and practice the personal conduct of every inhabitant. Living by themselves more than the people of most other places, they become more attentive to whatever is their own, and less to the concerns of others. Hence their own customs, especially those which have come down from their ancestors (and these are almost all that exist among them), have a commanding influence on their conduct.

Dwight believed that East Hampton had generally benefited from its cultural isolation. Other communities throughout America had succumbed to materialism, but in this village, one still found old-fashioned Christian values. But, less attractive, their lack of communication with the outside world meant that people of East Hampton sometimes accepted silly rumors as truth.

I must confess to a special fondness for Dwight's commentary. Unlike Gardiner and some of the other historians who told the villagers stories about themselves, Dwight did not actively contribute to the evolution of a local mythology. Rather, he was a listener who attempted as best he could to comprehend what today we might call the town's "historical identity." I have no way of knowing how he obtained his information. I suspect that he simply interviewed men and women he happened to encounter along the road, and, finding themselves confronted by an inquisitive stranger, the president of Yale College, no less, they expressed a bundle of inchoate beliefs about their own history. They seem to have possessed no precise image of change; theirs was a history without discernible topography. They assumed that in 1800, or, for that matter, in 1750, the local society had looked much as it did in 1650. They told the traveler from Connecticut a tale of ordinary farmers, a God-fearing people, untouched by commerce.

Who knows what ordinary men and women thought of this interpretive tradition. Perhaps they humored the likes of Timothy Dwight, and in the company of friends and neighbors told themselves stories about East Hampton's history, about their own families in East Hampton, legends that they did not bother to share with inquisitive strangers.

During the late 1830s another Gardiner took it upon himself to write a history of East Hampton. Unlike his older cousin John Lyon Gardiner, David never became a lord of the manor. This lawyer and successful New York State politician did manage briefly to lease the family's island estate, however, and it was during this period of his life that he probably composed a series of historical essays for a local newspaper. Twenty-seven years after David's bizarre death (he was killed in 1844 by an exploding gun on board the frigate *Princeton,* then anchored in the Potomac River), these articles were collected in book form under the title *Chronicles of the Town of Easthampton.* This work may have been the product of a long-standing rivalry between the two cousins. David seems to have regarded John Lyon as little more than an antiquarian, and in the *Chronicles* he observed that "local history is indebted" to John Lyon "for some curious and important information"—not exactly a ringing endorsement.

Whatever David may have thought about the other man's work, the two Gardiners shared many assumptions about the early history of their community. David imagined colonial East Hampton to have been an isolated society cut off from commerce and fashion. The first settlers found themselves on the end of Long Island "secluded from the busy parts of the world."

David's analysis of the town's early development sounds a great deal like Timothy Dwight's (Dwight may, in fact, have been David's professor at Yale). The farmers of East Hampton, Gardiner insisted, "were mostly upon a level in their station in life, and they were too remote from the other more populous settlements to suffer pride by comparison. Beauty unadorned, is adorned the most, and the good wives and young damsels were not so exposed to the temptations of exotic finery, as to violate this approved maxim." He based his conclusions about the character of early East Hampton on his own personal recollections of people whom he had actually encountered in the community. Gardiner maintained that his approach to the study of the local past was perfectly acceptable, since, in point of fact, East Hampton had not changed much in almost two hundred years. "Those who can recollect the aged of the last generation in the town," he explained, "can pretty accurately conceive what might have been the apparel in long gone days; since, changes have been little frequent, and eras of fifty years have produced till lately but trifling alterations."

David Gardiner also seems to have shared John Lyon's

contempt for any form of religion that elevated emotion above reason. From this perspective the early East Hampton settlers received high marks. Although they had been God-fearing men and women, they had contained their enthusiasm. The town records also demonstrated to David's satisfaction that the founders never attempted to mix the affairs of church and state. The idea of creating a Christian utopia in the New World, an American "city on a hill," held little appeal for these hardworking people. They did not require evangelical religion to appreciate the danger of excessive freedom, and, even in the earliest days of settlement, they established a local government strong enough to combat licentiousness. In fact, his reading of seventeenth-century documents convinced David that the colonists "were of too practical a character to believe in the perfectability of human nature, and too well acquainted with mankind to think that a community could be restrained from injustice by the mere light of reason."

Although the author of the *Chronicles* dismissed the perfectability of human nature, he had no difficulty accepting an evolutionary view of social progress. To be sure, improvement of any sort was hard to document in a pastoral community like East Hampton. The farmers of 1650 looked pretty much like those of the Revolutionary generation. When Gardiner spoke of progress, however, he took a much longer perspective than a mere two centuries. The European settlers who transferred to the New World represented "civilization," a higher and more desirable stage of social development than that achieved by the "savage" Indians. This historian told East Hampton a story of inevitable historical forces, and although he substituted progress for Providence, the structure of his narrative remained fundamentally the same as that of Beecher's account. "The settlement formed, the wilderness was now to be cultivated," wrote David Gardiner. "The grounds were to be cleared of the forest. The wild animal was to give place to the tame and domestic; the hunting grounds and wigwam to the arable field and pleasant cottage; the gutteral voice of the red man to the softened tones of the civilized white, and the pow-was [sic] of the savage to the worship of the Christians' God."

As in most of the early nineteenth-century histories of East Hampton, the Indians were central figures. Although Gardiner insisted that the Montauks were out of step with the upward course of social development, throwbacks to a primitive stage of evolution, he could not ignore their suffering. At the moment when he composed his *Chronicles,* a few Native Americans still lived in this community, desperate survivors in a community constructed by the "civilized white." For Gardiner, the Indians were not abstractions. He bore witness to a real dying culture. Their plight—the Montauks were "now reduced to three families of some six or eight individuals in the whole"—called into question the values of their more advanced neighbors.

Gardiner responded by pointing out that the people of East Hampton had tried to save the Indians from extinction. The whites warned the Montauks against excessive drinking. They lectured the Indians about the virtues of hard work. They shared the mysteries of the Christian faith. But the Indians showed no interest in benefiting from civilization. Indeed, they seemed more willing to die than convert, and cultural resistance of this sort was one thing that a historian like Gardiner could not comprehend. "The efforts in this case," he explained, "for regenerating the Indian character, were certainly a decided failure, and may be added to the thousand others in this western world, which have disappointed the general hopes of the philanthropist. To be never weary in doing well, is the divine injunction, but the expectation of ever redeeming the red man from his state of nature, would seem, from what has been the result of all previous experiments on this continent, a labor at least unaccompanied with any reasonable hope. From the progress of civilized life, they have either retreated or remained but to perish; and so rapidly have they disappeared, that no trace of them has been left, where but a few years since they were sole lords of the soil."

Henry P. Hedges carried local mythology to a much wider

audience. The Gardiners recorded their thoughts in publications that even in the nineteenth century must have been hard to find. By contrast, Hedges broadcast the story. If John Lyon Gardiner was an intellectual, Hedges was an evangelist. The energy he brought to the task helped legitimate the interpretation; enthusiasm enhanced credibility. Hedges was born into this culture, and during the middle decades of the nineteenth century, as a prominent local judge, he brought to the history of East Hampton a driving sense of purpose. What initially stirred his curiosity about the local past is not clear. It may have been an interest in genealogy. His family had been prominent in community affairs since the founding; when the town finally published its records, Hedges provided long introductory essays, telling readers exactly what they would find or, perhaps more accurately, what they *should find.*

The judge appeared as the featured speaker at major celebrations such as the observance of the Fourth of July. These ritual displays of nationalism called forth the man's full oratorical skills. Hedges must have sounded on these occasions like a Stephen Douglas or Daniel Webster. He brought the muscular "spread-eagle" style of nineteenth-century politicians to the history of East Hampton.

Hedges created a powerful interpretation. He told his admiring neighbors a story about themselves that contained no ambiguities, no doubts, and, certainly, no guilt. Holding forth on the brightly decorated bandstand, the judge assured the audience that history possessed meanings—grand meanings. Hedges linked what had happened in this little community to the development of a new nation and the rise of a great empire. "Back," he cried in his "Address of 1849," "far back in the early English settlements of this fair land are found the springs from whence its rich blessings flowed. But for the virtue, the piety, the self-denial, the wisdom, the genius of the fathers, this Nation in the largeness of its freedom, the breadth of its education, the universality of its equal rights, the solidity of its unbroken union, the grandeur of its territorial greatness, the march of its beneficent missions, could not have been." This was Beecher's Providence now decked out in patriotic garb.

Hedges urged his contemporaries to take pride in their past. Their ancestors had overcome great adversity to establish this community. "We are not unwilling to acknowledge our origin," he maintained, "we delight to honor the memory of our heroic fathers, our pious ancestry, who first planted religion, civilization and refinement upon these shores." To be sure, the seventeenth-century settlers—no mention was made here of African-Americans or Indians—had been humble men and women. They were the salt of the earth, these independent yeomen of Jeffersonian tradition. They had relied on no one but themselves. And that, Hedges insisted, was an important lesson for a current generation of nineteenth-century consumers. The farmer of early East Hampton did not run to the store every time he needed something. "How little he bought," marveled the historian, "and how much he contrived to supply his wants by home manufacture would astonish this generation." These people had been models of self-sufficiency. "Nothing was bought that could be made at home. The spinning wheel was constantly running and carried in visits to neighbors."

Unfortunately, on some aspects of life in colonial East Hampton the early town records were not entirely clear. Hedges argued that one point in particular was likely to cause misunderstanding. The colonial documents contained too much talk of common fields, of shared resources of various sorts, and, as a staunch economic liberal, Hedges wanted to make certain that the people of East Hampton did not get the wrong impression about their early history. The town fathers, he declared, had not been socialists; they had initially experimented with a common field system, but it had not long survived. How could it? "The failure of the experiment here under most favorable circumstances," Hedges lectured, "is in itself a strong testimony against commonism or any like system that seeks to substitute the common in place of the several improvements of lands by their owners." One wonders what inspired this outburst. Had someone actually suggested an alternative reading of East Hampton history? Were there other meanings to be found in the past?

Having exonerated the founders of "commonism," Hedges turned to politics, and here the town records spoke in a clear patriotic voice. The early settlers had repeatedly resisted the encroachments of grasping appointed royal governors, and on each occasion, they had defended their actions in terms that any Jacksonian could appreciate. Their foes had been formidable: "More insidious than the wily savage; more dangerous than the wild beast; more relentless than the venomous serpent, these robber governors were the mightiest foes of the Colony." But because of their uncompromising belief in the sanctity of representative government, the founders of East Hampton had preserved their freedoms. "Neither Thomas James or Samuel Mulford (mighty names!) would tamely surrender the rights of a free born people to arbitrary power," Hedges explained. "The angel of American Liberty was unfolding his wings preparatory to a flight above the power of servile Governors, base-minded Lords or irresponsible Kings." In these confrontations, Hedges was sure he could make out the first republican stirrings of the American people. The seventeenth-century town records anticipated the "Declaration of 1776" and the glorious victory "won at Yorktown."

Tradition of this sort provided an unassailable blueprint for future behavior. Hedges held out to his neighbors the possiblity of East Hampton's remaining what it had been in the past. History would shape things to come. East Hampton, Hedges thundered, had been founded by self-sufficient, independent capitalists who expected their political representatives to preserve property. There was no virtue in change. No reforms needed here. This was not a story in which slaves or indigenous peoples played a significant part. It served essentially to legitimate continued rule by the sons of the first families. In no other account of this community's past is the relationship between power and interpretation as obvious or as self-conscious. Perhaps it is not surprising that this particular reworking of the various elements of the local myth has proved the most enduring.

After about 1880 a new theme began to appear in the story of East Hampton. As we have seen, early historians such as the Gardiners and Hedges viewed the past as essentially unchanging. To be sure, sometime during the early nineteenth century, the Indians dropped out of the local chronicle, but white residents of East Hampton assumed that everyday life in 1800 or 1850 was not all that different from what they imagined it to have been in 1650. Tradition was a living force within this community, a conservative heritage powerful precisely because the people of East Hampton took it for granted. By the end of the nineteenth century, however, this long-enduring, pastoral society no longer seemed so secure. Outsiders who were not part of the story that local families told themselves about themselves began to arrive in ever larger numbers, and as the pace of change accelerated—or seemed to some of the keepers of the past to accelerate—the imagined past increasingly took on the characteristics of a lost Golden Age.

J. Franklin Jameson, a man without roots in East Hampton, may have been the first to sound the alarm. For him to have expressed such nostalgia seems odd. He is remembered today as one of this country's first professional historians. Jameson championed the use of archival sources and developed bold interpretive schemes. During a long and productive career, he helped organize and preserve thousands of early American records. Like so many other historians active at the turn of the twentieth century, he greatly admired contemporary German scholarship. Compared to that of the United States, it seemed more scientific, more carefully documented; most impressive, it laid out in painstaking detail the long evolution of important social institutions.

It was from this perspective that he interpreted the history of the common lands of East Hampton. As he read through the town records, however, Jameson did not fail to see the irony of his situation. He was spending hours in the local archives studying institutions that were about to become extinct, and in an article published in the then prestigious *Magazine of American History,* Jameson voiced his lament:

> One hears rumors of fine clubhouses and summer cottages, of iron piers and fast New York trains and European steamship lines; but surely one sees with some regret the breaking-up of an institution [the common fields of Montauk] which has lasted two centuries, and which carries the mind back far beyond the time of Wyandance [a seventeenth-century Montauk chief] or the coming of the Mayflower, far even beyond the coming of Hengist and Cerdic, to the days of our German forefathers and of the greatest of Romans, who first described the customs which they followed in cultivating their half-cleared fields at the edge of the solemn forests.

What East Hampton's ablest twentieth century historian, Jeannette Edwards Rattray, thought of Jameson's account is not known. It is probably sufficient to point out that she shared his misgivings about the corrosive effects of social change. But Rattray never pretended to be a professional scholar; she was an "insider," a child of East Hampton, a self-conscious guardian of its traditions. Of the many historians who searched the town records of East Hampton for meaning and who tried to explain what possible relevance the past could have for the living generation, none was more dedicated to the task than she.

Rattray set out simply to update the essentially genealogical history of Judge Hedges, a figure whom she seems to have admired. Although her *East Hampton History and Genealogies,* first published in 1953, was dedicated to that impassioned patriot of the nineteenth century, Rattray did not rehash the old narrative. Her book represented an original synthesis, and it is this finely-crafted account of the town's history that most members of the current generation regard as definitive. Here is the local mythology in its most developed, most sophisticated form.

As a descendant of what she called "Old East Hampton," Rattray did not pretend to be a neutral observer. She loved her community, and when she described local tradition, her tone became protective, as if she would brook no challenge to a way of life self-evidently superior to that found in any other part of the country. But her militant pride of place also contained a good measure of defensiveness. Absent from her history of East Hampton was the ebullient self-confidence of Judge Hedges's era.

The traditions that distinguished East Hampton from so many other American towns, she argued, had their roots in the earliest years of settlement. The local records demonstrated that the founders had been decent men and women, solid rather than flashy, certainly not the sort of people that would ever have set the world on fire. Indeed, their appeal seems to have derived in part from their having been slightly "above average." "East Hampton's first colonists must have been, by and large, intelligent, able, independent, and godly men," Rattray observed. "The pattern they set remained almost unchanged for two hundred years. Their descendants were long faithful to one church, while entertaining peaceably enough the occasional French, Irish, or Jewish arrival who might not conform to it. They depended upon agriculture, fishing, and domestic manufactures. They were above average in culture and comforts."

As Rattray also confessed, this traditional world had come under severe attack. Slowly, almost unnoticed at first, the character of the community had begun to change. Jameson had been correct. The fast New York trains had dumped a horde of strangers on East Hampton, and although these people shared with the "natives" a love of natural beauty, they were most certainly not interested in becoming farmers or fishermen. Rattray sketched out what had amounted to a wrenching social transformation. "Farming on eastern Long Island," she explained, "is a big industry now, a great change from the early settlers' subsistence farming. Fishing is no longer for food or fertilizer alone but has developed into a highly profitable sport. Neither farming nor fishing, however, is

East Hampton's chief occupation nowadays. The 17th and 18th century houses have, many of them, been sold to the 'city folks.' "

Faced with the challenge of absorbing so many "foreigners" into the long history of East Hampton, Rattray might have found a way to open up the past, to make it a vital element in shaping the future. She had an opportunity to reinterpret the story—to give it new meanings—and thereby to save local myth from ossification. Instead, Rattray retreated into the safe and familiar world of genealogy. Like the Gardiners and Hedges, she conflated the history of the town with the history of several dozen founding families. "The best reason for tracing back our own families to their roots," she explained, "is to deepen the sense of responsibility in each one of us."

There were obvious limits to the traditional genealogical framework. The Indians provide a good example. In a chapter significantly entitled "Friendly Indians," Rattray described the culture of the early Montauks with insight and sensitivity. She specifically condemned John Lyon Gardiner's crude racism. The European founders had learned from the Native Americans how to cultivate and cook unfamiliar crops. They had even borrowed words from the Montauks' vocabulary. But just as Rattray seemed prepared to explore the full range of interaction, she concluded, "To sum up the Indian phase of East Hampton history, it does not seem as sorry a chapter as that which might be written about some of the other Colonial settlements. According to the social consciousness of their times, the first settlers treated the Indians well." The founders were exonerated, much as Lyman Beecher had absolved them in 1806, and we are left wondering just why the Indians had been so friendly. In fact, in the context of seventeenth-century East Hampton, what could the word *friendly* have meant?

The elements of the local mythology should by now be obvious. In the beginning, East Hampton was an extraordinarily beautiful place inhabited by diligent, God-fearing families. The settlers created a democratic, essentially self-sufficient, society, and, unlike pioneers in other parts of colonial America, they treated the Indians generously and honestly. A pastoral community had endured virtually unchanged for more than two hundred years, and it was only with the coming of the "outsiders," however defined, that East Hampton belatedly and begrudgingly entered a threatening new age of development. Not surprisingly, as the world of the founders became part of what one might call "myth time"—the exact dates do not really matter—it acquired ever greater symbolic importance within the community, and the imagined traditions of an earlier period survive as powerful moral imperatives. It is against this historic background that contemporaries plan for the future.

It would have been relatively easy—as well as diplomatic—for me to have "discovered" elements of the mythic history in Mulford Farm. I should explain immediately that the word *myth* is not intended to suggest that the historians of East Hampton created their past out of thin air or that they purposely misread the town records. They simply filtered these texts through their own perceptions. In any case, few people in East Hampton would have been surprised to hear that seventeenth-century farm buildings reflected the values of a simpler, less commercialized society.

The perceptions that I carried to East Hampton, however, were not those of people who saw themselves as guardians of the past. Although I did not set out to contest a familiar interpretation, I inevitably read the town records from a fresh point of view. Mulford Farm took on new meanings. It spoke to me not only of the achievements of the old families, but also of a complex, commercial world in which the men and women of three races had struggled for survival. These ancient structures reflected an earlier, nearly forgotten attempt to convert a fragile physical environment into private profit. For me, the job of a Resident Humanist was not to debunk the founders, but neither was it to confirm historical stereotypes. Rather, it was to communicate the experiences of the first settlers to a modern, heterogeneous community anxious about its own ecological future.

V

$\mathcal{M}$y reinterpretation of the early history of East Hampton got off to an unpromising start. David Swickard, the Historical Society's development officer, arranged an interview with a reporter from the *New York Times,* and, on an especially warm summer afternoon, we talked with her in front of the Mulford house. As we chatted, a photographer busily snapped pictures while I tried to look like a proper Resident Humanist.

David was delighted that the Historical Society at last would receive what promised to be favorable publicity. He had been particularly annoyed by the failure of the local paper to cover this story. In any case, standing on Samuel Mulford's lawn, he took full advantage of the opportunity, telling the reporter about the work of the society, its recent successes in obtaining grants, and most important, its interest in providing the community with a new, exciting interpretation of Mulford Farm. He explained that my research might have radical implications for the history of East Hampton. He assured her that before my arrival, "There had never been an intellectually sound and legitimate look at the historical context of East Hampton from someone who was outside East Hampton."

This was strong stuff. After three hundred years, someone would at last set the historical record straight. "We really felt," David continued, "that it would be exciting to have someone with a comparative perspective on Colonial America come to East Hampton without any prejudice or genealogical relationship to the founding fathers. We wanted someone who could look at the town with a completely new, fresh and alive perspective." During the interview, I threw out some preliminary findings. The *Times* reporter seemed particularly surprised (as I too had been) to learn that a sizable African-American population had lived in late seventeenth-century East Hampton. The story eventually appeared with a large photograph on the front page of the second section of the Long Island edition. David and I were pleased.

But not for long. Carleton Kelsey, the town's official historian (according to New York State law, every community can appoint an official historian), shot off an angry response to the *East Hampton Star*. The opening line established the tone of his letter: "As Queen Victoria is said to have remarked, 'I am not amused.' " David's enthusiastic claims for my research had offended Kelsey. How, he asked, could any responsible member of the staff of the East Hampton Historical Society maintain "that local history, as so far written, is incomplete and prejudiced because the writers were genealogically rooted in the past"? This assumption, Kelsey asserted, "is baseless and therefore ridiculous. . . . Obviously, there has been no intelligent or really critical reading [at the Historical Society] of David Gardiner, Judge Henry P. Hedges, Harry D. Sleight, Jeannette Edwards Rattray, Everett Rattray, or Madeline Lee." Though some of these names were obscure by any standard, Kelsey seemed to regard his list as an honor roll of local historians. As for the work of the Resident Humanist, Kelsey announced, "Now, at long last, we are to be treated to the 'real' Colonial history of our Town! It will be 'complete' and 'unprejudiced.' Now we will be able to see the forest!"

David groans when he reads Kelsey's letter. He predicts that it will cause him trouble just when the Historical Society is trying to develop a more professional image. While David is considering whether it is worth continuing the debate, I decide to pay Kelsey a visit, eager to meet anyone who feels so strongly about the town's history.

A little distance beyond the Village of East Hampton, on the way to Amagansett, a local realtor has established an office in what appears to be a colonial structure. While the building is eye-catching, its sign is arresting. The company beckons vacationers who pass on Route 27 to "Share Our Traditions." Buy property and "Share Our Traditions." What a stroke of genius! Tradition transformed into a commodity. A sales pitch. I wonder how many local people appreciate the irony.

The meeting with Carleton Kelsey turns out to be a pleasant surprise. I had expected him to be a truculent, disagreeable

"Share Our Traditions"

fellow eager to humiliate a visiting scholar. But, in fact, he welcomes me into the Amagansett Public Library, where he has worked longer than anyone can remember. The library is a charming wood-frame building that has somehow survived the commercial development that encircles it. Its tiny rooms are cramped; even to negotiate my way among the stacks of volumes is difficult.

Kelsey greets the steady flow of people who on this bright August afternoon have driven up to the village to borrow books. It is clear to me in an instant that they adore Kelsey. He is a local institution. One woman came especially to introduce her young daughter to the librarian. As he stands behind the circulation desk smiling, she tells the girl that this man lent her a book more than a generation earlier. The daughter seems impressed. The mother is happy that an old friend is still in charge of the collection. More interruptions. A telephone caller asks for genealogical information. An elegant-looking gentleman wants advice about a recently reviewed book. Through it all, Kelsey maintains a running conversation, asking after relatives and remembering events that others have long ago forgotten.

As Kelsey goes about his business, I note the intensity of his eyes. They communicate rapid shifts of mood, a flash of humor, an inquisitive glance, a skeptical stare. In just a few minutes he runs through them all, including the raised eyebrows registering exaggerated surprise. Like Senator Sam Irvine, the savvy constitutionalist from North Carolina who insisted during the Watergate hearings that he was just a "poor country lawyer," Kelsey denigrates his own expertise. As we sit talking at a little table reserved for new books, I can hardly believe that this is the same person who so recently rebuked David and me for our ignorance of East Hampton historiography.

Our conversation proceeds slowly at first. I mention the sign I had seen in front of a real estate agency inviting passers-by to "Share our Traditions." I ask Kelsey what in the context of contemporary East Hampton that phrase might mean.

"Nothing," he snaps.

The sign itself is not the issue. Businessmen can say whatever they like in advertisements. Rather, the statement reminds him of another, more irritating, problem. Almost no one in East Hampton, he thinks, has the slightest interest in preserving what he calls the town's "real" traditions. People do not even know what they are.

For Kelsey, however, tradition matters a great deal. Unless a community knows what is good and useful in its own past, he explains, it lacks stability. It becomes a rootless society, subject to dangerous excesses. The only thing that could save

towns like East Hampton, he believes, is a genuine conservatism, a deep Burkean appreciation of the role of history in
shaping the future.

I observe Kelsey closely as he talks. His eyes express both
sadness and pride. He explains that the motivating force in his
life has always been the preservation of tradition. It was so even
before he moved to East Hampton as a young man. And although he was not a native, he attempted to educate anyone
who bothered to listen about the lessons of local history.

"What then are the traditions of this community?" I ask.

Conservatism, for starters. The first settlers, Kelsey states
confidently, had been self-reliant, tough men and women. As
farmers, they could not afford to take chances. If a crop failed
or if animals died, a family might not survive the winter. Such
people were not likely to chase after fads.

I mention J. Franklin Jameson's essay, which laments the
arrival of the railroad and the breakup of the town commons.
Does Kelsey think that the history of East Hampton should be
divided at the beginning of this century? Had there been a long,
virtually unchanging period followed by a sudden flood of com-
mercialization?

"No," he responds after a pause. The first period did not
extend into the twentieth century. The early decades of settlement had been an idyllic time in East Hampton. The founders
may have occasionally suffered personal hardship, but Kelsey
characterizes that society as a kind of "big happy family."

The Town Historian pauses again. He adopts a confidential
tone, as if he is about to say something quite scandalous. The
early seventeenth-century settlement, Kelsey states quietly, had
been almost "communistic." By that, he means only that the
founders established a system of common fields. They defined
themselves not primarily as individuals, but as members of a
community and, as such, had accepted responsibilities for the
common good. They looked after neighbors in need. But, according to Kelsey, their generosity hardly amounted to a great
sacrifice. During the colonial period, the soil was still so rich
that these self-sufficient families regularly generated surpluses.

They built up huge herds of cattle that grazed on the lush fields of Montauk. The sea increased their bounty.

As I listen to Kelsey, I wonder how these tough, self-reliant settlers managed to live with such prosperity. Had they not been tempted just a bit by luxuries? Had success not strained their native conservatism? I keep these thoughts to myself, and inquire instead about the alleged isolation of early East Hampton. What, I ask Kelsey, are we to make of John Gardiner's history and Timothy Dwight's diary? These early commentators had not exactly portrayed East Hampton as an economic success.

Kelsey seems torn. He cannot very well dismiss these early reports. After all, these were the kinds of sources that he had publicly chided David and me for not reading. No doubt, Kelsey admits, East Hampton experienced a certain cultural and economic insularity, but he also insists that the community had never been cut off from the rest of the world. During the nineteenth century, he notes, the men of East Hampton sailed out of Sag Harbor on great whaling vessels. In any case, focusing his attention specifically on Jameson's essay, Kelsey declares that the first period of local history ended with the Civil War. A second period extended from 1860 to 1914. This was the time when outsiders first began to change the character of the community. But the social pressures of these years were mild compared to what occurred after World War I. This was stage three, the period when the summer people transformed East Hampton.

With his letter to the newspaper still on my mind, I ask the librarian of Amagansett whether local history—at least, the kind of local history that he seems to champion—is not really just a celebration of genealogy. Does the story of East Hampton involve anything more than an account of the activities of a few favored families? Are these not the traditions he wants to preserve?

"No," he answers firmly. Tradition is more than the history of particular men and women. It can be taught to others. In any case, Kelsey explains with no obvious emotion, the founding families will soon be gone. Several surnames are already extinct. The children of the settlers have for the most part moved away, joining the great stream of rootless Americans who have lost a sense of place. They are now indistinguishable, he thinks, from the weekenders who rush past the Amagansett Library on their way to Montauk Point. They are all men and women without a history.

"Perhaps something like Mulford Farm could make the past come alive," I suggest.

Kelsey's arched eyebrows comment on my apparent naïveté. He doubts that the people who speed through East Hampton on Route 27 even bother to look out of their cars, let alone reflect on the history of this extraordinary community.

VI

It is early evening when I drive up to Trevor Kelsall's house. He lives in a section of the Village of East Hampton that has not yet been disturbed by new development. I understand now why someone during the day had commented that this was a part of town where "real" people still live. It seems a comfortable neighborhood, reminding me in the gathering twilight of places that I knew as a child.

Kelsall is waiting for me on the front porch. A middle-aged man with striking red hair, he gives me a strong handshake. I explain that I am pleased to meet the Historian of the Village of East Hampton (not to be confused with Carleton Kelsey, who is the Town Historian). Kelsall smiles a tired smile. His title has momentous quality.

"What does a Village Historian do?" I ask.

Kelsall responds with a laugh. Sitting on a wicker chair in the growing darkness of a warm summer evening, he seems a little apprehensive, as if he half-expects me to spring some impossible question about the origins of the community. Leaning forward, clenching his hands together, he tells me that he receives an annual budget of about $300 from the Village. He is supposed to answer questions about local history. Most of Kelsall's time is spent teaching seventh-graders at a school in Montauk. He also belongs to the Volunteer Fire Department and a number of community organizations. But it is the teaching that he loves. Unlike many middle-school teachers I have known, Kelsall is genuinely enthusiastic about his profession. He just likes working with young people, and as he talks about his history classes, he relaxes just a bit.

Kelsall loves history just as much as he loves teaching. He brings to it an almost boyish excitement. He collects stories as well as artifacts. It soon becomes clear that there is very little about East Hampton's past that does not arouse his passionate curiosity.

One thing bothers Kelsall, however, and he seems anxious to set the record straight. Just because he serves as the Village Historian, he does not want me to conclude that he is a member of one of the founding families. He is not related to the Daytons or the Hedges or any of the other major clans. His name does not appear in the genealogies that pass for history in this town. His father moved to East Hampton many years ago and took a position working on one of the local estates. Trevor grew up here, went to school here, and, as an adult, makes his home here.

He reminisces about earning summer money as a potato picker on fields just up the road that are now completely developed. He tells me about the scuffles that he and his friends sometimes had in school with local boys who thought they came from better families. The memory of these class divisions amuses Kelsall. The new residents who flock to the Hamptons are so much richer than even the wealthiest old families that it makes no sense now to maintain the social distinctions of his youth. The bullies of the past have become his friends. Since the war, in fact, the locals have had "to draw up the wagons," to preserve common traditions in the face of change.

Trevor—by now we have established a first-name relation—serves soft drinks. Just then, his son bounds out of the house looking for car keys and, discovering a visitor, immediately apologizes for the intrusion. When Trevor formally introduces us, I learn that the boy is studying art in a college located in Savannah, Georgia. We exchange pleasantries about living in the South. And then, with another flurry of apologies, he rushes off. As his car leaves the driveway, Trevor notes how difficult it is for a boy to remain in East Hampton after he grows up. "Too expensive now," he says. "Too expensive for ordinary people."

Trevor encourages me to ask questions. "Does local history really mean anything to the residents of East Hampton?" I inquire. He seems puzzled. The question is not well phrased. I try again. "How do people who share your interests and concerns maintain the old traditions?"

Trevor responds that a lot of his friends belong to the Lost Tribe of Accobonac. It is a club, he tells me, only open to men and women who have been raised and educated in East Hampton. The group is also called the Sons and Daughters of East Hampton, but Trevor clearly prefers the Indian name. No one apparently takes the organization all that seriously. They meet a couple of times a year in the Springs Fire House, and the old-timers tell stories. At a recent gathering a World War I veteran spoke to the Tribe. Trevor wants me to understand that this is essentially a social club. It is certainly not a stodgy group like the East Hampton Historical Society. Those people preserve artifacts, he states. "We keep oral history alive."

"How do you think East Hampton got to be the way we find it today?" I ask.

"You mean before Hamptonizing set in?" Trevor asks rhetorically.

Money, he believes, changed the character of the town. Before World War II, East Hampton "*really* was a community." If someone got in trouble—a wife or child needed an operation, for example—the men would place a jar in the bar with the person's name on it, and people would contribute to the fund. Such spontaneous generosity does not occur much anymore.

Before the flood of wealth weakened the foundation of Village society, Trevor continues, East Hampton was a much more desirable place. In that period—and his time frame was a little vague—the residents of the community had been independent-minded. They had also been tough. Before the 1880s, men had two choices: either they took to the sea or they worked the land. In those days, he says with an edge in his voice, "we were all Bonackers." This was truly a lost Golden Age. During those years, he asserts, none of the local residents had yet sold out their traditions. They still understood that the essential characteristic of East Hampton was "wryness."

It is my turn to look puzzled. "Wryness?"

"Sure," Trevor continues. "That is what one needs in this town, a canny quality."

Wryness sounds much like Carleton Kelsey's "conservatism." It is a deep, almost instinctual commitment to individualism, to self-sufficiency, to survival. It is a quality that the members of the Lost Tribe respect.

Trevor insists that even in the earliest days of settlement one encountered expressions of the "Bonacker" spirit. He is not sure of the details. In fact, as he candidly admits, he has not closely studied the seventeenth-century records, but that does not matter. The distant past merges in his mind with more recent events. History and memory flow together; imagination shapes the past. This myth-time with which he identifies is reflected in Mulford Farm and the other colonial buildings in the village. Even as a boy, Trevor assures me, he loved to walk down Main Street toward the Old Cemetery. The sense of the past that he felt so strongly then excites him still.

By now it is quite dark. As I get up to leave, Trevor invites me to see some of the "stuff" he has collected over the years. "I'm a dump picker," he adds with a touch of pride. We enter the living room, where he shows me a beautiful old drop-leaf mahogany table. Trevor informs me that he found it in the town dump. He has also salvaged from the trash pit the log of a nineteenth-century whaling ship, as well as numerous plates, bottles, and signs. Every room contains some treasure carted home and preserved. Sensing my curiosity, he brings out a small, brightly colored piece of cloth. This fabric, he announces, has survived from the eighteenth century. There had been a companion, which he presented to the Historical Society.

"You found this in the dump!" I exclaim.

He nods.

The newcomers, he insists, do not care about local history. To support his point, he tells me of an ancient barn that was purchased recently and moved to another location, no doubt to become a studio. The owner had no interest in the dusty contents of the structure and ordered them all hauled off to the dump. This impetuous decision led to one of Trevor's best days as a trash-picker.

"What will you do when the town closes the dump?" I ask. He seems surprised that I have heard that the present dump, nearly filled to capacity, is scheduled to be closed soon.

Trevor shrugs his shoulders.

As I walk toward my car, we hear a barn owl. "Been around here for the last couple of nights," Trevor notes. "Don't hear them much anymore."

VII

The *East Hampton Star* is a journalistic anomaly. On first reading, it seems to be just another small-town weekly. The paper carries predictable stories about local teams and social events. I remember in particular reading an account of the landing of a huge white shark off Montauk. In Wisconsin or Indiana a comparable piece might report the sighting of a large bear or the weight of a prize-winning bull.

Unlike many rural journals, however, the *Star* also runs sophisticated music and theater reviews. Perhaps even more unusual is the paper's willingness to do battle with powerful developers and politicians. Its editorials possess a feisty, no-nonsense quality, and, as one might expect, the adversarial tone of the *Star* seems to annoy a good many readers, especially those whose economic oxen are being gored. Even people who would experience culture shock without the morning *New York Times* know by the end of each Thursday—the day the *Star* goes on sale—what appeared in the local paper, and it is not uncommon to hear guests at dinner arguing about how the *Star* covered some local event.

Only after becoming a regular reader did I begin to appreciate how much attention the *Star* devotes to the history of East Hampton. It occasionally runs long serialized accounts of various aspects of the local past. The paper reminisces about a less complex, slower-moving society that once existed on the South Fork. And when various developers threaten the community with massive change, editorials rally the people of East Hampton to a defense of their historic character.

The voice behind these appeals is Helen Rattray, the journal's editor. She is obviously an important person for me to talk to about the history of this community. Unfortunately, Rattray is not at all eager to see the Resident Humanist. When I first contact her, I explain that I am writing a book about how East Hampton's past has shaped popular perceptions of its future. This meets an icy reception.

"Mr. Breen," she declares over the telephone, "we all have books to write."

At a later date, however, Rattray's attitude toward my research softens, and she agrees to meet with me and photographer Tony Kelly in the offices of the *East Hampton Star*.

The paper is located in the historic district of the Village. Tony and I are directed up a long, narrow flight of stairs guarded by an aging Labrador retriever. We eventually find the editor sitting at a large, cluttered desk. From the window she enjoys an excellent view of Main Street.

Helen Rattray seems relaxed as she motions to us to clear off a couple of chairs and sit down. It is a Friday. The week's deadlines have been met, and no one at the *Star* appears much worried about gathering copy for the next issue. With considerable reluctance she allows Tony to take her photograph. Tony assures her that he is an "old newspaperman" himself and, with a laugh, guarantees that she will like his work.

With that settled, she turns her attention to me. I ask how she had become so interested in the history of East Hampton.

Helen declares that she inherited it. She describes herself as a outsider in this society. She came here in 1960, a woman from New Jersey who happened to marry into one of the founding families of East Hampton. Her husband, himself a respected local historian, had been the son of Jeannette Edwards Rattray, the author of *East Hampton History and Genealogies*. And when her husband died, Helen not only acquired a newspaper, she also took on a certain responsibility for the history of the entire community.

Like Carleton Kelsey, Helen Rattray protests that she knows little about the details of the town's early history. She reads old books about East Hampton, and only when these fail to provide adequate information does she turn to people like Kelsey for assistance.

As pleasantly as possible, I indicate that I do not believe a word that she is saying. It is clear to anyone who reads the *Star* that the editor knows a great deal about East Hampton's historical development.

Without responding directly to my challenge, Helen states that she cannot tolerate sloppiness. There is passion in her voice. To sharpen the reporting skills of the younger members of her staff, she sometimes orders them to correct the press releases regularly issued by the East Hampton Historical Society. She claims that these releases contain a surprising number of errors. Nothing earthshaking, to be sure but, for Helen, every detail matters.

Helen is not the least bit apologetic. If the seventeenth-century records state that a certain piece of land was a "sheep fold," then it will not do to label it a "sheep pound." From her perspective, such seemingly minor mistakes betray a lack of seriousness about the history of East Hampton. But something more than mere sloppiness is involved here. Because the character of the local community is changing so rapidly and because so many new people take up residence in East Hampton every year, the public memory is inevitably short. Newcomers seldom even know the terminology of local history. For them, the very language of tradition is alien; unless someone systematically corrects errors of fact, even the smallest ones, then they will surely become absorbed into the history of the town. No one knows any better. That is why Helen believes that the *Star* has a special obligation to educate the people of East Hampton about their own history. In this community, she maintains, history is—indeed, it must be—news.

"Why bother?" I respond, hoping to draw her out. "What difference does it make to know a 'sheep fold' from a 'sheep pound'?"

"History is one of the joys of life," Helen replies immediately. In this sense, getting the details of a story right is its own reward. But there is more. She speculates that history may perhaps mean more to someone who is Jewish than to others in our society. Hers is a heritage that celebrates tradition; because of this, she suggests, she may have brought to East Hampton a heightened awareness of the role of the past in shaping social identity.

But history is more than that, Helen insists. Indeed, it "is the only thing that will save us from becoming Smith Haven Mall."

She refers to one of those large, sprawling suburbs that one passes on the way to and from New York City. I have heard it all before. Indeed, people here use Smith Haven Mall much as the Republican Party used the "bloody shirt" after the Civil War. Sell out local traditions and look what happens. Ugly little stores, fast-food outlets, tasteless housing developments. It can happen here, right here in East Hampton. Like the Baymen and the members of the L.V.I.S., like Carleton Kelsey and Trevor Kelsall, Rattray believes that a society that has lost a sense of its own past—lost a clearly articulated understanding of how it got to be the way it is—cannot possibly move with confidence and vision into the future. Without historical roots people drift through time, allowing themselves to be homogenized into a larger culture over which they exercise almost no control. History is a discourse of cultural resistance.

At the very least, Helen asserts, East Hampton must preserve its architectural heritage. For the editor of the *Star* this

Helen Rattray in Her Office

means more than fighting to preserve old buildings like Mulford House. Throughout the town, she believes, people should pay more attention to the relation between design and tradition. It is not simply the character of the architecture that offends her. Recent construction in East Hampton has changed the very appearance of the landscape. It no longer looks quite right to her. It does not even smell right. Everywhere one looks, one sees the same process at work. New owners buy up an old potato field, build a house as fast as they can, and then set about to plant trees and shrubs. Not just any trees and shrubs. They want trees and shrubs that complement the expensive house that they have just completed. They want designer trees and shrubs. No one pauses to consider whether the various species that transform the potato fields are actually indigenous to the East Hampton environment. Such decisions do not take into proper account the community's visual traditions, and for Helen at least, many of the carefully manicured lawns and gardens of the South Fork represent a disturbing retreat from history, a betrayal of the past.

At this moment, a man walks past the editor's desk. He wears a full white beard and a billed cap. Just as he starts up a flight of stairs leading to the third floor, Helen calls out, "You had something to say?"

He hesitates.

"You left a note, didn't you?" Helen says to the man.

He returns to her desk, and for a few moments they carry on an animated conversation about a certain window on the ground floor. He wonders whether the screen should not be secured. After a few minutes, Helen announces that the problem does not sound very serious and urges him to give it no further thought. The man—he was not introduced to us—hurries off.

"I wanted you to meet my uncle Morris," Helen informs us. He is a special person in her life, a link with a part of her family that does not come from East Hampton. He apparently brings to mind her own son, who shares his mother's love of history. She is certain that he would like to talk to me—apparently because I am a real historian—and she attempts to arrange an interview. After making several calls, however, she fails to locate the boy. We sit patiently. While dialing one number, Helen notes a little sadly that her son will probably leave the community. I do not press her on this point. Her comment reminds me of Trevor's son and Carleton's lament for a rootless generation.

It is time to leave. Helen wants to spend the afternoon gardening. Just as we are departing, she observes rather abstractedly, "I'm jealous of people writing the history of this community."

I am momentarily taken aback. At that moment her voice sounds wistful.

As I leave the offices of the *Star* and walk out onto Main Street, I realize that Helen is not alone. A lot of people take the history of East Hampton very seriously.

CHAPTER TWO

Inventing a Community

And as the moon rose higher the inessential houses began to melt away until gradually I became aware of the old island here that flowered once for Dutch sailors' eyes—a fresh, green breast of the new world. Its vanished trees, the trees that had made way for Gatsby's house, had once pandered in whispers to the last and greatest of all human dreams; for a transitory enchanted moment man must have held his breath in the presence of this continent, compelled into an aesthetic contemplation he neither understood nor desired, face to face for the last time in history with something commensurate to his capacity for wonder.

F. Scott Fitzgerald,
The Great Gatsby

*E*ast Hampton experienced a difficult birth. Other New England towns—and colonial East Hampton always identified more with Connecticut than with New York—appear to have sprung up fully developed communities. This, of course, is the stuff of legend. Whether the first landings occurred at Plymouth or Salem, we always seem to encounter men and women exuding a powerful sense of mission. For some, the process of community formation began even before they departed for America. In England they broadcast their intention to establish a more righteous society, and, once they arrived in the New World, they quickly drafted covenants pledging to the Lord and to each other to live according to Scripture. They knew their place in the social hierarchy and were prepared to work for the common good.

It does not seem to have been so in early East Hampton. And perhaps, if we investigated more closely, we would discover that it was not really so in those New England communities that have come to dominate our modern historical imagination. To be sure, the first settlers of East Hampton— those who took up residence in the early 1650s—shared certain assumptions and values not only with each other but also with their contemporaries in Connecticut and at Massachusetts Bay. They were children of the Protestant Reformation, Puritans who responded positively to the teachings of John Calvin. They spoke the same language, revered the common law, and in each other's company took for granted much about everyday English culture.

This shared cultural baggage not withstanding, the people of East Hampton did not immediately establish what historians would recognize as a classic covenanted village. In our terms they found it difficult in the beginning to "imagine" themselves as a community. The problem was that, unlike many colonists who settled the coastal towns of New England, these men and women had not thought out in advance what it meant to form a little commonwealth. So far as we know, before 1650 they did not produce a formal statement of purpose. They could not even draw upon the ties of kinship during the earliest days of settlement. With the exception of the Mulford brothers, John and William, none of the original inhabitants of East Hampton appear to have been blood relations. They were committed Christians, to be sure, but in their concern for material well-being, they seem not unlike the millions of migrants who for three centuries have been drawn to the American shore in search of a better life.

Within a short time the character of East Hampton changed. By 1664, the year when this village officially came under the jurisdiction of the government of colonial New York, it was clear that a group of relative strangers had managed to create something that we would today readily recognize as a community. An institutional structure was in place. Certain families had risen to the top of the social order, and, although some decisions reflected the peculiarities of an unusual physical environment, the community looked much like those that had developed in other parts of New England. The people of East Hampton—some of them—had belatedly achieved a sense of purpose.

The process of sorting themselves out would surely have gone more smoothly had early East Hampton drawn upon what contemporaries called "natural" leaders: in other words, upon men whose high social standing was so widely recognized that their neighbors immediately elected them to positions of authority. Governor John Winthrop of Massachusetts was such a person. But with the possible exception of Lion Gardiner—and his credentials were a little suspect—none of the first East Hampton settlers enjoyed obvious social superiority. They were too much alike, too equal, too concerned with the rewards of this life to create a loving commonwealth on the American frontier.

This difficulty had worried some Englishmen even before the great seventeenth-century migration to America. John Robinson, the respected Separatist leader who had fled from England to Holland, anticipated how hard it would be in the New World to establish authority upon a foundation of social equality, and when the Pilgrims departed for Plymouth under William Bradford, he warned, "Whereas you are become a body politic, using amongst yourselves civil government, and are not furnished with any persons of *special eminency above the rest,* to be chosen by you into office of government; let your wisdom and godliness appear." He urged the Pilgrims to elect men who would love them and promote the common good. And after these rulers had been installed in office, Robinson counseled, the citizens should give "unto them all due honour and obedience in their lawful administrations, not beholding in them the *ordinariness* of their person."

Try as they would, however, the early East Hampton residents do not appear to have been able to accept Ronsinson's prescient advice. The problem was by no means restricted to political matters. In ordinary exchanges these migrants contested each other's claims to social status, and of course, in the very act of challenging someone else more clearly defined their own. The process of sorting out a group of ambitious, though ordinary, people into a stable hierarchy sparked a series of confrontations, one of which came close to taking the life of an innocent woman.

These were truly formative years, and even though I have found different meanings in the past from those celebrated by the local historians, I am persuaded that the creators of the "origin myth" were absolutely correct to draw attention to the earliest years of settlement—in other words, to the doings of East Hampton's founding generation. Indeed, I would argue that the character of modern East Hampton owes much to decisions taken during this period about the physical environment. The founders struggled with conflicting imperatives. They wanted to create a Puritan community, one in which godly men and women shared corporate responsibilities. In this they were not unlike the people who settled the villages of Massachusetts and Connecticut. But quite by accident this group of colonists found themselves in possession of an area that promised to fulfill their fondest economic dreams. Rich grasslands stretched for miles, and occasionally a whale yielding barrels of marketable oil drifted onto a beach. The question was how to share these opportunities. Would some families profit more than others? Whom would they exclude? The Indians? The poorer inhabitants? The late arrivals? By the 1670s the answers were clear. East Hampton had become a Puritan "boom town," and for those people who defined themselves as the community, who in fact had "invented" it, the prospects for personal prosperity never seemed brighter.

I

*L*ion Gardiner remains an anomalous figure three hundred years after his death. Like other resolute, ambitious Elizabethans, he journeyed to America to find adventure and, with luck, a fortune as well. He reminds me of Captain John Smith or Captain Miles Standish, two more famous veterans of England's wars on the Continent who also took a chance on the New World. They too were swaggering, confident, worldly soldiers whose range of experience made it impossible for them to return to the quiet farm life from which they had escaped as young men.

Gardiner fought for the Prince of Orange, learned to speak Dutch, and earned a reputation as a capable military engineer. As a soldier, he appears to have been a skilled, imaginative leader. These attributes, coupled with a strong personal allegiance to reformed religion, brought him to the attention of Lord Saye and Sele and Lord Brooke, two English aristocrats who championed the Puritan cause and who also had received a grant of land in the area located in what is now southeastern Connecticut. The two noblemen were apparently so unhappy with the rule of Charles I that they seriously contemplated emigrating to New England. In any case, they dispatched Gardiner to the mouth of the Connecticut River with instructions to construct a fort at a place that became appropriately known as Saybrook.

Gardiner's activities in the New World inevitably brought him into conflict with the Pequot Indians, a proud, well-organized Algonquian people who did not welcome English settlement on English terms. In a joint military operation with soldiers from other New England colonies, Gardiner's forces destroyed the major Pequot encampment, really a palisaded stronghold. The fort was put to the torch, and, as the Pequots, men, women and children, rushed out to escape the flames, the Europeans killed them. Some were shot; others hacked to pieces. It was reported that the massacre deeply distressed the Narragansetts, who during this particular campaign had allied themselves with the English colonists. They did not believe that war should be so bloody, so total. Even Gardiner, who must have witnessed a good many atrocities in the Netherlands, found that in America he had no stomach for genocide.

Whatever happened after that terrible battle, Gardiner seems to have earned the respect and trust of the local Indians, especially those who inhabited the eastern end of Long Island. We can only guess at the psychological underpinnings of this relationship. These people may have feared that they too would die by fire and sword. An equally important factor in this cross-cultural conversation was probably Gardiner's own background. Because of his experiences on the Continent dealing with people of other religions and nationalities, he was less parochial than many of his countrymen, and though there was no doubt as to who was in charge at Saybrook, Gardiner never condescended to the Indians by treating them as simple savages or as detestable heathen. Again, like Captain John Smith, who won the begrudging respect of Powhatan and his famed daughter Pocahontas, Gardiner appears to have blended firmness and honesty, threats and generosity, and within a few years he had evolved a way of negotiating with the local Algonquians that was more successful than the high-handed approach of the more provincial Puritan leaders. It seems he even learned to speak the local Indian language, a tongue that almost none of his contemporaries was able to master. In 1639 the Native Americans of Long Island repaid his understanding by offering to let him purchase a large island they called Manchonacke, an Indian term meaning roughly "a place where many have died." It was renamed the Isle of Wight, and later became better known as Gardiner's Island.

We have no way of knowing what went through Gardiner's mind as he watched these Indians put their marks on documents transferring ownership of this vast piece of land. He may have felt like one of F. Scott Fitzgerald's Dutch sailors who for one dramatic moment came face to face with something commensurate to his capacity for wonder. Gardiner, a forty-year-old veteran of the Dutch wars, who migrated to the New World in the employ of two Puritan lords, a hireling in an expanding empire, a shrewd survivor, suddenly found himself a lord of the manor.

And on his island, in the company of his Dutch wife and growing family, Gardiner dreamed what one might call feudal dreams. This was no mythic frontier of rough-hewn American democrats. The island society was an echo of another age, an anachronism that fate had tossed unexpectedly into the hands of a restless soldier. Not surprisingly, once Gardiner had taken possession of his estate, he held onto it with the tenacity of a military captain defending a walled city. This was his ground. Around him he gathered his servants, slaves, and tenants, dependents of three races working together in an isolated society that looked very little like the textbook Puritan villages of New England.

The old English soldier never fully trusted the Indians who had transformed him into an American gentleman. In a curious autobiographical account, written in 1660, he chided the New England colonists about their complacency in matters of defense. They concerned themselves with military matters—building forts and militia training—only when confronted with the outbreak of hostilities. Gardiner regarded them as soft, illprepared, easy marks for an Indian conspiracy. He warned his negligent contemporaries of the terrible price they would surely pay. "I am old," he observed, "[and] I would fain die a natural death, or like a soldier in the field, with honor, and not to have a sharp stake set in the ground, and thrust into my fundament, and to have my skin flayed off by piece-meal, and cut in pieces and bits, and my flesh roasted and thrust down my throat, as these people, and I know [it] will be done to the chiefest in the country by hundreds, if God should deliver us into their hands, as justly he may for our sins."

The Gardiner family and their laborers were living on the island when the first group of settlers arrived in East Hampton, and although Lion eventually took up residence in the village center, he never fully became part of the local community. His estate remained a world apart, a massive, mysterious presence where people without an invitation ventured at their own peril. Over the years Lion added more land to his sprawling holdings: a large Indian purchase in what is modern Smithtown and more acres on Montauk. The Gardiner wealth increased, and although his neighbors in East Hampton, ordinary farmers who harbored less exalted ambitions, deferred to the local lord, they may have had some misgivings about this soldier who stamped his personality so powerfully on the landscape. They had all heard odd stories about the island. Former tenants and servants moved to East Hampton, and sometimes in the privacy of a kitchen or over a glass of rum, they talked about how Lion pushed his people. His estate seemed to generate rumor and conflict. Later in the century, long after Lion had died, there were tales of pirates such as Captain Kidd visiting Gardiner's Island. To this day people swear that treasure lies buried somewhere on the estate.

Whatever may have happened on the island, no one could deny that Lion Gardiner had succeeded in the New World. Not only had he carved a great landed estate out of the wilderness, he also managed to pass his wealth and position on to his son. And from that Gardiner on to the next. From generation to generation male Gardiners guarded the manor. The family persevered. Changes in the colonial government, minor rebellions, national independence, the rise of an industrial republic, and

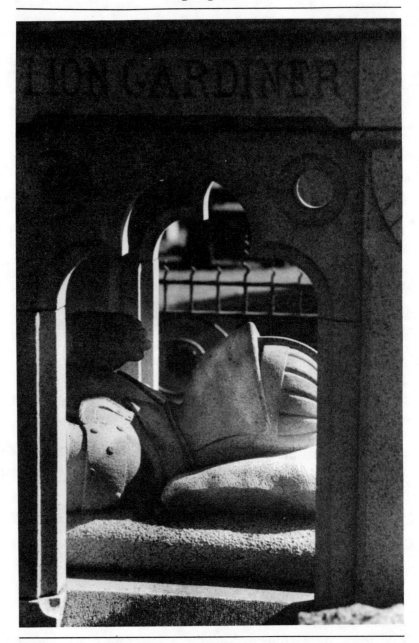

Lion Gardiner's Tomb

through it all the Gardiners hung on, feudal survivors in a modern society. A likeness of Lion in full armor lies on top of his tomb in the East Hampton cemetery. It is an appropriate remembrance. Amid the simple slate markers of his neighbors, the lord of the manor reigns still, an English knight at rest in American soil.

Lion's island still profoundly shapes how East Hampton imagines itself. It is a presence, like Ionesco's rhinoceros, too large to ignore and yet too alien to incorporate easily into familiar categories of description. For most modern inhabitants of East Hampton it is unknown ground, terra incognita, and it is said that the Gardiners employ watchmen to discourage strangers from exploring the manor. Fishermen told me of relatives and friends who had actually walked the island, but these tales almost always involved fleeting visits decades earlier. I suspect that even the most curious local residents would be disappointed if Gardiner's Island ever became a state park. Accessibility would destroy the mystery.

Robert Gardiner, the last of a long line of Gardiners, lives on Main Street in East Hampton, and although he professes to be extremely busy managing a shopping center located on Gardiner land in Smithtown, he agrees to talk to me about local history. The brownstone mansion that during the mid-nineteenth century served briefly as the summer White House for President John Tyler has seen better days. But although the stonework shows the effects of weather, the Gardiner house remains impressive.

Robert Gardiner shows me a collection of artifacts salvaged from Fort Saybrook. They are spread out on a great trestle table in the entrance hall. As we walk slowly through the spacious rooms, he draws my attention to the artwork. To the Thomas Moran, the Turner, the Salvador Dali, entire walls of paintings, some of them landscapes but most commemorating the Gardiners.

"We were rich a hundred and fifty years before the United States existed," Robert explains. His tone is matter-of-fact, as if he were commenting on the style of a particular piece of china. He asks no questions about my own background. The man seems anxious to demonstrate that later generations of Gardiners have fulfilled Lion's aristocratic ambitions. The island alone costs the family more than a million dollars in taxes, he states with undisguised pride. Such are the burdens of wealth. We make our way through accumulated objects, and, as I admire specific items, Robert reminds me, "We didn't do it with mirrors. We grew rich with America, and that is more than a lot of landed families did." One after another the American aristocrats have let down tradition, sold out, or simply faded into genteel poverty. For Robert Gardiner, each fall from wealth seems to represent a tragedy. Only a few families, like his own, have managed to resist the corrosive leveling spirit of our democratic society. "We have to survive," Robert warns, as if he expects to enlist me in the cause.

After a great while, I interrupt Gardiner's jeremiad. I remind him that I have come to East Hampton to discover how the past has shaped the present, how the town perceives its own history. Robert seems pleased. He has found most of the history that he has read—and here he appears to refer to all American history—fundamentally flawed. It has asked the wrong questions.

"I sympathize with you," he announces. "You do human history." We need no more histories of "fish and rocks and flowers," Robert explains. The challenge is "human history." By that he seems to mean a story of Gardiners. He is greatly annoyed, in fact, by local historians who in his estimation have denigrated the Gardiner contribution to the development of East Hampton. He clearly intends to set the record straight. Whatever period of East Hampton history we discuss, Robert immediately focuses on one of the many lords of the manor who have preceded him, from Gardiners and the governors of colonial New York, Gardiners and the pirates, Gardiners and the American Revolution, Gardiners in the White House, and Gardiners marrying into other aristocratic families.

"Do you know why East Hampton is two words rather than one?" he asks suddenly. I confess my ignorance. He wants to tell me the story. It seems that sometime during the nine-teenth century a sign painter was hired to make a sign for the local railway station. He had no idea how to spell the name of the town, and so he spelled it as two words, as East Hampton rather than as Easthampton. And East Hampton it has remained ever since.

We stroll through what once must have been an elegant renaissance-style garden. A path lined with Italian statuary leads back to a small pool. Robert tells me that many of the trees and flowering bushes were brought by his relatives to East Hampton from all parts of the world.

As I am about to take my leave, Robert tells me that not too long ago he traveled to England to meet the Queen. Un-fortunately, when he arrived at the banquet, he discovered that Elizabeth had gone off to Canada for some official function. No matter. Princess Margaret had taken her place. During the course of the evening a representative of the royal family ap-proached Robert, announcing that the Princess requested an introduction. An American aristocrat? How could there be such a thing? As they danced, Robert told Margaret the strange story of how a seventeenth-century Puritan soldier had acquired a lordship and manor on the eastern end of Long Island.

II

In the spring of 1648 the local Indians sold to a group of New Englanders the land that would soon become East Hampton. The exchange apparently pleased all parties. The governors of Connecticut and New Haven—then separate col-onies—and their "associates" acquired possession of most of the land east of the Southampton boundary. The Indians kept Montauk for themselves. Even so, there was no question that the New Englanders had purchased sufficient acreage for a new township. And the price seemed a real bargain. The sachems—as leaders of Indian bands were called—received an assortment of manufactured goods: twenty coats, twenty-four hatchets, twenty-four hoes, twenty-four knives, twenty-four looking glasses, and one hundred little metal drills known as muxes.

Though it would appear that the English negotiators pulled off a transfer rivaling the legendary purchase of Manhattan Island, the Indians knew what they were doing. In fact, they probably thought that they had got the best of the deal. The muxes were used to drill small holes in shells so that they then could be strung together as wampum, cylindrical beads manufactured from whelk shells (white) and quahog shells (violet). In other words, the Indians were quick to appreciate the value of European technology. Too often we see these exchanges as inevitably undermining traditional Native American culture, but in point of fact, so long as the Indians remained healthy, they perceived these trade items, especially the metal goods, as a way to improve a customary way of life. A change, to be sure, but not a threat. In this case, the sachems immediately realized that these metal drills would greatly expand the production of wampum.

The Indians also protected what today we might term their economic rights. Considering that they did not speak English nor probably understand the full common-law implications of signing a contract, they drove a hard bargain. The transfer of title, they insisted, would not deprive them of the liberty to fish in "the cricks and ponds" or to hunt "up and down in the woods." On their part, the Indians promised that while engaged in these activities, they would give the English "no just offense." It was a nice thought. They had no way of knowing that a "just offense" might mean something quite different to a European than to an Algonquian. The sachems claimed "the fins and tails" of whales washed up on the beaches and, perhaps most important, the right "to fish in all convenient places for Shells to make wampum." They had reason to be pleased. They had sold the land without compromising their traditional economic interests.

This contract and similar ones negotiated later in the century figure significantly in the historiography of East Hampton. The chroniclers take pride in the fact that the land was transferred from Indians to Europeans by means that in the official records at least seem to have been fair and generous. Presumably the colonists could have seized the land by force or employed strong drink to cheat the Indians out of their rights. Other New World settlers did so. Whatever may have actually occurred in 1648, the two governors and their associates quickly resold the land to a group of men described in a receipt as "the Inhabitants of East Hampton." These settlers paid a little over £30 for the land, a sum that apparently covered the cost of the goods that the two governors had already delivered to the Indians. It was this new group, of course, that would determine the meaning of "just offense" in future white-Indian relations.

We do not know much about the English background of East Hampton's first settlers. I was told repeatedly that many of the earliest inhabitants originated in and around Maidstone, a prosperous commercial center located in the county of Kent a few miles southeast of London. This may have been so, but the genealogical evidence neither confirms nor refutes it. To pin down the place of origin of families who happen to bear common English surnames is almost impossible. They might have come from Kent or, for that matter, Devon, Sussex, or the West Country. Moreover, names such as Mulford, which was unusual even in the seventeenth century, have generated a great, though inconclusive, tempest among family members who care about such matters. One faction traces the Mulfords to Devonshire; the other to Kent. In all probability these debates will never be resolved to anyone's satisfaction.

Except for the genealogists—a fierce tribe of researchers who show remarkably little interest in social history—such questions do not really matter. It is a good bet that the majority of the original East Hampton settlers came from southern England—in other words, from a region that in the reign of the early Stuarts already had a long history of commercial fishing and agriculture. The farmers of Kent sold their produce to the expanding metropolis of London. Even at this early date, the city contained nearly one-tenth of England's total population. This was also an area of the mother country that was swept up in the religious ferment known to its detractors as Puritanism.

Wherever their English homes may have been located, settlers traveled first to Massachusetts Bay, principally to Salem and Lynn. They were latecomers. Even during the first decade of American settlement, some communities complained of overcrowding. There was not enough land available in these established villages to allow new arrivals full grazing rights for their domestic animals. They grumbled about the "want of accommodation for their cattle." According to John Winthrop, the Bay Colony's first governor, many of these people were soon looking for new opportunities. "The occasion of their desire to remove was, for that all towns in the Bay began to be much straitened by their own nearness to one another, and their cattle being so much increased."

Some men and women migrated to the Massachusetts frontier or to the new colonies of Connecticut and New Haven. But for other families unhappy with conditions in Lynn and Salem, the towns of eastern Long Island seemed particularly inviting. Here were the large tracts of grazing land that had been denied them at Massachusetts Bay. During the 1640s many individuals who would eventually move to East Hampton took up residence in Southampton. We must assume that they were most concerned about their economic futures. None of them— at least so far as I know—expressed displeasure with the religious institutions of the Bay Colony. None was particularly distinguished. East Hampton attracted no Winthrops or Cottons, no Hookers or Mathers, indeed, probably not a single university graduate.

The "stockmen" who left Massachusetts wanted to share in the prosperity of the New World as well as to reform the Church of England. For them, there was no necessary conflict between meetinghouse and countinghouse. One could have both so long as one lived, or tried to live, according to Scripture. But however they worked out the balance, they must have found the commercial possibilities of East Hampton particularly alluring. These families had not traveled across the Atlantic in hope of creating a self-sufficient village, something they would

not have known in Kent or Devon, in any case. The simple life
held little appeal. In fact, these men and women had grown up
in a complex market economy in which farmers regularly sold
agricultural surplus. By searching out a locality where they
could raise large herds of livestock, in effect they were announcing their intention to produce marketable meat and hides.
They probably also anticipated making extra income from the
sale of whale products, oil and bone. Early colonial promoters
had promised a "great store of whales," and even before East
Hampton had been purchased from the Montauks, whaling had
become a minor industry in Southampton.

It is useful to remember that early East Hampton was not
originally conceived as a close-knit community. Some residents
had known each other in Southampton or in Lynn or perhaps
even in England, but these had not been necessarily close relationships. In fact, in a particularly bitter court battle involving
the Edwardses and the Prices, one witness hinted that Mrs.
Edwards had been as irascible in Lynn as she was in East Hampton. Whatever their differences may have been, they found
themselves largely for personal reasons settled on the eastern
end of Long Island. The point is that although the East Hampton
migrants were hardly strangers in 1650, they were as yet uncertain about just what sort of people their neighbors actually
were. Settlement was an experiment, a gamble, and during the
first years they had to learn to live with each other, a process
that involved testing and confrontation as well as what the New
England Puritans called "loving mediation."

Each original family received a house lot of several acres
located in the center of East Hampton. These were individual
holdings, private property, as important to the modest farmers
in providing them with recognized social status as was Gardiner's Island to the lord of the manor. It was only a question of
scale. Ownership of a house lot entitled each family unit to
additional strips of land in the common fields, which were
scattered over a wide area and included some pasture, some
arable land, and some woodlot.

The common fields, of course, required a different social

etiquette from the house lots. Within the village center one could essentially do as one pleased so long as it did not interfere with one's neighbors. Families were expected, for example, to keep their hogs from trespassing in other people's gardens; the character of each garden was determined solely by the farmer who actually put out the seed. Each owner decided what herbs and vegetables to grow, where to locate the woodpile, and how best to arrange the outbuildings. By contrast, the common field demanded constant cooperation. Such matters as the quality and design of fences, the number of cattle allowed each family, and the annual schedule for planting and harvest required general agreement, a product of discussion and compromise.

Village government provided a forum for making such decisions. It is not known exactly what the East Hampton settlers had in mind when they devised a local constitution. In all probability, they drew upon the experiences that they had had in England as well as America. The town records do not mention a searching debate into the character of magistracy or the nature of franchise. The system simply took root. The adult male inhabitants of East Hampton who owned house lots selected each year a group of "townsmen" to run local affairs. Their positions combined administrative and judicial functions.

From a modern perspective, it is easy to exaggerate the importance of these figures in determining the character of village life. We find it almost impossible not to think of elected officials as being "politicians," or at the very least as persons preoccupied with problems that we would label as "political." But that would be grossly anachronistic. The townsmen of early East Hampton focused most of their energies on making a living. They did not run for office or, for that matter, present rival visions for the development of the village. Like most people who find themselves in such situations, they dealt with problems as they arose and probably wondered in the privacy of their families why they had ever agreed to serve.

It is not surprising to learn that some men held office more frequently than did others. We have no precise idea why this was so. Perhaps they were richer than their neighbors, or more pious, or more talented, or more ambitious. Or perhaps they were temperamentally the kind of people who accept such responsibilities. Considering how few early records have survived, it would be crudely reductionist to assume that political leadership was merely a function of how many acres or animals a person owned.

Whatever the rules of selection may have been, contemporary Dutch settlers living in what would become colonial New York viewed this participatory form of government with unconcealed envy. It was reported that colonists living in towns like East Hampton "have an election every year and have power to make a change in case of improper behavior, and that, they therefore say, is the bridle of their great men." From the perspective of New Amsterdam, in those days an autocratically run company town, the government of the New England villages probably possessed considerable appeal. It certainly did so for later American historians who sang the praises of frontier democracy.

Curiously, however, the early settlers of East Hampton seem to have been reluctant democrats. Selection to public office appears to have been regarded more as a burden than an honor, and the town established stiff penalties for anyone who without "sufficient reason" refused to serve. Attendance at village meetings, "general courts" as they were called, was made mandatory, and the "townsmen" imposed hefty fines on neighbors who did not bother to show up for elections. It was not that inhabitants did not appreciate their political rights or that they would have accepted a less open system. Rather, the founders of East Hampton took participation in local affairs largely for granted. If they had a particular grievance, they could make a fuss. If not, as they quickly discovered, village government could be a little tedious.

Even more remarkable than the establishment of democratic forms—and neither the founders of East Hampton nor their co-religionists in New England were the least bit interested in what today we would call a genuine democracy—is the settlers' insistence on due process. Their sense of the common law did not involve specific statutes or English court decisions. Indeed, there is no reason to believe that anyone in East Hampton had received formal legal training. The founders thought of the common law as a vague, though powerful, guarantee of the rights of property against arbitrary authority. Unlike some other colonial American settlements, such as early Jamestown, East Hampton set up clear legal procedures. The elected constable had to issue warrants in the proper manner. There were witnesses to be called, forms to be observed, and records to be kept. When one particularly difficult case was carried to the high court at Hartford, the Connecticut judges gratuitously commended the "townsmen" of East Hampton for the care that they had taken in gathering depositions. The local magistrates knew their own limits; they refused to hear criminal matters involving "life and limb": in other words, major offenses that traditionally called for capital punishment.

I am not suggesting that officials in East Hampton did not make mistakes or that they did not on occasion act in a high-handed manner. They surely did, but, admitting this, it is not very productive to focus on their failings. Rather, we should appreciate how much what might justly be called the spirit of the law pervaded daily affairs in this town, structuring human relations and determining access to economic resources. Insomuch as there were winners and losers in early East Hampton, they were winners and losers before the law. However loosely defined, it was the glue that kept an amorphous community from becoming a Hobbesian reality.

Most issues coming before the townsmen did not require the attention of a keen legal mind. The members of the local government spent most of their time monitoring an annual agricultural routine. This involved not only setting dates for moving the town herd or planting the common fields, but also making certain that no one took advantage of a neighbor by cutting too much wood or by neglecting to construct adequate fences.

The language of the regulations has a marvelous precision.

The men who wrote them knew every feature of the landscape, the habits of their animals, and the shifting demands of an agricultural calendar. A local ordinance passed in 1653 ordered "that the cows, calves, and oxen shall be put into the plain, first the new plain and then the little plain and then the great plain and last the Eastern plain, and this is to be done when the herd breaks up." On another occasion the wording of an order revealed irritation. "No Cattle of what kind soever," the townsmen declared, "shall be kept or turned into the Common land within the general fence belonging to the plain to be baited [fed] during the time of this late part of this Summer until the Constable and Overseers give liberty for the town to turn their Cattle into the plain." The sheep had to be removed from Montauk so "that the feed might be preserved for the relief of other Creatures."

Fences, even more than the menace of what the town fathers labeled "unruly swine," dominated the agenda of town meetings. It may be true that good fences make good neighbors. What the poet did not consider is what sort of fences. This matter was the subject of intense debate in early East Hampton, and well it should have been. If even one man's share of the fence around the common field was not built properly, then the harvest of every inhabitant was at risk.

One of the earliest local regulations ordered each man— that is, each man who possessed a home lot—to fence the land he "enjoyed." The more land he owned, the more fence he constructed. Town officials soon levied fines against delinquents. The question quickly escalated, raising sticky problems of tort law. In fact, although they did not use the phrase, the settlers of East Hampton developed a doctrine of "contributory negligence." According to an order of 1651, a man who failed to protect his corn with an adequate fence could not demand damages from the owner of a hungry cow who wandered uninvited into the field. But if a hog—really a tank of an animal— leveled a strong fence to reach the corn, the farmer could seek compensation.

Bucolic concerns, to be sure, but however close to nature

the early East Hampton settlers may have been, theirs was not a world that we should romanticize. The lost preindustrial villages that have been so lovingly recreated as living museums throughout modern New England required a firm regulatory hand. The common good—even in the seventeenth century— never took care of itself. Whatever expressions of public cooperation we encounter in early East Hampton depended as much on the will of the townsmen as it did on shared religious values or a common English background. There is no question that such elements helped promote smooth relations within the village, but even in the covenanted communities of New England, someone in authority had to prod reluctant farmers to contribute to the general welfare.

These same villagers confronted each other every Sunday in the impressive local church, which they constructed within a few years of the founding of the village. Although we have almost no direct information about religious practices in early East Hampton, we assume that the church figured centrally in the life of the town. Other New England villages, Salem and Boston, for example, organized the community around the meetinghouse.

The town's first minister, the Reverend Thomas James, seems to have been a great success. His parishioners voted to give him a generous salary; they excused him from paying taxes. But no list of his church members has survived. We do not even know how one became a member of the East Hampton church or who selected the minister or if the congregation elected elders. Did James possess what a New Englander like John Cotton might have regarded as autocratic powers? These were precisely the kinds of issues that divided other congregations, and, during the early years of settlement, they may have created factions within East Hampton.

The absence of such information can lead to all sorts of unwarranted claims about the founders of East Hampton. It tempts us to forget that these were the theological children of John Calvin. In fact, by concentrating our attention on the political events recorded in the town records, we tend to transform the men and women of East Hampton into secular beings, into persons who would sooner talk about the price of cattle than about eternal damnation. They become in our imaginations modern folk—no brooding Puritans here.

Such a conclusion would involve an understandable lapse of historical judgment. This is the type of problem that long bedeviled Etruscan scholars. Since most of the information about these mysterious pre-Roman people came from tombs, interpreters insisted that the Etruscans must have placed greater significance on the rituals of death than on other aspects of life. But, of course, the Etruscans played and loved, gossiped about trade and politics, acted pretty much like members of other ancient cultures. The interpretation reflected the survival of a particular kind of evidence, not how the Etruscans actually lived. By the same token, our apparently "political" or "economic" East Hampton settlers were also God-fearing Puritans, men and women who if they had remained in England would surely have flocked to the standard of Oliver Cromwell.

One historian calls attention in a powerfully evocative phrase to early East Hampton's "densely collective existence." Perhaps it is an accurate description. My reading of the surviving records suggests, however, that it lays too much stress on the "collective" and not enough on the "individual." Even in the initial years of settlement, there were structural strains that like great fault lines divided neighbors who regularly worked side by side in the common fields. It would be excessive to claim that East Hampton's inhabitants had been touched by the spirit of modern capitalism. But there is no doubt—and here I risk sounding like the great Fourth of July orator Judge Henry Hedges—that each family in this village knew exactly what it owned, each animal, each piece of land, each tree. They defined the landscape through personal possessions, and although the farmer was compelled during the earliest years to follow regulations established ostensibly for the common good, he kept an eye out for the main chance, for the particular interests of his own family. The townsmen understood the tensions. In 1652 they ordered every man to demarcate his plot with "four sufficient stakes or land marks in their meadow between man and man." Between man and man; *meum* and *tuum*. That was a language of private property that the founders of this village could fully appreciate.

But it was not the whole story. The early settlers of East Hampton *did* enjoy a rich collective existence. There was no necessary conflict between the individual and the group at this early stage of the town's development. After all, they faced common problems, such as defense, that they could not solve as individuals. The adult males of East Hampton served in the village militia, and although they were never called upon to fight, they feared that the Dutch might stir up trouble among the local Indians. If they were like the militia of the other American colonies, they probably viewed training more as a social event than as an activity vital to the security of the village.

III

The whales crystallized the tensions between individual and community. In the winter months, smaller species migrated from the Arctic Ocean to the waters off Long Island. During the seventeenth century, the most common whale in this region was the Atlantic right whale, sometimes called the "whalebone whale." In *Moby-Dick* Melville described the various kinds of whales, including the "right" or "true" whale. The name apparently distinguishes this particular baleen feeder from other types of whales that do not yield so much oil. They must have been friendly, rather slow-swimming creatures.

From time to time during the winter, a dead whale would wash up on one of East Hampton's ocean beaches. These were termed "drift whales," from which the Montauk Indians claimed the fins and tails. For the farmers of East Hampton the right whales represented a marvelous bonus. In most New England towns the winter months were a largely unproductive season, a period of waiting between the autumn harvest and the

View of Northwest Harbor

spring planting. But here, there seemed to be the promise of a harvest of another sort.

The founders treated the drift whales as an extension of the commons. Since the beaches of East Hampton belonged to the landed inhabitants, it seemed reasonable that a dead whale became the possession of the village proprietors. In any case, the town quickly exploited this opportunity to bring in extra income. It organized regular "whale watches" that were physically far more demanding than militia service. In 1650 local officials divided the householders of East Hampton into two groups. As soon as a beached whale was reported, one of two teams of men was supposed to turn out immediately. Even in the winter, the body of the whale decomposed rapidly, and the cutting of the blubber could not be long postponed. It was nasty, smelly work; the men were probably cold and wet. There was considerable risk of being slashed by one of the long knives as the villagers hacked away.

It is worth examining the precise language of East Hampton's first whaling regulation: "It is ordered that if any whales be cast up within our bounds that every householder shall do his part of the work about cutting them out according as his turn shall come." The word *householder* is of particular interest. Every able-bodied male was expected to participate in military training. Whaling, however, was from the very beginning a more exclusive activity. One had to own property—just how much is not defined—in order to share in the profits from the oil and the bone.

I doubt that in 1650 anyone in East Hampton could predict how much money the winter harvest would yield. Whatever the expectations may have been, the town records reveal that officials took the disposition of the drift whales quite seriously. Rewards were established for anyone discovering a carcass, and men who did not respond to the lookout's call were fined five shillings. "If any Englishman of the Town do accidentally find a whale," the town announced, "and do bring the first tidings of it, he shall have a piece of whale 3 foot broad." The finder, of course, need not have been a householder. He could be a servant or a tenant, and there is the suggestion in the wording of this regulation that town leaders suspected that some people in the town might be tempted to keep the "first tidings" of a drift whale to themselves.

In December 1653—for reasons not stated in the records—the town passed what may be termed a "whale code," a series of ordinances setting forth the precise obligations of every man in East Hampton. The regulations represented a tightening of control over the drift whales. The code was divided into three separate sections, and I quote them in full, if for no other purpose than to share with the reader the peculiar syntax of the earliest town records.

It is ordered that every man do look out for whale as his turn comes, being lawfully warned by the man authorized by the town for that work and for the neglect herein to forfeit five shillings and to stand the censure of the court.

Secondly, the town being divided in two parts are to have two overseers to see that every man do his work, and that all [whales?] be cut so near as may be, and if any man do neglect his labor in cutting, he shall be censured by the overseers and his company, according to the nature of his offence.

Thirdly, that the whale being divided, every lot that the town gives out, from thirteen acres and upward shall have his share, being possessed and inhabited: the division of the town for this work is between Thomas Chatfield's and Ralph Dayton's and Thomas Tomson's and Thomas Baker's, the overseers for the South end are John Hand and Robert Bond and for the North end, Thomas Baker and Benjamin Price.

These regulations contain curious elements. It is not clear, for example, if the "men" mentioned in the first and second sections—in other words, the people who were expected to labor on the beaches—were the same persons who were entitled to a share of the whale. My reading is that every man, regardless of his status in the village, was obliged to turn out for whale duty but that only inhabitants who owned a developed, thirteen-acre homelot actually profited from the find. The phrasing is ambiguous, and it is possible that the town secretary, fatigued by sitting through a long public meeting, simply took the meaning of certain words for granted. Still, it would seem that these regulations substantially revised the ordinance of 1650. Even more interesting is the assumption that men could be shamed by their neighbors into participating in the butchering of the whales. The censure of one's company, used here in the sense that one belongs to a fire or militia company, could shape conduct as powerfully as a five-shilling fine.

We have no direct evidence about the income actually generated by the drift whales. I have found no receipts or production figures. But there are hints that the whales were becoming an ever more important facet of the local economy. In 1657 the townsmen ordered that "whoever shall desert his lot and leave the town destitute of an inhabitant by that means, he shall lose his part of whale." A few people were apparently willing to hold onto vacant land in East Hampton simply to gain a share of the blubber and bone.

We do not know how the settlers during this period transformed "pieces" of whale into marketable oil. The heating process, known as trying, would have required a large, strong metal vat, and although each man may have tried his own oil, it seems unlikely that he did so. For one thing, the purchase of a huge kettle would have represented a substantial capital outlay, and at the very least, we might expect families of East Hampton to have shared the necessary implements. Moreover, there was obviously a problem of quality control. The larger the number of separate triers, the greater the chance of many separate failures. If the East Hampton oil acquired a reputation for unreliability, merchants from New Amsterdam or Boston would not have bothered to purchase it. Nor do we possess any information from this early period about coopers, the men who would have made the barrels in which the finished oil was shipped.

There is something to be learned from this declaration of ignorance. The production of whale oil, even when the animals conveniently washed up on the local beaches, was a demanding process, one that required a sizable capital investment, expertise in the trying of blubber, and access to finished, liquid-tight barrels. Put simply, this was not, as it first appeared, an activity that fit smoothly into the routine of the family farm. Stated in different terms, the local economy suffered from a structural problem, and although the settlers of East Hampton attempted to treat the processing of the drift whales as a collective venture, much like tending the common herd or drilling the militia, they were moving rapidly toward a moment when these strains would have to be resolved. Some men would be farmers engaged in mixed animal husbandry, some would be whalers, and a few managed to be both.

*   *   *

That moment had not been reached by 1662. In that year the town reorganized the harvesting of drift whales. It set up three companies, eleven men each, under the direction of two overseers. Presumably the blubber was still to be divided among the owners of the home lots, but if everyone in East Hampton was involved in the winter business, some were clearly more equal than others. The regulation announced that "it is fully agreed that Mr. James and Mr. Gardiner shall give a quart of liquor a piece to the cutters of every whale and be free from cutting." This was probably a good deal for the shivering men who hacked away at the water's edge. The whiskey at least warmed the blood. For Gardiner and James, it was a gamble much like that taken on by baseball players who promise to give a certain amount of money to charity every time they hit a home run. In a good year the local minister and the lord of the manor might have to provide their neighbors with a case or more of "liquor."

One point about the drift whale in early East Hampton requires additional clarification. Some historians describe the communities of colonial New England as "preindustrial." By that, they seem to mean that the people who inhabited these villages were not what we would recognize as capitalists. They apparently did not produce goods for profits alone. Nor, for that matter, did they allow market forces to determine work routines. Much of this kind of thinking has been incorporated into the mythology of East Hampton.

It would be ludicrous to claim that the settlers of East Hampton did not worry about feeding their families. There were minimal levels of security that had to be reached before one could consider selling grain or livestock. But even accepting these conditions, this sort of reasoning turns ultimately on a false dichotomous proposition: *either* the town was a close-knit, cooperative society not yet penetrated by the market economy, *or* it was a collection of capitalists eager to maximize return on investment. In point of fact, the two positions are not mutually exclusive. The farmers of East Hampton cooperated in cutting up the whales that washed up on the beaches, *and* they also tried to sell the oil produced from these creatures for a good price on the world market. Even in 1650 this was not a self-sufficient economy. It would be more accurate to describe early East Hampton as a rural society characterized by its commercial activities, or even better, by its preindustrial capitalism.

The townspeople seem to have understood the subtle mechanisms by which the market establishes price. In the records of East Hampton one does not encounter set or rigid prices for goods. Local producers sold their harvests for whatever the merchants happened to be offering. Indeed, the farmers seem to have appreciated just how rapidly these figures could fluctuate. When East Hampton engaged a man to build a mill, for example, the townsmen promised him £50. Several payments were to be made in goods, not cash. "The corn and pork," they stated, "[are] to be paid at the price current upon Long Island and in the Eastern part of it, and for cattle as two indifferent men shall value them." In 1657 all the inhabitants of East Hampton at a full town meeting voted to pay the Reverend Mr. James's salary "in good merchantable pay as it will pass current to the merchant." Another example comes from a complex indenture negotiated in 1664. One party in this contract pledged to deliver a sum of money, "in good merchantable wheat, corn, beef, pork, oil, or cattle, as two indifferent men shall prize them according as wheat at 4s. 6d. per bushel, Indian [corn] at 3s. per bushel, pork at 3£ 10s. per barrel, beef at 50s. per barrel, and [whale] oil at [the] price current with the merchant." The whale products were obviously the most volatile. Even in the earliest years of settlement, the local economy reacted to the markets in England and Holland.

Again, the point is not that the farmers of East Hampton failed to develop a rich collective existence. Of course, they did. But by the same token, the settlers were also integrated into a larger market economy. During the early years, both features of this society—its traditional forms of economic cooperation and its growing dependence upon an expanding Atlantic market—helped shape the organization of local oil production.

Neighbors did work together on the "whale watch." They endured physical hardship and danger in part because they cared about what other villagers thought of them. They could be shamed into diligence. At the same time, the driving engine of this particular activity was the expectation of obtaining a good price at a distant market.

IV

*L*ittle is known about the pre-Conquest history of the Montauk Indians who sold the land that would become East Hampton. The Algonquian Indians of this region did not have a written language, and therefore, our only knowledge about their culture comes from two equally unsatisfactory sources. Archeologists have uncovered various Indian artifacts at what appear to have been camps and grave sites. Although these materials are valuable in reconstructing some aspects of the Indian past, they do not provide much insight into what these people actually thought. The arrowheads and stone tools are disappointingly silent about an emotional universe that must have involved love and hate, joy and envy, pain and ecstasy. Descriptions of Indian life provided by the settlers are somewhat more helpful, but they also present us with severe interpretive problems. They show us the Native American as seen through European eyes. The bias is a function of the source. Even the most sympathetic observers of seventeenth-century New England, such as John Eliot of Massachusetts Bay and Roger Williams of Rhode Island, depicted the Indians in ways that their white readers could comprehend. The very categories of print analysis were alien to the culture of the Native Americans.

Still, we must do the best we can with what has survived. The Montauks were Algonquians. On the eve of the conquest of North America, these people were found along the Atlantic coast from North Carolina to eastern Canada. While the Algonquians were not a tribe in any meaningful, political sense, they have been grouped together by scholars largely for linguistic reasons, much as the Romanians and the Portuguese are today. The Indians of eastern Long Island spoke Monegan-Pequot, a language they shared with the Indians living in southeastern Connecticut.

The Montauks apparently maintained regular contact with the Pequots and Narragansetts who occupied southern New England. With the other Algonquian bands living on Long Island, they developed even closer ties, and it is said that Wyandanch, an important Montauk sachem at the time of the purchase of East Hampton, exercised political hegemony over these neighboring Indians. The Long Island bands never formed a confederacy, and in all probability Wyandanch's powers were nominal.

The Montauks migrated with the changing seasons. The town records of East Hampton mention "wigwams," portable housing that the Indians must have carried from place to place. They did not own horses. However, they did construct huge canoes, and the sea seems to have figured centrally in the development of the Montauk economy. One scholar suggests that they were not very good farmers. Perhaps the sandy soils of the eastern end of Long Island were to blame for their poor performance. Whatever the explanation, the Montauks were apparently forced from time to time to buy food, and to do so, they used wampum, money made from the abundant local shells. Even before the arrival of the English settlers, the Montauks had begun to specialize in the manufacture of this bead currency, and by the late 1620s the production of wampum had become the chief winter activity of the Indians of eastern Long Island. Other Indians, located as far away as Albany, accepted wampum in trade; even the early European colonists employed it. In fact, the Montauks seem to have established a successful Native American mint. It should now be clear why the local Indians were so eager to obtain a supply of muxes. Quite literally, they intended to make money with western technology, and although the term is probably anachronistic, it is not surprising that some historians have referred to the members of Wyandanch's band as "entrepreneurs."

The Montauks do not appear to have regarded the English settlers as potential enemies or, for that matter, as a serious threat to their way of life. The records suggest that the Indians of eastern Long Island thought that they were in control of the situation. After all, it was Wyandanch who initially approached Lion Gardiner, who was then the officer in charge of the small English fort at Saybrook. The Indian leader had apparently heard rumors that the colonists were planning a major military campaign against the Pequots, a powerful tribe that demanded and received tribute from the weaker Montauks. Wyandanch thought that Gardiner and his Puritan allies might help liberate the Long Island Indians from Pequot tyranny. The Montauk sachem was also eager to establish regular trade with the English outpost.

In his "Relation of the Pequot Warres," published in 1660, Gardiner records the details of his first conversation with Wyandanch. The sachem allegedly "came to know if we were angry with *all* Indians. I answered No, but only with such as had killed Englishmen. He asked me whether they that lived upon Long-Island might come to trade with us." Gardiner sensed immediately that he had the upper hand in these negotiations. How, he asked Wyandanch, could he open trade when in all probability the Pequots would murder the English as soon as they landed on Long Island? How could Gardiner be sure that the Montauks were not in league with the Pequots? A murder, even if not committed by one of Wyandanch's band, might spark a war between the English and the Montauks. To this argument the Indian countered, "If we may have peace and trade with you, we will give you tribute, as we did the Pequits [sic]." Gardiner was after tribute of a different sort, however, insisting, "If you have any Indians that have killed English, you must bring their heads also. . . . So he [Wyandanch] went away and did as I had said, and sent me five heads."

As we have seen, New England troops nearly exterminated the Pequots. The destruction of such a formidable group convinced the Narragansetts, the Pequots' oldest enemies, that the European presence in New England had radically transformed the character of war and commerce. The English were not normal trade partners. They defined relations with the Indians in terms of domination rather than reciprocity, and, even at this early date, it was becoming clear, at least to the Narragansetts, that alliances with the whites only served the interests of the settlers, for as soon as the Europeans achieved their goals—be it land or furs—they turned against their Indian allies. That was the lesson of the Pequot War. Whose turn would be next? The Narragansetts'? The Montauks'?

These were questions that Miantonomi, a Narragansett sachem, asked a Montauk assembly in 1642. Lion Gardiner recorded this Indian's remarkable speech:

> We are all Indians as the English are, and say brother to one another; so must we be one as they are, otherwise we shall be all gone shortly, for you know our fathers had plenty of deer and skins, our plains were full of deer, as also our woods, and of turkies, and our coves full of fish and fowl. But these English having gotten our land, they with scythes cut down the grass, and with axes fell the trees; their cows and horses eat the grass, and their hogs spoil our clam banks, and we shall all be starved; therefore it is best for you to do as we, for we are all the Sachems from east to west.

This proposal for pan-Indian cooperation fell on deaf ears, for Wyandanch did not trust the Narragansett spokesman. Ancient animosities, suspicions that probably predated European settlement, made the prospect of an alliance seem more a threat than an opportunity. The Montauk leader threw in his lot with the English. Indeed, he betrayed the Narragansett sachem. But Wyandanch badly misplayed his hand. In a series of battles against the Narragansetts, the Long Island band took a terrible beating. A great armada of war canoes that the Montauks dispatched to the mainland was destroyed at sea, and soon Narragansett raiding parties were attacking Montauk fortifications near East Hampton with relative impunity.

Faced with almost certain annihilation at the hands of their old enemies, the Montauks begged their English neighbors to come to their assistance. For the settlers of East Hampton, this does not seem to have been a difficult decision. To some extent, their own security was at risk. The Narragansetts had killed a Southampton woman and damaged property throughout the South Fork. Once the Europeans joined the fight, the marauders were easily driven off. The status of the Montauks, however, was never the same. Commissioners from the three English towns—Southampton, Southold, and East Hampton—informed the local Indians that the English would defend them "provided that the said Indians on Long Island do not begin new Quarrels, but behave themselves quietly without provocation."

Their military misadventure effectively reduced the Montauks to clients of the white community. It was a change that would undoubtedly have taken place in any case. The Narragansett war merely accelerated a process that brought the Native Americans into dependency upon the European colonists. Other factors contributed to the erosion of the status of the local Indians. As other currencies began to circulate throughout the region, the demand for wampum fell off rapidly. And so, by the late 1650s the Montauks had nothing else to offer the settlers of East Hampton except land and the drift whales found on the beaches still owned by the Indians.

It was an indication of their growing marginality that the Montauks gave special favors to men in the village whom they identified as potential patrons: in other words, to individuals who seemed to be the sachems of the English settlement. In November 1658 Wyandanch announced, "Of my own voluntary motion and upon consideration known to myself, [I] do give unto Mr. Thomas James, Minister of Easthampton, the one half of all the whales or other great fish [that] shall at any time be cast up upon the Beach from Napeague eastward to the end of the Island." The other half of these whales went to "my friend" Lieutenant Lion Gardiner. The weakness of Wyandanch's position must have been obvious to all parties involved. All he could demand in return was that the two Englishmen "shall give to me or to my children and successors . . . what they shall judge meet, and according as they find profit by them." Perhaps the sachem realized that the men of his band did not have the technical expertise necessary to try whale oil. Whatever his reasoning, his successors would soon discover that the colonists did not judge it meet to give the Indians much of anything at all.

The local Indians were in time decimated by contagious diseases such as smallpox and measles, against which they possessed no immunity. From an account of Native American culture written by Daniel Denton in 1670, we obtain an appreciation not only of the destruction of the Algonquian bands of Long Island, but also of how the English interpreted the extraordinary death of so many Indians.

> To say something of the Indians, there is now but few upon the Island, and those few no ways hurtful, but rather serviceable to the English, and it is to be admired how strangely they have decreast by the Hand of God, since the English first settling of those parts . . . and it hath been generally observed, that where the English come to settle, a Divine Hand makes ways for them, by removing or cutting off the Indians either by Wars one with the other, or by some raging mortal disease.

With regard to the Montauks, Denton probably exaggerated the numbers involved. They did not die off as rapidly as those Indians living closer to Boston or New York City. The climate of the South Fork may have contributed to better health. Whatever factors may have been involved, the survival of a good number of Montauks—exact figures are of course impossible to obtain—meant that East Hampton would remain a genuine biracial society for at least the rest of the seventeenth century. Later the colonists introduced African-Americans into the town, but during the first two decades, it was primarily whites and Indians who had to learn to live with each other.

During the earliest years of settlement, the English looked upon the Montauks with suspicion. Although Wyandanch pledged his friendship, some colonists apparently feared that the Indians might ally with the Dutch and attempt to drive the English from Long Island. In this situation, the inhabitants of East Hampton thought it prudent to keep the Native Americans at a distance. They were not welcomed in the village center, and when they did appear, the settlers watched their movements closely. In 1653 the Townsmen ordered that "no Indian shall come to the town unless it be upon special occasion, and none to come armed because . . . the Dutch hath hired Indians against the English and we not knowing Indians by face." One can only guess how long it took an Englishman to identify an Indian by face.

The boundary between the two cultures was even more tightly drawn in 1656. The whites passed what might be termed a code of racial etiquette. It is a revealing statement.

> It is ordered that no man shall let any ground to any Indian for to plant on, upon penalty of 2£ for every acre.
>
> It is also ordered that no wigwams shall be set up by any Indian whatsoever within our bounds without leave of the town on the penalty of paying 2£ 10sh.
>
> It is ordered that whatever Indian do set any traps, if he or they be found that set it shall pay the sum of 2£ 10sh.
>
> It is also ordered that no Indian shall travel up & down or carry any burdens in or through our town on the Sabbath Day & whoever be found so doing shall be liable to *corporal punishment* according unto the nature of the offense.

As one reviews these regulations, one should recall the original agreement transferring ownership of the land from the Indians to the English. The Montauks promised not to give the newcomers "just offense" in the territory that they had just purchased. The Indians clearly thought that they retained use of the land, the right to catch fish and hunt for animals. Only a few years after they had signed this contract, however, they found themselves warned off the land. One also notes that East Hampton officials were loath to administer corporal punishment to an English person. Legal matters of that nature were taken to Connecticut. A different standard was in place, however, for Indians who wandered about the village on Sunday.

None of this is unusual. The story was repeated throughout colonial America. The idea that the two races developed a special relationship in East Hampton simply does not stand up. The Indians of the South Fork were "friendly"—the word comes from a twentieth-century history of the town—largely because they had no other choice.

The Montauks had gambled that their alliance with Gardiner and the other settlers would translate into power over the Narragansetts; when that strategy backfired, they found themselves even more dependent upon the English. Local Indians occasionally accepted minor jobs such as watching the town herd. They petitioned for favors. Mostly they became shadowy figures, constantly interacting with settler families but somehow always a little out of focus. A few years before Wyandanch died (poisoned, it is said, by the members of his own tribe), he gave a large chunk of land to Lion Gardiner. The wording of this deed poignantly reveals how the once powerful sachem now addressed his English patron. Or perhaps it reveals how the Englishman who created the text thought that a fallen sachem should address a triumphant patron.

> We had great comfort and relief from the most honourable of the English nation here about us; so that seeing we yet live, and both of us being now old, and not that we at any time have given him anything to gratify his fatherly love, care, and charge, we having nothing else that is worth his acceptance but a small tract of land.

Actually the Montauks had one other thing to give, the labor of their bodies, but until the English discovered that the right whales could be successfully pursued offshore, they showed no interest in promoting the well-being of this dwindling Algonquian band.

V

*A*nyone reading a modern genealogical history of East Hampton cannot but wonder how certain names came to be included, others excluded. The selection process represents a greater problem than might at first appear. We must consider the claim of certain local families to be the legitimate founders of this community. We know that families with particular surnames—those of the great East Hampton clans—somehow acquired special historical standing within East Hampton. How did they do it?

The answer involves a dialogue between the past and present. The chroniclers of the nineteenth and twentieth centuries surely made decisions about who did and who did not deserve inclusion as charter members of this community. To some extent the selection process—one that occurs in every community—reflected social realities at the time when the lists were actually compiled, but this line of thought can be pushed only so far. Although later generations may have manipulated the past for their own ends, they did not invent the names. The original settlers also had a say in the process of inventing a community.

During the earliest years of settlement, East Hampton consisted of a collection of relative strangers, migrants who did not really know very much about their neighbors' backgrounds. With the exception of Lion Gardiner, these colonists began as social equals. Some families may have been slightly richer than others, but initially these distinctions do not seem to have been very great. After all, each householder received a sizable home lot and a share in future land divisions.

Social equality, however, was not their goal. Within two decades the settlers of East Hampton had created a rough hierarchical order. Expressed in more familiar language, they had determined who were the winners and the losers of early East Hampton. In mythic accounts, the history of the town takes this process for granted or begins the story after it had already run its course, but this approach is wrongheaded. What we today call the original "community," the very core of any historical interpretation that posits the existence of a lost Golden Age, was in fact a group of families who managed to rise to the top of East Hampton society and who in a later period would dominate its economic resources.

The ordering of any society is a cooperative activity. One can always claim a certain status, but if others refuse to recognize its legitimacy, the claimant is exposed as something less than he or she maintains. How those who settled in early East Hampton actually sorted themselves out is a murky business. Modern historians often assume that wealth is always the critical variable: the richer the family, the higher its social standing. But the evidence supporting such claims frequently turns out to be nothing more than the accidental survival of records related to the accumulation of property. Government bureaucracies from the ancient Greeks to the present day have sedulously recorded people's names for the purpose of generating revenue; as a result, we often discover that the only information we have about someone is where he (rarely she) stood on a tax list. Other elements that gave meaning to the lives of ordinary people in the past have generally been lost. In East Hampton, therefore, we find ourselves at an extraordinary disadvantage. There is only one document from the earliest years that could possibly be labeled a tax list, and it is grossly incomplete.

At this point we must confront the limits of our own historical knowledge and admit how we have been radically cut off from the past. We have no way to determine exactly why the town secretary occasionally referred to Joshua Garlick and his wife as *Goodman* Garlick and *Goody* Garlick. These deferential terms of address do not appear to have been a reflection of Garlick's wealth. His name stood near the bottom of a list of villagers who contributed to the construction of a new meetinghouse. Lion Gardiner and Thomas James almost always appear as "Mr." Gardiner was clearly the richest man in East Hampton, but the Reverend Mr. James did not own a manor. Why then does he fall into the same category as Gardiner? And what of the apparent inconsistencies in the town records? Some-

times a person is listed only by a surname, other times as Goodman. These may be mistakes, or they may indicate that a man's
status, like the price of common stock, could dramatically rise
and fall within only a few months.

On the basis of such fragmentary records, there is no sat-
isfactory way to answer these questions. The rules for ranking
families in East Hampton must remain obscure, and that in itself
may be revealing. The procedures governing social standing
may not have been very clear even to the original inhabitants.
The confusion may help to explain why the local magistrates
spent a remarkable amount of time hearing disputes involving
slander and defamation. These were essentially status contests,
public challenges among families unsure of where they stood
in the local hierarchy.

What makes the cases both unusual and significant is the
participation of the women of East Hampton. When other formal town business was under consideration, women rarely appeared in the records. They exist just outside our field of
historical vision. We encounter them as wives, mothers, and
occasionally as inheritors of property. They remain obscure
figures; they do not have distinct personalities at the distance
of three centuries. The defamation trials are a dramatic exception. Here the women of East Hampton come alive. We see
them circulating through the village, visiting neighbors, chat-
ting about their families, and carrying tales.

Another curious feature of the slander and defamation cases
is the frequency with which they came before the justices of
East Hampton. Between 1650 and 1665, this type of dispute
appeared in the town records significantly more often than any
other form of legal action. To be sure, the local judges struggled
with several lengthy contests involving alleged breaches of contract, but those suits did not match the defamation cases in
complexity and number. At one time or another, almost everyone in the town seems to have participated in the trials. No one
was exempt; Lion Gardiner, Thomas James, and William Mulford accused others of defamation. So too, did John Wooley, a
young indentured servant. The thin-skinned quality of East

Hampton society appears to have been a function of a general uncertainty about where other people stood. In a sense, the magistrates found themselves arbitrating social status. The results of each challenge brought a greater measure of legitimacy to an evolving social order. During the mid-1660s, cases of this type suddenly disappeared from the records of East Hampton. One still encounters disputes over property, usually charging trespass, but no more involving slander and defamation. The disappearance, I suspect, is related to the invention of community.

These disputes involved a bizarre range of alleged insults. A woman's garment sparked one acrimonious suit. A servant insisted that his honor had been impugned by persons who claimed that he made unseemly noises behind his mistress's back. And one particularly ugly action raised the possibility of witchcraft, a capital offense in this society. It is this case that has attracted most scholarly attention. For local historians it is an unhappy anomaly; others view it as part of the larger story of seventeenth-century New England witchcraft. I have chosen, however, to interpret this particular case solely within the context of East Hampton. Like the other slander and defamation disputes that turned family against family, this one was basically a contest over social status within a loosely defined community. The major difference between it and other actions such as the "petticoat" case or the "pumpkin porrage" case was the possibility that the defendant might die.

In order for a case to come before the local magistrates or, if necessary, before a jury, an aggrieved party had to accuse another person formally of slander. In other societies the disputants might have resorted straightaway to violence. A duel was once a recognized means of defending one's honor, in America as elsewhere. In East Hampton, however, such matters involved the institutions of the law. The plaintiffs and defendants stated the facts before elected judges who were also their neighbors. Witnesses were summoned and damages assessed.

What initially sparked enmity between the Edwardses and the Prices will probably never be known. Whatever the origins may have been, their differences first came to the attention of the local magistrates—that is, in their official capacity—early in 1652. Benjamin Price accused his neighbor William Edwards of overcharging him in some sort of business transaction. Both men were "inhabitants of East Hampton": in other words, owners of home lots. As the testimony in a later, separate dispute reveals, both families had apparently lived briefly at Massachusetts Bay before moving to Long Island. Even in Lynn there seems to have been no love lost between the two men and their wives. Because of the abbreviated character of the town records, we cannot tell exactly what goods were involved in the transaction. In any event, Price maintained that Edwards received three pounds more than he deserved. The townsmen found for Price, but the small amount of damages that they actually awarded could not have been very pleasing to the plaintiff.

Price pressed his suit at a time when the Edwardses seem to have been particularly vulnerable. The Edwardses certainly do not apper to have adjusted well to their new social environment, and the outspoken Mrs. Edwards made her disappointment with East Hampton known to just about everyone in the village. A month after Price brought his action for overcharging, the local justices fined her three pounds and ordered her to "have her tongue in a cleft stick for contempt of a warrant." This was a punishment usually meted out in early New England for common scolds. Again, we do not know what brought the constable to the Edwards house, but when he arrived Mrs. Edwards informed him that the warrant he carried was not worth the paper on which it was written. East Hampton, she insisted, possessed no legitimate government. It lacked proper magistrates and a governor, and until the local officials obtained the necessary authority—just what she had in mind she did not make clear—she vowed to burn any warrants that the constable attempted to deliver.

While Mrs. Edwards questioned the town's legal foundation, her husband grumbled about the quality of the land that he had received. Indeed, he raised such a fuss that town leaders warned him and two unhappy neighbors to "quietly enjoy their land that they now possess without any more questioning." One has the impression that William and Ann Edwards, both of whom were what we would now describe as middle-aged, may have had second thoughts about migrating to East Hampton. Perhaps they believed that they deserved better treatment. Perhaps their lives had not worked out quite as they had once planned.

Whatever their frame of mind, the Edwardses could not endure the nettlesome Prices. During the summer of 1653 the smoldering animosities burst into flame. First the two men asked the town to arbitrate a difference, and instead of finding for either party, the magistrates fined both Edwards and Price ten shillings. Such impartiality, however well-meant, could not resolve such a long-standing personal controversy. Both participants wanted a clear victory.

Only a week later, Edwards and Price were back in court. This time it was Edwards who brought the action. In a passionate statement before the magistrates, Edwards accused Mrs. Price of slandering his wife. At issue was apparently the origin, perhaps even the existence, of a petticoat that Mrs. Edwards claimed that she had once transported from England to America. The two women bickered about the history of the garment, and when she left the Edwards home where she had been visiting, Mrs. Price announced that Mrs. Edwards was a liar. When asked to retract her words, Mrs. Price stoutly maintained her position. Mrs. Edwards, she exclaimed, was "a base lying woman" and she pledged to "prove her a liar in many particulars."

Neither woman testified before the local justices. In fact, all that we know of their controversy comes from their husbands and from witnesses whom these men summoned to court. As the plaintiff, William Edwards insisted that Mrs. Price had defamed not only him and his wife, but also his "posterity." In a rhetorical burst, he asked members of the local jury composed of his fellow "inhabitants" to imagine what future townspeople might say about his children: "Here go the brats of a base liar." It was more than he could bear; all Edwardses had lost face. At stake in this case, William declared, was his wife's very life. He warned that not even a settlement of "a hundred pounds"— three times the original cost of East Hampton—could now restore his wife's sullied reputation. He demanded public exoneration of the Edwards name.

Interestingly, Edwards did not mention the petticoat. If it had not been for the testimony of the various witnesses, we would not have the slightest idea what actually had occurred during Mrs. Price's visit. Instead, William appealed to traditional patterns of deference. Since she was a much older woman than Mrs. Price, Mrs. Edwards could justly have expected her younger guest to mind her tongue. Age demanded deference; so too did anyone who entertained a visitor in her own home. Finally there was the matter of recalcitrance. When Edwards had gone to see Mrs. Price, urging her privately to withdraw her "grievous" slanders, she had defiantly declared that she would "maintain them in all the courts in New England."

Benjamin Price responded to every charge. One senses from the tone of his statement that although he was sorely annoyed by Edwards's suit, he found the whole event strangely amusing. This may be reading too much between the lines of the town records, but Price does seem to have recognized that hyperbole had undermined Edwards's credibility before the local magistrates. Price turned each of William's complaints against him. To say that Mrs. Price had caused Mrs. Edwards "a deep wound" or that her "life was at stake" was nonsense. Moreover, there was a question of semantics. Price argued that his wife had never actually declared that Mrs. Edwards was a "base, lying woman." Rather, the younger woman only claimed *that if* Mrs. Edwards publicly denied the truth of what Mrs. Price had said—presumably about the origin of the petticoat—*then* she was indeed a liar. Third, if Edwards was so worried that villagers would say that his children were "the brats of a base liar," he should have settled the dispute in private. It had been his decision to go before a jury, and now his "posterity" would just have to live with "a blemish" on their honor. Finally, Mrs. Price had gone to the Edwards home not as a guest but to buy some things, and in such a commercial situation, she had every right to assume that the "ancient" woman would treat her properly.

Each side produced three witnesses. Edwards's supporters were a disappointment. Those who came forward for the Price family, however, had a great deal to say, all of it damaging to the Edwardses. "Goodwife" Simons remembered that Mrs. Edwards had bragged about a petticoat that she had "brought out of England," but strangely, no one had ever seen the petticoat. Even more peculiar, at least in the eyes of his neighbors, William Edwards altered his wife's story, claiming that it was the money for a petticoat, not the petticoat itself, that they had carried to Lynn. The constable also reminded the justices that when he and a deputy had attempted to bring Mrs. Edwards to court, she physically attacked them and screamed that "her husband had brought her to a place where there was neither magistrates nor ministers. Also, she said that he brought her to live among a company of heathens and she would hang him when he came home."

The jury awarded Price damages of twopence. The entire affair had been a nuisance, a waste of time for farmers who would have preferred to be tending their fields. Or was it? This trial involved in one capacity or another representatives from at least half the families in East Hampton. What they witnessed was a contest over status. Benjamin Price, a man who was to become a leader in the community, had successfully fended off a challenge by a person whose future was behind him. To be sure, Mrs. Edwards was a difficult woman, but she was not crazy. She seems to have been fully aware of the symbolic significance of the mysterious petticoat. The issue was not simply the existence of this garment, but her claim to the social standing that the possesion of such a luxury item implied. When the younger woman exposed the lie, the position of the Edwards family dropped in the local hierarchy.

To be dishonored in this society was to lose face. Even obviously marginal people in East Hampton, those who did not own a home lot or were not likely to inherit one, were sensitive to the slightest insult. A servant's chances of being allowed to remain in the village depended in large measure on his or her maintaining a good reputation. Personal honor was often the only thing that a dependent person possessed. Such considerations helped make this a prickly society in which ordinary conversations could suddenly take an unexpected turn and lead to confrontation. To interpret such legal proceedings as a form of class war, however, would be a mistake. It was as common for less wealthy members of this village to challenge their more prosperous neighbors as it was for leading figures in the town to haul smaller landowners into court for having defamed their reputation. The poorer men and women also sued their social peers, since in the scramble for position in this still loosely defined hierarchy, it was as important for a humble farmer or indentured servant to maintain his honor as it was for the lord of the manor.

A peculiar case of this type came before the local justices in the autumn of 1654. Anthony Waters entered an action of slander against John Davis in behalf of John Rose, his seventeen-year-old servant. Waters specifically contended that Davis had gone about the village accusing Rose and others of being notorious masturbators. These charges were no doubt related to a particularly disagreeable matter that had embarrassed the entire village earlier that summer. Four men—Daniel Fairfield, Foulk Davis, John Davis, and John Hand, Jr.—had been convicted of "spilling their seed." What made this case especially peculiar was that Foulk and John Davis were not young men. Foulk seems to have been nearly forty at the time. John, who may have been Foulk's brother, was even older, and both were married men. Hand and Fairfield were probably in their twenties. Fairfield, an indentured servant in the Garlick household, had acquired a reputation as a troublemaker, but Hand came from a substantial family. Indeed, his own father sat as one of the judges. After conferring with authorities in Connecticut, the East Hampton magistrates decided that however serious the offense may have been, it was not "worthy of life or limb." They sentenced Foulk to the pillory as well as to some form of "corporal punishment." John Davis and Fairfield received a public whipping; and Hand escaped with a good scare. Apparently, John Davis later attempted to implicate others in his crime, and, as Anthony Waters must have realized, such loose talk had to be silenced immediately. At risk was John Rose's future standing in this village. Since the town secretary neglected to record the judges' decision in this case, we shall never know whether he successfully defended his honor.

Rumor fed upon rumor. Soon William Mulford lashed out against neighbors who were whispering unkind stories about his wife. What, exactly, they were saying is not clear from the records. The culprit may have been Daniel Fairfield, the servant who had just received a good whipping and who would later come before the court for seducing the Reverend Mr. James's daughter and his maid. We know that after leaving Joshua Garlick's service, he became Goody Mulford's servant. William Mulford was a leader of the village, a frequent officeholder, and a substantial landowner. In July 1654 he charged the Garlicks with having "uttered scandalous speeches" against his wife. They may have assumed that Fairfield was up to some of his old tricks in the home of his new employer. A few months later Mulford also sued William Simons for defaming his wife, and on this occasion the records clearly show that the court found for the plaintiff. It fined Simons ten shillings plus court costs.

By this time Mulford was anxious to put an end to the affair. Somehow he persuaded Simons to sign a formal contract pledging that he would never again speak ill of Mrs. Mulford. It was really a kind of peace treaty, and its very existence says a good deal about the increasingly fractious quality of everyday life in East Hampton.

> It is also firmly agreed and each party, both plaintiff and defendant, doth by this obligation bind themselves in a bond of 20 pound sterling not to renew the action . . . either here or in any other place: and so the declaration and the depositions to be burned: and so all differences to be ended between them and theirs in all cases whatsoever that have been between them for the times past: also each party doth

bind himself in the same bond: not to speak of any differences that have been between them and their wives in the disparagement of each party.

Neither man was apparently literate. In the presence of Luke Lillie, the witness, they carefully affixed their marks to the agreement. From the fragmentary records of East Hampton, it is impossible to tell if other slander actions generated documents of this type. Such covenants would, of course, help to explain why more depositions have not survived.

Even Lion Gardiner was not exempt from the backbiting that swept through the village. It is surprising that a person of such eminence in East Hampton would have bothered with the likes of Garlick and Simons, but Gardiner was not a man to let an insult go unchallenged. He may not have felt as socially secure as modern historians imagine. However he interpreted his position in this society, his management of the tenant farms on the island created friction. He even sued two of "his" farmers for trespass. On another occasion some local men allegedly threatened to "strike Mr. Gardiner . . . if he stood to help the Dutchmen." At the time England was at war with Holland, and Gardiner's Dutch connections may have made him a suspect figure.

During the summer of 1654 Gardiner charged two villagers—Goodwife Simons and Joshua Garlick—with having defamed his reputation. The records do not describe the character of the alleged slander. Gardiner's actions seem to have been connected in some way with Mulford's problems with the two people. All these cases came before the local magistrates during the same session of the village court. The lord of the manor may have withdrawn his complaint before the judges rendered a verdict. He and Garlick took out a bond of ten pounds sterling "never to stir in this action . . . neither here nor elsewhere." A few months later Lion's son David accused John Davis of slander, possibly an echo of the masturbation trial.

We should note that we are encountering the same characters. The Garlicks and Simonses persisted in saying things that clearly annoyed their betters. We shall never know whether their statements were accurate. Perhaps Mrs. Mulford had in fact been too familiar with the high-spirited Daniel Fairfield. Maybe David Gardiner did hang out with the wrong sort of friends. The point is that Gardiner and Mulford felt compelled to respond to these gossips. The Garlicks and Simonses were in effect protesting their own importance. These were people who owned just enough land to have developed a sense of their independence. Like the feisty yeomen who throughout English history have defended their rights against high-handed author-ity, they found it difficult to defer to men whose background was not so very different from theirs. The major problem was their noisy insistence that they were as good as most of the other families in East Hampton. Of course, their techniques were crude. Mrs. Edwards kicked the constable in the shin. Simons was fined for "his provoking speeches to the 3 men in authority." To label them cranks or misfits, however, would be to misunderstand how a frontier society of nearly equal peo-ple sorts itself out. Gardiner and Mulford could not ignore their challenges precisely because their own standing in this village was not that secure.

The society had not cohered as the inhabitants might have expected. Neighbors charged neighbors with all sorts of mis-behavior, and, to make matters worse, such challenges seemed to be escalating. Although no one in East Hampton had read the works of Thomas Hobbes, his spirit must surely have hung over the troubled village. The situation was spinning out of control. Early in 1657 the townsmen addressed the growing crisis by passing a series of ordinances—more Old Testament than common law in spirit—designed to discourage the kind of contentious behavior that had divided the settlement.

> It is ordered that whosoever shall rise up as a false witness against any man to testifie that which is wrong, there shall be done to him as he thought to have done unto his neigh-

bour, whether it be to the taking away of life, limb, or goods.

It is ordered that whosoever shall rise up in anger against his neighbour and strike him, he shall forthwith pay ten shillings to the town and stand to the censure of the court and if in his smiting he shall hurt or wound another, he shall pay for the cure and also for his time that he [has] thereby hindered.

It is ordered that whosoever shall slander any [person], they shall be liable to pay a fine to the value of 5 pounds, if the men in authority see meet or any sum under that [that] they see good to inflict, but not above.

These were stiff punishments. A five-pound fine represented ten percent of the Reverend Mr. James's entire annual income. Such a sum was sufficient to purchase a good horse. However harsh the penalties, they do not appear to have dissuaded people from saying unkind things about their neighbors. A few months after the passage of these regulations, Charles Barnes, the local schoolteacher, entered an action of slander against Samuel Parsons, Roger Smith, and John Wooley. As is so often the case with these records, we do not know the nature of the "speeches" that Barnes found so insulting. What is certain is that the three "men in authority" took the matter very seriously. This was precisely the type of uncivil behavior that the townmen had hoped to curtail. After interviewing seven witnesses, they found for Barnes and fined each of the defendants four pounds "to be paid forthwith." Moreover, the three were made responsible for the court costs, an additional bill of more than eight shillings. This was an extraordinarily heavy penalty, especially when one considers that these were young men who probably could not easily raise that kind of money.

In January 1658 John Wooley appeared before the local magistrates in another action involving defamation. On this occasion, however, he claimed that it was he who had been wronged. This action—the aforementioned "pumpkin porrage" case—is surely the most bizarre trial to be found in the records of early East Hampton. Wooley, a servant on Gardiner's Island, insisted on a full hearing before a jury, and it is probably for this reason that the justices collected depositions from everyone who might have witnessed the central event in this odd drama. The facts, such as they are, seem clear enough. Mrs. John Hand accused Wooley of making strange noises behind the back of Mrs. Lion Gardiner. The sound was described by one person as a "bow wou [wow?]." Exactly why Mrs. Hand would have taken such an interest in this matter is obscure; she was not even present when Wooley allegedly made "a noise with his mouth." Still, she gratuitously insisted that this behavior—she had no doubt that he had barked—mocked the wife of East Hampton's leading citizen.

The witnesses who appeared in Wooley's behalf testified that Mrs. Hand had got it all wrong. To be sure, there had been a domestic argument in which Mrs. Gardiner lost her temper. The records state that she was scolding or "talking thick." She apparently set some of her "pumpkin porrage" in a room, and when she returned, it had been eaten. Goldilocks was soon found. Two members of her own family confessed to the crime. Mrs. Gardiner berated the pair, and if Mrs. Hand's story was correct, this was when Wooley jeered his mistress with a "bow wou." Arthur Howell, Gardiner's son-in-law, and Goodwife Simons explained to the magistrates that Wooley had been out of the room when the fight over the "pumpkin porrage" had occurred. Others—Mrs. Garlick, Mrs. Veale, and John Osborn—reported that they had heard Mrs. Hand defame Wooley. Indeed, Mrs. Veale specifically remembered telling Mrs. Hand to maintain her sense of humor. After all, said Mrs. Veale, everyone knew that Wooley was the kind of fellow who would "mock his friend in a merry way."

By contrast, Mrs. Hand's defense seemed feeble. Her own son spoke up, but offered only hearsay evidence about Wooley's merry carriage. Others declared that they did not think that the servant was in attendance when everyone in the Gardiner household was "discoursing about the pumpkin porrage."

How are we to interpret this episode? It would seem that

in conversation with friends Mrs. Hand had clumsily attempted to demonstrate her concern for Mrs. Gardiner's reputation in the village. Like the "men in authority"—and her husband served in that capacity from time to time—she may have been agitated about the lack of deference displayed in ordinary social relations: between the young and the old, servants and masters, and men and women. She probably never bargained that Wooley would take the matter to court. After all, she may have really believed that this servant made insulting "bow wou" sounds. And after the decision in the Barnes case went so dramatically against him, Wooley may have seemed an obvious mark for such criticism.

John Wooley, however, had powerful supporters of his own. The Gardiners clearly did not believe that their good name had been slandered, and in any case, they let the meddlesome Mrs. Hand—and, for that matter, the entire village—know that they were fully in charge of their own affairs. From the perspective of the Gardiners, her loose talk represented a greater threat to the proper ordering of society than did Wooley's silly noises. The jury found for the plaintiff, awarding him ten shillings plus court costs.

Early in February 1658 the inhabitants of East Hampton harvested a decade of ill will. The bad feelings, always stirring just beneath the surface of ordinary relations in this town, burst forth suddenly and dramatically, and almost cost one unfortunate woman her life. Because the incident involved allegations of witchcraft, a capital offense that still exercises a powerful hold on the modern imagination, historians have linked this case to those that occurred in other seventeenth-century communities. The appropriate context for this particular trial is not the long story of New England witchcraft, but rather the short, local history of slander and defamation. For in this society nothing could have been more damaging to a person's reputation than a charge of witchcraft. It is as if all the previous cases of slander and "false witness" were merely a rehearsal for this explosion of mean-spiritedness within a town that did not quite hold together. We shall never be able to reconstruct the psychological underpinnings of this event. Human motivation is a murky affair, and most of what ultimately sparks violence and love, ambition and envy, remains forever hidden from our view. Insofar as this case was part of a sorting-out process in this society, it produced winners and losers. It is also clear that witchcraft dealt a fatal blow to the political autonomy of East Hampton.

The incident began innocently enough. Elizabeth Howell, the daughter of Lion Gardiner and a young mother, announced one afternoon that she was not feeling well. The illness, which she did not believe to be serious, appeared to have an obvious cause. She had not dressed warmly and had experienced a chill, and that chill soon brought forth a severe headache and a slight "fever." In other words, during the first hours of her discomfort, Elizabeth's own explanation for her sickness was based on common sense. She grew worse, however, and complained constantly of intense pain. By evening the woman was occasionally delirious. The loss of her reason apparently frightened Elizabeth. At one point, she confided to her husband, Arthur, "I pray God it may not be with me as it was with you when you were at your mother Howell's and were senseless." She breast-fed her child. Someone summoned Lion Gardiner.

As Elizabeth's condition deteriorated, she offered another explanation for her illness. She had been bewitched. Neighbors who had begun to gather in the Howell home stood amazed as Elizabeth stared off into space, shrieking, "Now you are come to torture me because I spoke 2 or 3 words against you." She saw a menacing "black thing" at the foot of the bed and tried to strike it; she claimed that the witch was pricking her with pins.

It was decided that Goody Simons—a woman we have encountered before—should sleep in Elizabeth's bed. Her husband and a friend slept nearby. They were shaken by the charge of witchcraft, and, perhaps because of the power of suggestion, the two men spent a fitful night. They later claimed that a "doleful" sound emanating from the back of the fireplace had disturbed them. Arthur described it as "the noise of a great stone thrown down among a heap of stones, and kept a great rumbling." They lit a candle, but they saw nothing out of the ordinary. Mrs. Simons slept soundly through it all. Elizabeth died the next day.

The men never learned the identity of the witch from Elizabeth. Mrs. Simons, however, knew better. She told the local magistrates that the dying woman had laid the blame on Goody Garlick. The justices may not have been surprised. Garlick and her husband had a long history of not being able to get along with their neighbors. They carried tales about things they had seen on Gardiner's Island before moving to the village. According to Mrs. Simons, Elizabeth had been severely upset by something that happened when she visited the Garlicks' farm. She had been looking for Arthur, and when she asked Joshua Garlick where her husband might be found, he answered sharply, so sharply in fact that he made Elizabeth cry. In her delirium she begged Mrs. Simons to bring Mrs. Garlick— though, strangely, not Joshua—to her bedside. Elizabeth vowed to "tear her to pieces." Mrs. Garlick, she ranted, was "a double tongued woman," and during her illness she had attacked Elizabeth with pins.

Before she died, Elizabeth told much the same story to her mother. Unlike Mrs. Simons, Mrs. Gardiner's instincts were to discourage this kind of talk; she suggested that it was all a dream. In a deposition Mrs. Gardiner recounted that "Bettie" protested that "she was not asleep. And I asked her who she saw, and she said Goody Garlick in the further corner." Gardiner urged her child "not to tell her husband, nor no living soul." But of course it was too late. Elizabeth had already told Mrs. Simons. Soon everyone in East Hampton knew the story.

It is difficult not to admire the local justices—John Mulford, John Hand, and Thomas Baker—who gathered evidence in this case. At a moment when the villagers had perhaps begun to panic, the justices maintained calm, insisting that the town follow normal legal procedures. Indeed, these depositions are the fullest to be found in the colonial records of East Hampton. None of the three "men in authority" had formally studied the

law, but they had a deep, almost reflexive, sense of the importance of due process. Whenever possible they supported the
testimony they had received from one person by calling in other
witnesses. After hearing Mrs. Gardiner's story, for example,
they interviewed Goody Brooks. She told the justices that she
had heard Mrs. Gardiner say "that her daughter was bewitched
and that it was a woman." The magistrates seem to have wanted
to determine to their own satisfaction that the charges against
Mrs. Garlick were not something invented after the fact, in this
case by a distraught mother trying to explain her daughter's
sudden death. But Mrs. Brooks put those concerns to rest. Mrs.
Gardiner had done what she begged Elizabeth not to do; she
told "a living soul" about the possibility of witchcraft and she
had done it while the girl was still alive.

The three men then turned their attention to Mrs. Garlick,
and at this point they opened a Pandora's box of unpleasant
memories. Various women came before the local court with
stories that initially seemed quite prejudicial to Mrs. Garlick's
defense. This phase of the investigation commenced a little over
a week after Elizabeth's death.

Mrs. Edwards, the woman who had assaulted the village
constable, testified about a series of strange coincidences involving Mrs. Garlick and breast milk. She explained that Mrs.
Garlick had sent to Mrs. Edwards's daughter, then a new
mother, a request for milk. The woman obliged the neighbor.
No sooner had she done so, however, than her own child took
sick. These events had made Mrs. Edwards uneasy, and she
shared her concerns privately with Mrs. Foulk Davis. What she
heard from Davis only increased her anxiety.

Some years earlier, it seems, Mrs. Garlick had asked Mrs.
Davis for breast milk, and after Mrs. Davis had provided it,
her own child fell ill. In fact, the child died. Mrs. Davis told
Mrs. Edwards that the same thing had happened to Goody
Stratton. Perhaps Elizabeth herself had heard these stories. She
too was a lactating mother, and just before she first raised the
possibility of having been bewitched, she fed her own infant
daughter. The sequence of events paralleled almost exactly what

had happened in these other households. Arthur Howell asked Elizabeth "if she would suckle the child, and she said, 'yes.' So I [Howell] gave her the child, and she said, 'Ah, my poor child. It pities me more for thee than for myself, for if I be ill, to be sure thou will be ill.' So having done suckling of it, I took it from her, and presently . . . she turned a Psalm and shrieked out several times together very grievously and upon that cried out, 'a witch, a witch.' "

The second witness to be interviewed during the long session of February 27 was Goody Bishop. She also had a curious story to tell about events at least ten years in the past. Once, when Mrs. Bishop learned that Mrs. Simons was sick, having "her fitts" according to the town record, she went to Mrs. Garlick's to fetch some healing herbs. When Mrs. Bishop brought the "dockweed" into the sick woman's presence, Mrs. Simons ordered it burned. Mrs. Davis, who just happened to be there, carried out the order.

While the dockweed crackled in the fireplace, Mrs. Davis and Mrs. Simons told Mrs. Bishop that they remembered someone carrying such plants into a house in Lynn, and there soon followed "a black thing." Then, when Mrs. Simons really did experience a seizure, Mrs. Bishop heard her say "that there came a black thing into the house, and somebody of the house inquired who had a black cat, and somebody said Goody Garlick." Mrs. Bishop offered one last piece of evidence. When Mrs. Simons was "in her fit," she cried out that "she would not have Goody Garlick nor Goody Edwards come near her." Elizabeth had not accused Mrs. Edwards. The contagion was spreading.

The next witness, Goody Hand, was not only the wife of one of the sitting justices but also the woman who had recently been fined by the court for defaming John Wooley's reputation. Much of her testimony focused on Mrs. Davis. She recounted a conversation that the two women had had at least five years earlier. At the time, Mrs. Davis lived on Gardiner's Island, as did the Garlicks. Mrs. Davis informed Mrs. Hand that she had heard that the Garlicks were planning to move to the village. There were rumors that they had obtained "a house lot" in East

Hampton. Mrs. Davis predicted that the townspeople would come to regret this decision. Goody Garlick brought misery wherever she lived. The catalog of unexplained happenings on the island was enough to frighten anyone: a hurt ox, a "man that was dead," a neger child . . . [that] was taken away . . . in a strange manner," and a "fat and lusty" sow that died in a peculiar manner while delivering piglets. Mrs. Davis associated these events with Mrs. Garlick, although Mrs. Hand appears to have taken these stories with a grain of salt. In any case, after the Davises themselves had transferred to East Hampton, Mrs. Hand noticed that Mrs. Garlick and Mrs. Davis saw a good deal of each other, and Hand could not resist asking Davis "how she dares to be so familiar with Goody Garlick as she was, since you have spoken so of her formerly as you have." The magistrates must have taken special note of Mrs. Davis's cynical response: "[Garlick] brought many things to me [such] as malt for one thing and is very kind to me. And to the best of my [Mrs. Hand's] rememberance, she said she were as good [to] please the Devil as anger him."

Goody Birdsall also concentrated attention on the Davis-Garlick relationship. She not only confirmed the "dockweed" story, but also added several new details about Mrs. Davis's troubled life on Gardiner's Island. She apparently told Mrs. Birdsall a pathetic story about the death of her own child. Mrs. Davis had just dressed the baby "in clean linen" when suddenly Mrs. Garlick appeared at her door. The visitor admired the little girl, saying to the mother "how pretty the child doth look." No sooner had these words been uttered than Mrs. Davis saw "death in the face of it." And within five days following this exchange the child was dead, an event from which the mother seems never to have recovered. During this painful conversation, Mrs. Birdsall also learned of a fight between Joshua Garlick and Lion Gardiner. Garlick apparently lost his temper. Mrs. Davis remembered "some threatening speeches." No doubt, this was the controversy that the two men pledged "in a bond of ten pounds never to stir . . . neither here nor elsewhere." The lord of the manor may have been willing to forgive Garlick, but not Mrs. Davis. According to Mrs. Birdsall, she was sure that Garlick had somehow broken the leg of one of Gardiner's oxen. This stream of calumny closed with the observation "Goody Garlick [is] . . . a naughty woman."

Late in the afternoon of February 27, after these women had given their testimony, the magistrates must have realized that the case against Mrs. Garlick was falling apart. To be sure, there was "a naughty woman" in East Hampton, but increasingly the evidence suggested that it was Mrs. Foulk Davis and not Mrs. Joshua Garlick. There was no question of Elizabeth Howell's sincerity; she really did believe that Garlick in the form of "a black thing" had tormented her. The notion that Garlick was capable of doing such things, however, seems to have been suggested by Mrs. Simons, who in turn was Mrs. Davis's close friend and next-door neighbor. The investigation into witchcraft had uncovered no witch; rather, it had exposed once again a pattern of slander and defamation. Discontented people in East Hampton who had come to this isolated extension of New England culture looking for a fresh start and some possible bettering of their lives had in their ambition turned on each other. As the witnesses poignantly revealed, no one in East Hampton seems to have experienced more disappointment than did Mrs. Foulk Davis.

By the end of the day the tide of local opinion appears to have turned against Mrs. Davis. Neither she nor Mrs. Garlick testified before the local justices—at least, I have found no depositions—but Jeremiah Veale and his wife, both of whom had lived on Lion Gardiner's troubled island, demonstrated that the star witness had feet of clay. Not even the lord of the manor, Elizabeth's father, had much use for Mrs. Davis. The Veales recounted a conversation with Gardiner in which they asked whether he really believed that Mrs. Davis's child had been bewitched. "Goody Davis," Gardiner snapped, "had taken an Indian child to nurse, and for lucre of a little wampum had starved her own child." Joshua Garlick concluded that Mrs. Davis had invented the whole business about witchcraft on Gardiner's Island, and on March 15 he "in the behalf of his wife has entered an action of defamation . . . against the wife of Fulke Davis."

These developments left the local justices in an almost impossible position. The charge of witchcraft had been made. It could not be simply dismissed, especially since it involved a capital offense. Even with the case crumbling, the justices decided to push ahead. The hearsay evidence gained from Mrs. Davis was clearly of no use. What they needed was the seventeenth-century equivalent of a smoking gun. In an effort to salvage the investigation, the magistrates recalled two witnesses who had actually attended Elizabeth Howell during her final hours. Mrs. Birdsall rehearsed the business about Garlick having "jeered" Elizabeth when she came looking for her husband. But Mrs. Birdsall also claimed to have seen "a middling pin" taken out of Elizabeth's mouth. Mrs. Edwards offered an even more a graphic account:

> The deponent said [that] she saw a pin pulled out of Mrs. Howell's mouth, and it was given to Goody Simons. Goody Simons said she was sure there was no such pin in the house, and the Deponent said [that] to her best remembrance, Mary Gardiner [Elizabeth's mother] said there was no such pin in the house. And a little before this pin was taken out of her mouth, this Deponent said that she did put the handle of a knife into her [Elizabeth's] mouth, and gave her solitt [?] oil and sugar and did look into her mouth, and she did not see, nor discern any pin there.

The problem was that the pin could have been planted by Mrs. Simons, who bore a grudge against Mrs. Garlick. Still, the discovery of the pin was enough for the three "men in authority." They dispatched Mrs. Garlick to Connecticut to stand trial for her life.

Whether the justices suspected a frame-up is impossible to determine. Whatever private doubts they may have entertained, they had other, more pressing issues before them. Until this time East Hampton had defined itself as nominally under the jurisdiction of Connecticut. No one had bothered to work out the details of this relationship. The Garlick case forced the villagers to formalize the union or, to put the point differently, to surrender a measure of local autonomy. In May 1658 a delegation from East Hampton agreed that the town would henceforth be part of Connecticut and would observe the laws of that colony. Everyone at the meeting recognized that communication between Hartford and East Hampton would be difficult. They decided, therefore, to allow the town to elect two magistrates to administer the law. The "freemen" of East Hampton were instructed to nominate annually three men from their own number with the understanding that the general court of Connecticut would select two of them to serve. The document also contained some discussion of who would pay for defense.

If we stand back from the finely textured detail of this particular case and consider the larger implications of formally merging with Connecticut, it is clear that the agreement was in fact a declaration of failure. A little village had proven unable to control the petty animosities among its inhabitants that surely occurred in other towns. This is a disturbing thought for anyone who believes that individuals in small groups, expressing their wills through democratic procedures and having access to resources sufficient to maintain their families, can coexist in peace and mutual understanding. In East Hampton this did not happen. By 1658 the vitriol had escalated to the point where the justices were forced to seek external assistance. No one foresaw that Elizabeth Howell's charges against Mrs. Garlick would lead to a constitutional change. Indeed, if the local magistrates had been willing to hear the case themselves, they might have preserved their autonomy, at least for some years longer. The ultimate lesson of all this was clear. Social tranquility at the local level was not supportable. Village harmony—then as today—requires higher authority, external bodies capable of arbitrating among contending parties. The reason most "covenanted" villages of seventeenth-century Massachusetts Bay avoided East Hampton's experience was that they existed within a well-defined chain of authority, with courts of appeal reaching from the little communities all the way to the general court.

When this chain was disturbed, as it was by the Glorious Revolution of 1688, many Massachusetts towns turned in on themselves, and it is not surprising that in one of them—Salem Village—the grumbling and backbiting generated horrible violence.

The East Hampton witchcraft case ended in Hartford. The Connecticut judges found the evidence insufficient to convict Mrs. Garlick of witchcraft. The Connecticut authorities praised the Long Island magistrates for their care in gathering depositions, and, perhaps because they knew something of the riven history of this town, they added, "Also we think good to certify that it is desired and expected by this court that you should carry it neighborly and peaceably, without just offense to Joshua Garlick and his wife, and that they should do the like to you."

To a remarkable degree this is exactly what happened. Although Joshua never held important office in the village, he built up a modest estate. There is no compelling evidence that the Garlicks—or for that matter their son—were treated as pariahs in this society. Indeed, the most unusual thing about the Garlicks was that they both lived to extraordinary old age.

Mrs. Davis seems to have died soon after the Connecticut verdict. Her husband married again, but he never amounted to much. It is reported that a family history contains this description of the hapless Foulk Davis, "Apparently he was a wanderer and left children in his wake wherever he went." He drifted from town to town on Long Island, searching pathetically for the opportunities that had never come his way. The Simonses also left East Hampton, although the exact date of their departure went unrecorded. Early in 1661 the Reverend Mr. James sued the Birdsalls for defamation. We do not know what precipitated this action, but the matter must have been quite serious, since James demanded a whopping £30 sterling. The court awarded the minister £10, one of the largest settlements ever awarded by the justices. The local society, like a liquid suspension that had been shaken violently, was beginning to settle out. In this sorting-out process, the Garlicks found a place. Those who had challenged them, the scramblers on the margins, do not seem to have survived the ordeal.

During the early 1660s the "men in authority" heard several other suits involving defamation. With the exception of the James case, all were relatively minor actions. No doubt, men and women in the town continued to say unpleasant things about their neighbors, but these exchanges no longer generated disputes that came before the local magistrates. The structure of the town had crystallized, and in this changed social environment individuals knew fairly well where they stood in the East Hampton hierarchy.

VI

In the town records for March 11, 1661, a striking phrase appears. The words are unprecedented in the early history of East Hampton. The "men in authority" chastised a person who had sold a piece of land contrary to local ordinance and had thereby caused "great damage . . . to this little commonwealth or town in which we are." The words betray uncertainty. For more than a decade this group of settlers had struggled to become a "little commonwealth." For reasons that we have already reviewed, they repeatedly fell short of the mark. Now, however, community seemed within their grasp; they could at last imagine themselves a "commonwealth."

John Lyon Gardiner, who in the last decade of the eighteenth century wrote a history of East Hampton, provided a clue as to what was happening. At the time of the original settlement, he explained, there were "35 purchasers, [and] the names of 13 of these are now entirely extinct in the town. The Christian and Sur names of many of the Original settlers are now found in the town, removed to the 4th, 5th, and 6th degree counting the first as one. Lands that were at first 'allotted' have descended in the family and are after a space of 150 years occupied by one of the same family and name." Although not all of the thirteen names disappeared during the first full decade, many of them did. Moreover, some people—John Wooley, for example—passed through East Hampton without making much of an impression on this society. They left the village looking for other, perhaps even smaller, ponds. They faced the same sort of "stinted" conditions in East Hampton that had driven the first group of settlers out of Lynn, and perhaps even out of England.

What we perceive today as the historical "community," therefore, was a social invention. It consisted not of all families living in East Hampton, but only those who survived the competition for place. It is the surnames of the winners that appear in the genealogical histories. In later decades other newcomers arrived in East Hampton, looking for the same kinds of opportunities that first had brought men and women to this isolated tip of Long Island. With rare exception, these people did not become members of the "community." They were *in* East Hampton, but not *of* it. To claim that community became a synonym for class would be an exaggeration as well as an anachronism. The "little commonwealth" increasingly became an exclusive body, a sort of tribal organization in which membership passed through the loins of the elders.

During the years following the Garlick trial, those who had invented this community moved decisively to tighten their control over the resources of East Hampton. In 1659 a general meeting of all the inhabitants of the town ordered "that all the lots given out *after* Stephen Hand's shall have no propriety in the whales, nor any part in the next division of land, nor any other privileges whatsoever in division of land or purchase of the plantation."

In 1664 East Hampton, along with the other towns on eastern Long Island, were officially absorbed into colonial New York. This political realignment would change little in the everyday lives of the property owners of East Hampton. They would continue as stockmen, raising herds of cattle and sheep and taking advantage of the occasional drift whale that appeared on the beach. This was the recipe for a largely self-supporting community that would participate in an expanding regional economy whenever it could. Nothing pointed to the creation of unusual wealth. In fact, one might have predicted that East Hampton would turn out like the settlements on the Maine and New Hampshire frontier, a backwater in an increasingly commercial empire.

That is not the way it turned out. The whales made the difference. These docile winter migrants brought some East Hampton inhabitants a level of personal wealth that no one could have anticipated in 1660. No sooner had they created a "little commonwealth" than they found themselves involved in a world market that radically transformed how the peoples of East Hampton—red, white, and black—dealt with one another. Participation in the Atlantic economy also changed the physical environment of this community in ways that only the current generation of East Hampton residents may fully appreciate.

CHAPTER THREE

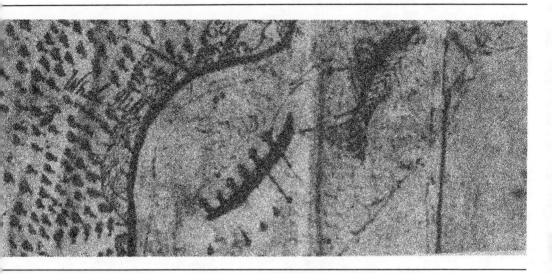

The Whale Design

I noticed some fishermen pursuing a whale. I took great pleasure in watching them. . . . There were small fishing-boats, each containing six or seven men. These followed closely in the fish's wake; when it raised its head . . . they moved up beside it and hurled a harpoon into its body. . . . They held fast, while he dove toward the bottom to break off the harpoon. As this was impossible he rose again. . . . He turned his head down and raised his tail out of the water and beat about with such violence that it was terrible to behold. . . . The fishermen moved closer with long lances or spears and inflicted innumerable wounds until he grew weaker still and began to spew blood instead of water. This elated the fishermen, who yelled with joy, for it was a sure sign that the fish was dying. They towed him ashore, greatly pleased, for they had earned more than a whole farm would bring us in an entire year.

Dr. Felix Christian Sporri,
description of offshore whaling near Newport,
Rhode Island, March 1662

"They've closed the beaches," I exclaim. "All of them. All the way from Southampton to Montauk."

"What?" Kelly responds in disbelief. It is the kind of bright August morning that makes people in East Hampton forget the hassle of Long Island traffic. Or, for that matter, any of the other problems that they might have on their minds, including gathering material to write a book.

Radio bulletins explain that because of a "shark alert" the local authorities have closed all of the town beaches until further notice. The decaying carcass of a dead whale has apparently drawn huge numbers of hungry sharks to the area. Sometime during the night the body of this great mammal, or what was left of it, washed ashore near Nepeague, just beyond Amagansett on the road to Montauk Point.

Later that morning, while Kelly and I have breakfast in a local café, we overhear the conversation of a group of guys who do not look as if they had come to East Hampton for a tan. The talk is of sharks and the dead whale.

"You should have seen it!" one exclaims. "The sharks were coming right up on the beach. They were snapping and biting, trying to get a piece of that whale. You could see their teeth. Some of them were almost out of the water."

Another patron confirms the story. "I'll bet there were ten or twenty sharks swimming around. They wouldn't give up. They wanted to clean that whale right down to the bone."

Two men claim to have spotted at least three different kinds of shark. No one thinks that the local police overreacted by closing the beaches.

On our way toward Nepeague, we stop at the offices of Lisa Liquori, the East Hampton town planner. As we discuss the role of history in making decisions about East Hampton's future development, our discussion soon turns to the whale.

"There's not much of it left," she tells us. The large finback whale had died several days earlier, and the body is rapidly decomposing in the August sun. When the town planner went over to Nepeague, she saw pieces of blubber floating in the water. By late morning the whale threatens to become a health hazard.

"It's sort of disgusting," the town planner adds, making a face.

Town workers had been trying for some time to get a rope on the carcass so that they can pull it up onto the beach with a bulldozer and bury it in the sand. According to the town planner, they have had a terrible time. The whale keeps slipping off their line. She seems slightly amused by the whole episode. After all, for almost two centuries the fishermen of East Hampton butchered drift whales on the local beaches. Using only knives and horse-drawn wagons, they somehow managed to get the job done. The arrival of this dead whale, however, presents an extraordinary problem. Modern, sophisticated equipment is not designed for this type of work.

Heading down a small road that leads to the beach from the main highway, Tony and I find that the whale has become a major attraction. Cars are everywhere. People who obviously do not live here are milling about. Several teenage boys ask excitedly where they can find the whale, worried that it will be gone before they see it. We point toward the beach, and they rush down the road. We can hear them telling each other stories about the sharks. After a few minutes, we follow, uncertain exactly where we are going.

The whale has drifted onto a beach near one of the more recently developed sections of East Hampton. The houses are large and expensive, and their owners seem to view the whale hunters with irritation. This is the kind of intrusion from which they thought that they had escaped by coming out to the end of Long Island.

Eventually we find a path leading over a huge sand dune. People returning from the beach tell us that the whale is a hundred yards or so ahead of us. A woman sitting in a folding chair in front of one of the houses watches the whale watchers. It has apparently been an exasperating day for this particular resident. As we begin our climb up the dune, she calls out, "There's nothing to see, already."

But there is. To be sure, by the time we reach the beach most of the body has been dragged ashore and buried beneath the sand. The flukes, however, are still clearly visible. A man dressed in bathing trunks attempts to place a rope around the tail. A policeman stands near him.

Although the area around the whale has been roped off, Kelly pretends that a newspaper sent him to cover the whale story. He walks over to the men on the beach, obviously intent on taking a photograph. The other people—including me—keep our distance. I half expect a shark to come crawling up out of the Atlantic, and mention this fear to someone who assures me that all the sharks have been driven off.

The scene that next unfolds before us is hard to interpret. The man in the bathing trunks, rope in hand, has edged up to the flukes of the whale. He stands in shallow water. It is a calm day. Whenever a wave breaks near him, even a small one, he jumps back violently. Then, anticipating a space between the waves, he again gingerly approaches the whale. Another wave. Another panicky retreat. This goes on for some time. Suddenly the man leaps from the water, drops the rope, and runs full speed down the beach.

"What's going on?" I ask Kelly, who has himself pulled back from the water in a hurry.

"Whale poison!" he responds.

"Whale poison?"

"That's what the policeman said," Kelly reports. "It's really dangerous. It can kill you if you swallow even a little bit of the stuff."

According to the policeman, a dead whale gives off potentially lethal toxins that float on the water. The man in the bathing trunks knew this and desperately tried to avoid being splashed by a poison-bearing wave. But some water

Fluke of a Dead Whale

had splashed into his mouth, and he ran off to get a disinfectant. The town planner was right; the whole thing is disgusting.

On the drive back into town Kelly is uneasy. "Think you got any of that whale poison on your boots?" I ask.

"I don't know." The policeman told Kelly that the previous summer a whale had drifted up on one of the East Hampton beaches. A worker assigned to bury it happened to be smoking a cigarette. He tried to be careful, but some contaminated water got on the cigarette, and from there into his body. According to the policeman, the man was critically ill for months. He was lucky to have survived.

"I bet they were pulling your leg."

"Yeah, you're probably right," Kelly admits.

Still, one cannot be too careful when it comes to "whale poison." At a drugstore, we purchase a bottle of disinfectant, and, standing on the sidewalk in front of the East Hampton library, Kelly pours the liquid all over his boots. As a young mother and her child pass by, the woman eyes Kelly nervously. There would be no use in trying to tell her of the close call we have just had at Nepeague.

I

Between approximately 1670 and 1730, East Hampton became a community quite different from what anyone would have predicted at its founding, or, for that matter, from what anyone would remember it to have been from the perspective of our own century. It is one of the vanities of modern times to imagine that social change—at least, change that radically transforms the character of society—is something new, and that to compare our situation with that of people in the past only distorts our understanding of their slower-moving, more integrated preindustrial world. For better or worse our lives are fundamentally different; we have the bomb, cities, penicillin, and factories. But the assumption that we are cut off from those who have gone before and face economic, ecological, and racial problems of an unprecedented kind simply does not hold, as the case of East Hampton clearly shows. Indeed, a most profound transformation of East Hampton society may have occurred at the end of the seventeenth century, as wrenching in many ways perhaps as that recorded during the decades since World War II.

In that earlier, largely forgotten period from 1670 until about 1730, the white people of East Hampton were rapidly incorporated into a large, increasingly complex market economy. Many of them probably enjoyed a higher level of material comfort than their fathers and mothers had ever known. These were good years, prosperous years. As the inhabitants of East Hampton reached out to participate fully in what David Hume called a "commercial society," they redefined the structures of village life. They looked for ways to maximize private profits; as they did so, they dramatically altered the character of race relations. The Montauk Indians, who had become almost invisible as they were marginalized and pushed aside by the founding generation, were suddenly invited back into the mainstream of the village economy. Montauk laborers risked their lives chasing the right whales, and, for a fleeting historical moment, it was conceivable that the Native Americans could have become, if not full members of this commercial society, then at least, members of a sort of New World peasantry. But it was not to be. And, perhaps not surprisingly, it was during this period of commercial expansion that African-Americans arrived in East Hampton, as slaves.

The English settlers squeezed a fragile environment for everything that might be turned to profit. They drove too hard, too fast; like the miners of some Western gold town who played out the mother lode, the inhabitants of early eighteenth century East Hampton found themselves living in a curious triracial society that showed some of the scars of its own past.

One qualification must be advanced immediately. Even during the most revolutionary transformation of society, during the French or Russian revolutions, for example, many aspects of daily life are virtually unaffected by the swirl of events. That was certainly true of the changes that occurred in late seventeenth-century East Hampton. For most families in this community the focus remained on agricultural pursuits, on raising enough food, on the preparation of meals, on fetching wood and water, on quotidian responsibilities to which people in any society must attend. The town records for this period testify to the jealous concern of ordinary farmers for the welfare of their animals and the allotment of land.

But local records testify to much more. They speak to a complex fit between production and consumption: in other words, to complementary aspects of a village economy. The claim that people in colonial times were consumers as well as producers seems on the face of it quite unobjectionable. In point of fact, however, economic historians have concentrated attention on the productive activities of the early American settlers. The colonists are portrayed as cultivating familiar staples such as tobacco and rice, or, if the person happened to live farther north, as growing the wheat and catching the fish needed to feed the sugar plantations of the Caribbean. Consumption in these descriptions gets shortchanged. It is as if deep in the American psyche is lodged the belief that consumption is weak and morally compromising, while productive work is strong, virtuous, and ennobling. This view is central to our mythic reverence for the self-sufficient Jeffersonian yeoman and the independent frontiersman.

There is no need here to contest the existence of this moral baggage; its genealogy can be traced back to ancient Greece and Rome. Whatever the philosophers may have said, however, ordinary people for centuries have purchased items that made them feel healthier, happier, and warmer whenever they had the opportunity to do so. In the late seventeenth and early eighteenth century such opportunities occurred in the Anglo-American economy as never before. To be sure, England was not yet an industrial nation; that economic transformation would not take place until the 1770s. Still, during this earlier period, thousands of small shops scattered throughout England were able to supply an expanding consumer market with an impressive range of goods that could make life just a little more pleasant.

Changes in everyday material culture are often difficult to document. Like most people today, the colonists tended to take for granted routine acquisitions. One seldom reads in early American diaries of the purchase of earthenware, pewter, or cloth, goods that we know from other probate records were beginning to flood into the homes of English and American families of even modest wealth. Perhaps as the purchase of such items became more commonplace, it no longer generated special comment. Whatever the psychology of consumption may have been, there is no question that imported items appeared in increasing quantity and variety in late seventeenth-century East Hampton. They turn up in probate inventories, for example: ironware, books, pewter goods of all sorts, brass pots and kettles, a pudding pot, chamber pots, a cream pot, tin lamps, metal tongs, chopping knives, and dripping pans. The list could easily be extended. No doubt the diaper napkins and tablecloths that show up so frequently were European imports as well. So too was much of the cloth that went into what one man called "my wearing garments." Some imported items were clearly a little out of the ordinary and a source of pride for their owners. When Thomas Diament died in 1682, for example, he made certain that his eldest son James received his "great looking glass."

Scattered customs reports also provide a tantalizing glimpse of East Hampton's nascent consumer economy. Unfortunately, these records are incomplete; they cover only a few years of the early eighteenth century and deal only with the commerce that flowed through the port of New York. Nevertheless, they reveal regular deliveries of "small parcels of European goods," some valued at only a few pounds. While we can only guess at the contents of these particular boxes, they probably contained the same items that appeared in the probate inventories. New York was not the only port that supplied East Hampton with European manufactures; far more of these "parcels" were shipped to Long Island by way of Boston.

*Leather-Covered Shipping Trunk Used in the Late Seventeenth Century
(Courtesy of the East Hampton Historical Society)*

The character of consumer demand in early East Hampton
would in fact remain something of a mystery were it not for a
remarkable document that Jay Graybeal, curator of the Historical Society, recently discovered in the manuscript collection of
the local library. The document provides a complete inventory
of the estate of Abraham Schellinger, a man who by the turn
of the century had become one of the town's more prosperous
merchants. This detailed listing of the goods that Schellinger
had on hand at the time of his death in 1712 allows us in our
imagination to wander through a colonial store. As we do so,
we should remember that if Schellinger had not known what

his customers wanted, he would not have been so successful.

On our tour we encounter first pans and skillets and a variety of cooking ware. Then come a number of dyes and thousands of nails in several different sizes. There are guns and gun locks. A little more than two pounds sterling would buy a huge kettle, perhaps of the kind used for trying whale blubber. Schellinger carried an impressive selection of pewter: plates, platters, pots, drinking pots, tankards, saltcellars, and cups. Near the pewter he might have displayed knives and forks. His customers could also buy books in this store (except for small portable Bibles, the inventory mentions no specific titles), penknives, spectacles, shoe buckles, earthenware, and a striking choice of textiles ranging in quality from fine silk to coarse drugget. For the East Hampton seamstress, there were thimbles and thread, hooks, metal and horn buttons. There were "wimmens" gloves and men's gloves, and thirteen pairs of knitting needles.

On and on the items went, shelf after shelf, container after container. By later standards the Schellinger selection may not seem impressive. But for the people of late seventeenth-century East Hampton the store—or, as it was probably called, the "warehouse"—offered a marvelous display of manufactures. Although they would not have expressed themselves in such terms, one might state that for the villagers these imported goods possessed transformative powers. Schellinger's customers were just beginning to discover the excitement and liberation inherent in choosing from among contending possibilities in a marketplace offering a choice of colors, designs, and textures, all of which the individual could employ to fashion and sustain a new sense of self.

But perhaps I exaggerate. This description may be a projection of the excitement of more modern times back onto a drab provincial world. It may be that the Schellinger warehouse looked something like the small dingy stores that V. S. Naipaul knew as a boy growing up in another colonial society. He recalls that on the main square of Port of Spain in Trinidad there were "emporia as dull as the emporia of those days could be,

suggesting warehouses for a colonial population, where absolutely necessary goods . . . were imported and stored in as un-
attractive and practical a way as possible." I do not think the
warehouses of Northwest Harbor looked like this, but such
interpretations are a matter of perspective.

Whatever magic the warehouses possessed, we must keep
in mind that in colonial East Hampton imports and exports
went hand in hand. As early as 1668 the town had its own
customs collector, one Thomas Chatfield, whose job it was to
take "an exact account of all such goods & merchandizes as shall
be imported or exported to & from the Towne or Port of *East
Hampton.*" Since his ledgers have not survived, we do not know
what quantities were involved, but his very presence in the town
at this early date suggests how rapidly the people of East Hampton were becoming integrated into a vast Atlantic economy, an
almost incomprehensibly large field of commercial transaction
linking them to the sources of those much-desired "parcels of
European goods." As time passed, reliance on the merchants
increased. For example, in 1672 the towns of eastern Long Island—East Hampton, Southampton, and Southold—sent a petition to the English government demanding to be made either
part of Connecticut or a "free corporation," for otherwise the
intolerable restrictions New York authorities placed on their
commerce would force their inhabitants to emigrate, a decision
bound to "be of damage [to] sundry Merchants to whom they
stand indebted for their Trade." Although one might question
the sincerity of this statement, it does demonstrate that the
people of eastern Long Island understood how much trade had
shaped their relations with the outside world. Colonel Robert
Quary, an English official who visited the area at the turn of
the eighteenth century, put the point rather tersely: "They cannot subsist without trade."

As for many other Americans, then as now, the demand
of the people of East Hampton for imports threatened to surpass
their ability to pay. Stated bluntly, without exports they could
not participate in this enticing consumer market. The goods
that flowed through New York and Boston were often expen-

sive. It has been estimated that during this period colonial merchants sometimes marked up the price of imports by as much
as 225 percent. One Boston merchant instructed his contact on
Long Island to sell his goods "for the most your market will
affoard, pray sell them as quick as you can."

East Hampton's prospects of finding marketable exports
did not appear promising at first. The soils of East Hampton
have never been particularly rich, and, in any case, once the
thin layer of topsoil has been disturbed, the land does not quickly
renew itself for agriculture. Although the winters in this area
were not usually severe, the climate is too cold to sustain the
production of staple commodities such as rice and indigo.
Nevertheless, confronted with such limited resources and driven
by the desire to purchase the goods that they saw in the local
warehouses, the people of East Hampton displayed impressive
creativity in finding ways to make what one New York governor called "returns to England."

Indeed, I suspect that the market itself powerfully shaped
the settlers' perceptions of East Hampton's physical environment. It is not that they did not appreciate the beauty of the
beaches and the sea; rather, they increasingly viewed the land
and the water as fields for economic activity. The market generated its own imaginative categories. The landscape promised
new possibilities for harvest, production, and exploitation.
Only later generations would describe this mental transformation in tragic terms. For those who were personally involved in the
process, who actually effected it, the opportunities presented
by the marketplace called forth a genuinely creative response.

By almost any standard, the town developed an impressive
range of exports. The great herds of cattle that grazed at Montauk were sold off as barreled meat and hides. The local woods
yielded shingles and planking as well as turpentine. There was
money to be made from feathers, bayberry candles, and tallow;
from the skins of small fur-bearing animals like muskrat, fox,
raccoon, wildcat, and otter. All these items entered a flow of
commerce that also included the more traditional cereal crops
such as wheat and oats. Almost no contemporary observer or

participant commented on this burst of market activity. We know of its occurrence largely from evidence provided in scattered receipts, an account book, customs records, and probate inventories. One exception worth noting, however, is the diary of Samuel Sewall, a sort of puritanical Samuel Pepys of Boston. On April 14, 1714, Sewall visited the city docks to talk with the crew of an East Hampton sloop appropriately named *Success*. What particularly caught Sewall's attention was the ship's rich and varied cargo: "600 Bushels of Wheat: 280 Barley: 40 Rye: 40 Indian [corn]: 50 Oats . . . 70 Barrels of Pork, 40 Barrels of Beef, 16 firkins Butter, 19 Boxes Candles, about 80 pounds a Box, Some Tallow and Bay-Berry Wax, 500 Weight, Few Feathers, Furrs."

II

Shipments like this, however frequent and abundant they may have been, did not ultimately transform the face of East Hampton. It was the whales that made the difference. During the early decades of settlement, the townsmen had waited for the drift whales to wash up on the Atlantic beaches. Their arrival represented a kind of bonus for a farming community, whose villagers exercised no effective control over the quantity of oil and bone produced.

All this changed sometime during the late 1670s. People in small boats began to chase and kill the right whales as they swam in the relatively shallow waters just off the East Hampton shore. The villagers had discovered a means to make "a return to England," to pay for the manufactured items that they so desired. It would be an exaggeration to describe late seventeenth-century East Hampton as a Puritan "boom town." There were no whale oil barons in the town. Nevertheless, those who were active in the trade did well for themselves. Edward Hyde, Lord Cornbury, royal governor of New York during the early years of the eighteenth century, estimated that "a Yearling [whale] will make about forty Barrils of Oyl, a Stunt or Whale two years old will make sometimes fifty, sometimes sixty Barrils of Oyl; and the largest whale that I have heard of in these parts, yielded one hundred and ten barrils." The average seems to have been about sixty barrels in addition to 750 pounds of bone. A price list drawn up in 1679 helps put these figures in perspective. A barrel of marketable oil fetched one pound, 10 shillings. At the time, beef brought only twopence per pound, winter wheat 4s per bushel, and Indian corn two shillings threepence per bushel. A decade later, oil sometimes sold for as much as £2 per barrel. In 1687, a year for which there are records, the villagers produced about 2,000 barrels; the income from whaling was obviously considerable.

The region's good fortune sparked contemporary comment, which was sometimes tinged with envy. Daniel Denton reported in 1670, "Upon the South-side of Long-Island in the Winter, lie a store of Whales . . . which the inhabitants begin with small boats to make a trade Catching to their no small benefit." And in his *General History of New England*, published in Boston in 1678, William Hubbard informed Puritan readers that the inhabitants of East Hampton "of late have fallen upon killing of whales, that frequent the south side of the Island in the latter part of the winter, wherein they have a notable kind of dexterity; and the trade that ariseth therefrom hath been very beneficial to all at that end of the Island."

Both statements stress innovation. At the time when these men were writing, the whaling "trade" had only just begun in East Hampton. *Trade* is a descriptive term that is all too easy to take for granted. It is, after all, an imaginative concept, a mental category that one employs to distinguish a certain type of economic activity. The problem is that our meanings are not necessarily those of the seventeenth century. For Denton and Hubbard, trade seems to have represented a positive achievement. Indeed, East Hampton had reached a stage of economic development that had apparently eluded many other colonial settlements. The self-conscious organization of production made all the difference. By skillfully exploiting a salable commodity, the lucky whalers of East Hampton had entered the world of trade.

One wonders why it took the fishermen of East Hampton so long to take to their boats since the monetary returns appear to have been substantial. In part the answer seems to be that the "Whale Design" was more difficult than they at first realized. Although the people of Southampton apparently organized whale hunts as early as 1644, the enterprise was by no means an immediate success. In 1672 the various towns on the eastern end of Long Island confessed in a petition to the king that they had "spent much time, pains, and expense for the settling of a trade of whale-fishing in the adjacent seas, having endeavoured it above 20 years, but could not bring it to any perfection till within the past two or three years."

The problem with this statement is that it suggests that ultimate success was just a matter of trial-and-error. If you chase enough whales in a small boat, you eventually get the hang of it. But "perfection" involved more than that. In addition to a certain amount of luck, the breakthrough required a fundamental restructuring of the relationship between individual enterprise and the general welfare. The founders of East Hampton regarded the drift whales as belonging to the entire village, at least to the owners of the home lots. As long as men had to share the returns, they grumbled about the hardship of having to butcher these animals. It was cold, nasty work. Everyone got something from the whales, perhaps a few pounds sterling for each family, but, whatever the amount, it apparently was not enough to inspire enthusiasm. The town threatened them with fines; it organized the "whale watches" as much to watch the workers as to look out for dead whales. It is not surprising that under these conditions "perfection" proved so difficult.

After the mid-1660s all this changed suddenly. A major contributing element was undoubtedly England's return to political stability after its long civil war. A restored monarchy and an ambitious parliament created a vital new commercial system that Adam Smith a century later labeled "mercantilism." This new system guaranteed that the raw materials of the New World would be transported to the mother country. From England flowed the consumer goods; no commercial rivals were tolerated in ports of colonial America. Indeed, Charles II threw the Dutch out of New Netherlands and renamed it New York in honor of his overbearing brother, the Duke of York. These military and political changes opened up new markets and created new possibilities. The local whalers simply took advantage of developments that they probably did not fully understand and certainly did not control.

A second factor contributing to the success of the Whale Design was the arrival in East Hampton around 1666 of a man who actually knew something about the whaling trade. James Loper is not the kind of man whose name appears in history books. He was not a political figure, nor a soldier, nor even an intellectual. His claim to inclusion in our story is that he was an entrepreneur of considerable talent. This young Dutchman was related to the Schellinger clan, and soon after he had taken up residence in East Hampton, he married Elizabeth Howell, the girl whose dying mother had accused a neighbor of being a witch. East Hampton was extremely fortunate not only to attract Loper, but also to keep him. "Headhunters" were at work in colonial times just as they are now. The settlers of Nantucket had offered Loper an extremely lucrative deal if he would agree to train the local fishermen in the mysteries of offshore whaling. He accepted the invitation but then, for reasons we will never know—perhaps his wife was not too keen on leaving her family—he changed his mind. By staying in East Hampton, Loper helped to organize an industry and, in the process, to reorder a society.

Even with Loper's advice, the "stockmen" of the village must have found it difficult to raise the capital required to establish themselves initially in the Whale Design. It is hard to place a precise figure on the cost of setting up in this trade. A whaler needed at least one boat, sometimes referred to as a "canoe." These small but sturdy vessels had to carry four rowers, a harpooner, and a steersman: six men in all, plus their equipment. One probate inventory included a "whale craft" valued at three pounds, which seems like a low appraisal; perhaps this particular boat was in poor shape. In addition to the whale craft, the fisherman needed strong lines, a harpoon, several metal lances, oars, an anchor, a drogue (a sea anchor, a flotation device used to tire a wounded whale), and a huge kettle for trying the blubber. Each man engaged in this trade probably owned a set of knives as well as other tools. The total outlay, therefore, must have been at least twenty pounds sterling, a major investment for an ordinary East Hampton farmer. Moreover, even if he owned the necessary equipment, he still had to pay a crew, an item that could be a major financial burden (three shillings per day per man), depending on the type of labor contract that the whaler had negotiated. (These figures are based on the predecimal system; in Loper's time there were twenty shillings to the pound, twelve pence to the shilling.)

The people of East Hampton, perhaps with Loper's guidance, responded to this challenge by forming private "whale companies." These small partnerships provided local men with a way to share costs as well as risks. No doubt the parties to these agreements recognized the economies of scale involved. It made little sense, for example, for each individual whaler to purchase an expensive iron kettle. These companies, which began to appear in the town records around 1670, seldom involved more than three partners. The large number of partnerships formed during these years suggests that these arrangements worked quite well. Indeed, this structural innovation seems so sensible, so businesslike, that it is easy to overlook just how extensively the companies transformed the character of local society.

The central term here is *company*. In the early period of settlement, the adult males of East Hampton were gathered into small, neighborhood companies. These were *public* bodies; their goal was not individual profit. However, the companies of the later years in which we encounter such familiar names as Gardiner, James, Mulford, Loper, and Schellinger were *private* concerns. However one characterizes the economic transformation of East Hampton during this period, one must recognize that it had the effect of creating a new set of relationships within the community. In plain terms, some became partners in the Whale

Design; others did not. It is not clear from the records whether this division generated social tensions.

However this "private" system operated, it is clear that the market itself had begun to determine the structure of society. In his eighteenth-century history of East Hampton, John Lyon Gardiner commented on this shift from common to private exploitation of natural resources, and although this passage is not as clear as one would like, it shows an awareness that this was a critical moment in the town's development.

> It appears from the records that the business of killing Whales at the South side of the town in the Atlantic Ocean was regularly followed by the town & profitts of the Whale divided among the Inhabitants in proportion to their rights in the town as Original Purchasers. . . . But as soon as their lands & stock required much attention; this business was carried on with profitt by Individuals.

That is nicely put. The measure of "perfection" in the East Hampton Whale Design was "profitt by Individuals." That may have been what those first settlers from Kent and Devon, from Salem and Lynn, those men who complained that they had been "stinted" in the Massachusetts Bay Colony, those people who had had such problems sorting themselves out into acceptable social hierarchies had always wanted: a new world for men and women who dreamed material dreams. That may explain why those Narragansett Bay fishermen described at the opening of this chapter "yelled with joy" when they killed a whale: "They had earned more than a whole farm would bring . . . in a whole year."

Each form of wealth generates its own type of larceny. If slander and defamation were the most common antisocial acts in the founding years, and thus our key to the cultural values of everyday life, then the theft of property associated with whaling became the antisocial acts after the rise of the private companies. As early as 1667 the governor of New York complained that people on the end of Long Island were taking whales found on the beach that rightly belonged to the entire community. In other words, they were claiming that what were in fact "drift" whales were whales that they had killed offshore. He intended to put an immediate end to the practice "of some men seeking their owne ends without regard either to the benefit of the towns & proprietors of the beach or to the just duties reserved to his Royal Highness." And within the town itself people began to accuse neighbors of stealing barrels of oil from their own front yards.

The Whale Design affected the community in other, more subtle, ways. The trade led to a specialization of work that the settlers would not have known during the earliest years of colonization. As farmers, the men had spent their days doing pretty much the same things: they planted crops and kept track of the great herds of cattle. Whaling required several quite different jobs, however, and few men in East Hampton excelled at them all. Of course, to obtain the oil and bone, one had first to kill a whale. This was a dangerous, unpleasant task. The right whales visited East Hampton in the dead of winter, the so-called whaling season. The crew of the whaling boat would row out into the cold Atlantic, harpoon a slow-swimming mammal, and then follow the wounded beast until it died. The drama could last for hours. It involved short, extremely fatiguing bursts of rowing. The goal was to keep the whale constantly in sight, while at the same time staying safely out of its way. If all went well, the men eventually dragged the whale ashore, where they cut out the bone and sliced the blubber into long strips.

For most crew members, that was the end of the job. Other men carted the blubber and bone to the trying works. Boiling blubber may not have been as dangerous as hunting, but it required an expertise—controlling the temperature, for example—that came only from experience. The smell of the boiling blubber was overpowering. Little mistakes could greatly reduce the value of the oil on the London market. In one case a leading British importer informed a local producer that only thirty barrels of oil in a shipment of 180 had been any good. The rest were "blacke and red & very fowle with dirt." The merchant wrote that he was attempting to dump the inferior oil on the

Dutch market, but he was not certain that he would be able to cover his expenses. The Americans would just have to do a better job.

The whaling business also generated opportunities for the local coopers. We do not know much about these men. In all probability, many were farmers who made a little extra money working for one of the whaling companies. Sets of cooper's tools frequently appear in the probate inventories of late seventeenth-century East Hampton. These people guarded the resources of their trade with a jealous eye. In 1672 they protested to the English government that the Dutch had threatened to cut down the forests of eastern Long Island, "which is but little [that we] have to [make] Casks for oyle." A few years later the town itself announced that only those persons who had obtained a "lycence" could harvest trees "fitt for building or fenceing, or for the use of Coopers in making of Cask." But what angered the East Hampton coopers most were the itinerant coopers from New England who traveled to Long Island each winter looking for work. The local artisans labeled this unfair competition, and in a hotly worded petition dated October 13, 1675, they begged the government of New York to protect them from these transients who neither paid taxes to East Hampton nor bothered to instruct the youth of the community in the mysteries of the cooper's trade.

The various activities involved in whale oil production came together at the warehouses that the whaling companies operated at Northwest Harbor, a small, well-protected landing area near Gardiner's Bay. It was probably here that the coopers constructed the barrels, that men spent long hours in the malodorous and tedious task of trying the blubber, that packers prepared the products of East Hampton's fields and forests for shipment to distant ports. Some vessels moored in Northwest Harbor were bound for the major mainland markets in North America, such as Boston or New York. A few would sail for the sugar islands of the Caribbean. And occasionally one would transport whale oil and bone directly to London. In other words, by 1700, and perhaps even before that, East Hampton had transformed itself from an isolated farming village into a modest provincial port.

It is important not to overstate the case. There was not the slightest possibility that East Hampton would overtake New York or Boston as a mercantile center. It was not even a serious rival to New London. Yet, by almost any measure, its commercial achievements during the last four decades of the seventeenth century were impressive. And in 1711, a year for which we possess some reasonably reliable figures, Samuel Mulford's company employed twenty-four men at Northwest Harbor, and John Gardiner listed eighteen on his payroll.

There is another way of looking at the commercial activity that drew so many men to Northwest Harbor. It was through this little port, through those warehouses scattered along the shoreline, that the people of East Hampton maintained links with a rapidly expanding Atlantic economy. What drew them to this place, as workers as well as customers, was not simply the chance discovery of a market for whale oil and bone, nor the sale of meat and hides and grain and feathers. Rather, what we see dramatically expressed in the physical transformation of Northwest Harbor is the interface between production and consumption, between supply and demand. Without the desire for English manufactured goods there would have been no incentive to chase the whales through the frigid waters, no reason for entrepreneurs like James Loper to organize the private whale companies, and few employment opportunities for the local coopers and packers. Contemporaries understood these connections. As Colonel Robert Quary, a customs officer, explained to his superiors in the British government, the inhabitants living at the "east end of Long Island . . . are concerned in whale-fishing, and do make good quantities of oyle & bone, the greatest part of which is bought up by the people of New England government, who trade there with sloops, and do supply them with all sorts of European goods, and allso with that of the West Indies."

Adam Smith would have understood the social and economic transformation taking place in East Hampton. Whatever doubts the Scottish economist may have had about the moral implications of consumption—and when it involved no more than a mindless accumulation of baubles and trinkets, he condemned it in no uncertain terms—Smith recognized that the desire for possessions, for a life somehow made better by the purchase of goods, was the ultimate spark of industry. The man who tried to comprehend the spirit of capitalism wrote in his *Theory of Moral Sentiments:*

> It is this which first prompted them to cultivate the ground, to build houses, to found cities and commonwealths, and to invent and improve all the sciences and arts, which ennoble and embellish human life; which have entirely changed the whole face of the globe, have turned the rude forest in agreeable and fertile plains, and made the trackless and barren ocean a new fund of subsistence, and a great high road of communication to the different nations of the earth.

But however much we agree with Smith's argument, we would do well to consider just what happens when the drive that so marvelously improves the forests and the waters goes out of control and begins to turn the fertile places into deserts, the living ocean into barren seas.

In this developing local economy some men rose above the others and claimed the title "merchant." This is a difficult term to define accurately. One Englishwoman who traveled from Boston to New York in the fall of 1704 complained that the New Englanders used the word promiscuously: "They give the title of merchant to every trader." These sentiments were shared by Peleg Sanford, a governor of Rhode Island, who in 1680 explained to English authorities, "Wee have severall men that deale in buying and selling, although they cannot properly be called merchants." Sanford, who himself was a successful businessman, believed that a person could not properly refer to himself as a "merchant" unless he owned ships that carried goods from port to port.

If we accept this definition, we discover that at least two

men associated with the whaling companies of East Hampton deserve to be called "merchant." Abraham Schellinger, whose Dutch father, Jacobus, had emigrated to the village from New York City around 1670, became the town's most successful merchant. His major vessel, a sturdy sloop called the *Endeavour,* sailed regularly out of Boston and New York City bound for Northwest Harbor. Schellinger sometimes carried hides and other local produce to the smaller Connecticut towns, but the major focus of his business seems to have been the wholesale merchants of New England and New York. It was from them that he acquired his parcels of European goods.

A more important figure for our purposes was Samuel Mulford, a man who by the end of the century described himself as a "merchant" of East Hampton. Unlike the Schellingers, the Mulfords had helped found the town. Samuel's father and uncle, John and William, had been among the original purchasers. William seems to have concentrated on familiar argicultural pursuits, and there is no evidence that he became a partner in one of the whale companies. His brother John, however, seems to have been more enterprising. His name appears in the records regularly as a local official. He also served as an Indian com- missioner, and on one occasion he angered the governor of New York by trying to purchase land from the very people he was pledged to protect. However aggressively he may have pursued his own real estate interests, John remained throughout his long life what he had been in his youth, a stockman. When he died in 1686, he provided well for his family. There was land and cattle for everyone, but most of his estate went to Samuel, his eldest son.

One could fairly state that Samuel grew up *with* East Hamp- ton as well as *in* it. His lifespan, 1644 to 1725, coincides almost exactly with the economic transformation of this community. He played a major role in bringing about the changes in the whaling trade. Samuel established one of the first private com- panies, and although he maintained an impressive herd of cattle and purchased large amounts of land, he styled himself "mer- chant" in the records of the town and colony. A small account book that Samuel kept during the first decade of the eighteenth century follows the journeys of his sloop *Adventure*. Although most of his business was transacted in Boston, where he purchased a house during the 1690s, he occasionally loaded his ships with oil and bone and sent them all the way to London. It was Samuel who purchased the property, in the middle of the Village of East Hampton, still known as Mulford Farm.

It was in this period too that a "community" developed in East Hampton. In the early years of settlement East Hampton was made up of individuals who happened to find themselves living in the same location. They had not yet sorted themselves out; they had not agreed upon rules as to who was and who was not a member of this little commonwealth. It was because of this gnawing uncertainty that they had to endure so many charges and countercharges involving social status.

After the 1660s these problems largely disappeared. The community consisted of a group of families—really a complex network of local clans—who managed somehow to survive. Their names appear in the partnerships of the private whale companies: Gardiner, Mulford, James, Dayton, Osborn, and Stratton. We also occasionally come across an Edwards or even a Garlick. To put the point somewhat differently, we are not talking about the formation of a ruling class, or about the creation of a self-conscious local elite, but rather about a body of men and women, some wealthier than others, who were more certain than their mothers and fathers had been of their place in this society and who thus could convincingly "imagine" that they *were* the community. Significantly, it was not a closed corporation. Newcomers with expertise or money—a Loper or a Schellinger, for example—could become full members of the East Hampton community. However they got here, these people determined how the town allocated its economic resources, responded to external political challenges, and dealt effectively with internal dissension. In the genealogical history books, it is they who dominate the story that East Hampton most often tells itself about itself, although no one much bothers to discover how these people came to hold such a privileged position.

Many who lived and worked in East Hampton were excluded from this core community. Even a casual reading of the town records during this period reveals a number of surnames that have neither history nor future in this town. They are the names of transients, men who were drawn to East Hampton in search of opportunity. The coopers who signed the petition complaining about outsiders were in fact outsiders themselves. These were not persons who received land in the village. They appear in the town records largely as troublemakers or as laborers hired by one of the local whaling companies.

In the spring of 1686 some of these people apparently rose up against the community. The background to their protest is not well documented, but, whatever happened, ten citizens, who described themselves as local taxpayers who had lived in East Hampton for at least four years, wrote to the governor of New York demanding a share of the town lands. They knew that they were fishing in troubled waters. Governor Thomas Dongan was just then insisting that the inhabitants of East Hampton pay him a quitrent, really a small annual land tax. In this matter, the town leaders dragged their feet a little more stubbornly than they normally did when dealing with officials of colonial New York. Perhaps to show them that he meant business, Dongan ordered the town government to give each of the ten men thirty acres of land.

This decision precipitated a minor crisis. How dare these outsiders appeal for land over the heads of the leaders of the community! Samuel Mulford called out his neighbors by the beat of a drum and marched them to the center of the village, where he nailed to the meetinghouse door a paper attacking the governor. The Reverend Mr. James, himself a leading member of a private whale company, delivered an intemperate sermon allegedly based on the twenty-fourth chapter of Job, second verse: "Cursed is he that removes his neighbor's landmark. . . . And their order for it . . . is no excuse, though it were an edict from the King himselfe . . . they . . . cannot be excused from the curse." After the attorney general of New York issued warrants for their arrest, Mulford and James had second thoughts, and the town leaders eventually compromised with Dongan. Although the ten petitioners received their land, it is doubtful, especially after Mulford's quasi-military demonstration, that they felt as if they belonged to the community. But this is speculation; we cannot really know what was going on in their minds. Perhaps these people resented Mulford and his friends. Or perhaps, in the context of their lives, as men and women on the move looking for economic opportunity, they were happy to have acquired finally a piece of property that they could call their own.

III

*T*he problem with the economy of colonial America, as contemporaries never failed to observe, was that no one was willing to serve as a common laborer. The prospect of working for wages held no appeal for the ambitious immigrant. Even men who had been common laborers in England or Holland became independent yeomen in the New World, or, at least, they tried to do so. There was no holding them back. As one New Yorker explained to uncomprehending royal officials in London, "North America containing a vast Tract of Land, everyone is able to procure a piece of land at an inconsiderable rate and therefore is fond to set up for himself rather than work for hire. This makes labor continue very dear, a common laborer usually earning 3 shillings by the day & consequently any undertaking which requires many hands must be undertaken at a far greater expense than in Europe."

This was precisely the situation confronting the independent whale companies of East Hampton. Each vessel employed in the offshore trade required a crew of six men. Chasing whales out into the Atlantic in the dead of winter was difficult and dangerous work.

Fortunately for the men who organized the whale companies, a supply of labor was close at hand. In fact, it had been there from the start. It was just that before the creation of the private companies, none of the English settlers had seen the Montauks as much more than an annoyance. The villagers had purchased their lands, piece by piece, until by the mid-1660s the Indians had been pushed to the margins of East Hampton. Out of sight, but not, of course, out of mind. The colonists regulated the movements of the Indians, restricted "their Powowing," and even determined the number of dogs they could keep, and yet, somehow, the Indians hung on. They survived the Narragansetts' raids, the introduction of alcohol, and the spread of European disease. But they were survivors without an economic future.

The rapid development of the whaling trade in East Hampton changed all this. It was not that the white settlers suddenly discovered hidden charm in the local Algonquian culture. Like the sugar planters of the Caribbean and the tobacco growers of the Chesapeake, the East Hampton whalers needed strong bodies, and for that reason alone, they negotiated labor contracts with the Native Americans. It all happened very fast. As Colonel Francis Lovelace, governor of New York, reported with considerable insight in 1672, relations between the whites and the Indians were no longer what they had been "in the infancy of time, before the Whalefishing was in Practice."

These labor contracts are extraordinary documents. If nothing else, they reveal just how much of seventeenth-century English life, even on the Long Island frontier, was bound up by traditions of the common law. It was central to the settlers' sense of cultural identity, and, perhaps not surprisingly, the people who organized the whale companies—and, for that matter, the town itself—insisted on maintaining proper forms, on observing due process, on getting it all down in writing.

During the long months before the start of the whale season, groups of Indians and whites came together to sign formal, binding contracts, which were then entered into the town records. For the English such acts were not all that unusual; even those men who were not fully literate had prepared deeds and wills.

But what of the Montauks? They did not have a written

language, and it is doubtful that they understood the workings of English common law. There is no indication in the records that anyone bothered to read the contract to the Indians in their own tongue. One might have expected it. Even at the time, colonial authorities in New York recognized the difficulty of communicating with the Indians in English, and they advised local officials to explain government regulations to the Montauks in their own language.

Whatever the limitations of the negotiating process, the Indians do not seem to have been physically coerced into becoming whalers. At least, not initially. The Montauks placed their marks on the contracts next to the signatures and marks of the members of the independent companies (a good number of the English, it should be noted, could not write their own names either) and, by doing so, the Indians agreed to "go to sea a whale killing . . . next winter." In addition, they promised to labor for their employers—one contract called them "co-partners"—"at all times and seasons till the full time be over for killing whales." The season, as it was called, ran from late December to the first of April. The colonists supplied the Indian laborers with the basic equipment from boats to harpoons. How the Montauks actually went about catching the whales was left up to them. They pledged only to give a "true and faithful performance."

The great majority of the surviving contracts promised the Indians one half of all the right whales that they managed to catch. At first, some Montauks apparently demanded a small signing bonus, but clauses of this sort disappeared from what rapidly became the standard East Hampton whale contract. On March 5, 1681, for example, five local Indians pledged: "each man for himself to go upon a whaling design for Benjamin Conkling or his assignees the next whaling season which will be in the year 1681 upon half share as is usuall between the English and the Indians."

The descriptive categories leap out of this agreement. It is a contract in which the language of identity, the representatives of a nation dealing with the representatives of a race, has become absorbed into the forms of the law. Such terminology helps us to comprehend how the Englishmen who actually wrote these documents must have perceived their world. For them, it was "we, the English," who have entered into an agreement with "you, the Indians." The mental categories the Indians brought to these arrangements we cannot know. Did they think of themselves as the representatives of something like a nation? The Montauks, as opposed to the Narragansetts or the Mohawks? Or perhaps they signed the contracts as individuals who happened to need work.

The wording of the standard contract raises another problem. What exactly constituted half a whale? The language suggests that the colonists defined half a whale as what was left of the great mammal after it had been tried and after the deduction of various other production costs, such as carting strips of blubber from one part of East Hampton to another. In one contract the Indians accepted a percentage "of all *profit* that shall be gotten or obtained." One wonders just what the concept of "profit" could have meant to these local Algonquian whalers. Profit may have meant to Indians something different from what it did to the English. But I am not sure. A word that looks so familiar, so contemporary, so representative of our own capitalist society, eludes interpretation in the context of these contracts. We are not certain how the men who organized the whale companies calculated their own profit or to what degree they had been integrated into a sophisticated market economy. Fully enough, it would seem, to discuss commercial affairs in terms of profit. But perhaps they were not yet so businesslike that they calculated the annual depreciation of whaleboats.

The whaling companies seem to have gone to a lot of trouble drafting and recording these contracts. It would be comforting to conclude that such scrupulous behavior reflected a concern for the welfare of the Indians, but I have not encountered a single recorded case in which a Montauk sued a villager for noncompliance. The contracts do not appear to have been written for the benefit of the Indians at all. The whaling companies were most concerned with their rivals. Put more force-

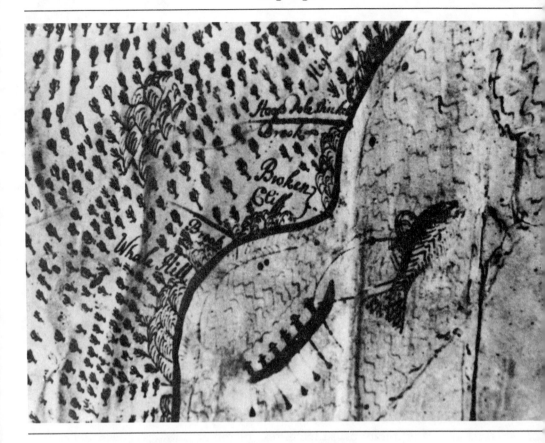

Colonial Whaleboat off Gardiner's Island (Courtesy of the East Hampton Historical Society)

fully, the possibility of making large profits caused the English inhabitants of East Hampton to look upon their neighbors as competitors. The stakes in this game were the Indians; there were simply not enough of them to go around. The prospect of a free labor market was totally unappealing, however, and, like some corporations in our own times, the whaling companies appealed to the government to restrict competition, in this case by setting limits on what an individual could offer an Indian for his services. In 1672 the governor of colonial New York confirmed a Southampton ordinance: "That whosoever shall Hire an Indian to go a whaling, shall not give him for his

Hire, above one Trucking Cloath Coat for each whale he and his Company shall Kill, or half the Blubber, without the Whale Bone, under Penalty." The governor added that if the whaling companies of East Hampton found this ordinance "practicable amongst them," they also could set maximum wages for the Indians. In other words, local employers wanted an outside authority to prohibit them from entering into bidding wars for Algonquian workers. It was the type of collusive regulation that the winners in these kinds of dealings often call "fair trade."

Not surprisingly, such arrangements did not work out well in practice. Competition for Indians led to sharp bargaining among the colonists, and the members of a successful whaling company could not afford to take the loyalty of their laborers for granted. There was always somebody prepared to offer a better contract. Even the local minister, who happened to be one of East Hampton's most ambitious whalers, did not fully trust some of his own parishioners. In April 1678 the Reverend Thomas James warned them to watch their step around his Indians:

> I, Thomas James of East Hampton, having together with my copartners for the whale design made several contracts and agreements with the Indians . . . I do by these presents both in my own name and name of my copartners enter a solemn protest against any person or persons who have or shall contrary to all law of God or man, justice or equity, go about to violate or infringe the above mentioned contracts or agreements without our consent.

Sometimes people had doubts about the integrity of their own partners. In 1679 the six organizers of one company announced publicly that they had pledged to "bind and engage ourselves to each other that what man or men doth take away his Indian out of the company to the hindrance of the design shall forfeit five pound sterling for the use of the company." The temptation to cheat, to gain a temporary advantage over a rival, to obtain an extra barrel or two of oil was obviously very great, and although it would be an exaggeration to claim that competition in the whale trade had transformed a Lockean village into a Hobbesian jungle, there is no question that the growing interest in individual profit affected the character of everyday life in late seventeenth-century East Hampton.

One might conclude from this discussion that the Montauks held their own in this competitive economic environment. After all, they still received half a whale for their pains. The texts of later contracts, however, suggest a different story. The villagers who invested their capital in boats and kettles demanded a labor force that was both stable and secure. Indians who moved from place to place or who decided suddenly that they no longer wanted to go "awhaling" could not be relied upon. When the season started a man had to be certain that his crew was ready to work. Enslavement and liquor were obvious instruments for controlling a labor force, and colonists in other parts of the New World used both devices to erode worker independence. There is not much evidence in East Hampton of actual enslavement of Indians. We know that one young Indian girl from New England was sold to a resident of East Hampton for "her natural life." (James Loper, the town's most skilled offshore whaler, gave the child to his wife as a present.) There may have been others. Moreover, at least two colonial governors issued the whaling companies special liquor licenses designed to help recruit the Indians into what English authorities described as an "infant industry."

The local companies, however, found a more subtle and ultimately more effective device for controlling the Indian laborers than liquor or enslavement. They systematically drew the Montauks into debt, and from a dependency on credit into economic bondage. On this point, the language of the whale contracts is unambiguous.

April 14, 1675: we the aforesaid Indians do engage ourselves to go to sea from year to year at all seasonable times for these our Copartners a whale killing till we have discharged to their satisfaction all former arrears or debts we stand engaged to them: and shall not take advantage of them to defraud or deceive them in the due performance of what we stand engaged to them by former agreements upon any pretense whatsoever. We also engage to the aforesaid Englishmen, our Copartners, that what goods any or all of them shall supply us with . . . the oil and bone we get this year shall be payment of the same, & so from year to year till all old debts be discharged. . . .

[March 10, 1683] . . . further I [Hector, a Montauk] bind myself that if I do not get so much by my half share this next season as will pay the said Robert Kedy what I shall be indebted to him, then I do hereby engage to go for him the next ensuing season until such time as I have paid him whatsoever I shall be indebted unto him. . . .

[March 5, 1681] . . . in case at the end of the said voyage, we or any of us [five Montauks] shall be indebted unto the said [Benjamin] Conckling or his assigns, then we do oblige ourselves to go to sea for him again the season that shall follow upon the same terms and so from year to year until we shall have wholly paid what we are indebted to him. . . .

[March 14, 1681] Also we [whose names are] underwritten do covenant and agree that we will continue under the said [John] Wheller's employ from season to season . . . until such time as we shall fully balance our account with the said Wheller or his orders in respect to what he shall betrust us with all. . . .

[January 6, 1681] I, Harry, alias Quauquaheid, Indian of Montauk, do firmly bind and engage myself to John Stretton, Sr., of East Hampton upon consideration that I am much indebted to him upon former accounts and his present supply of my present necessity do, I say, bind and engage myself to go to sea awhaling. . . .

From contract to contract the phrase "from year to year" reappears. Even to enter a whaling agreement the Indian had to post a bond of ten pounds sterling. The Montauk was in debt before he had killed even a single whale. It is difficult to characterize this labor system. The Indian found himself suspended in a kind of unfreedom, nominally an independent worker, but in fact bound to a specific Englishman for a period of time. The people who drafted the contracts were uncertain how best to describe the status of the Indians. The Montauks were sometimes referred to as "Stretton's Indians" or as "James's Indians." In April 1679, for example, a crew of six Indians pledged to go whaling for a company organized by Jacobus Schellinger "so long as we shall be indebted unto *our said owners or employers.*" Owners or employers? Slaves or freemen? Schellinger probably would have had a hard time explaining what in practice had become a clouded distinction. It is perhaps not surprising that one leading twentieth-century historian described the Montauk as "friendly" Indians. Reading the whaling contracts, it becomes clear why the Indians may have appeared so amiable to the white settlers; they had no other choice.

From the perspective of modern historiography the tragedy of this story is that the Indians were the victims of an economic system not of their own making. But this judgment, it seems to me, is somewhat condescending. If the Montauk whalers were victims, then they were eager ones. They too wanted the consumer goods that flowed through the warehouses on Northwest Harbor. And they demanded more than rum. Indeed, one of the two best preserved pieces of seventeenth-century glass in East Hampton comes from an Indian grave. (It is virtually identical to the so-called Loper bottle pictured at right.)

We should not forget that the Montauks had established wampum factories in this area long before the English arrived, and although there is no evidence that they transferred skills learned in that enterprise to the whaling trade, it is certain that they appreciated how the competition for laborers among the white settlers had improved their own bargaining position. After all, they were occasionally successful in playing one company off against another. In 1680 one local official reported to the governor of New York that he had received many complaints from East Hampton:

> . . . that they are like to be much disappointed and damnified in their business of whaling by the deceits and unfaithfulness of the Indians with whom they did contract the

James Loper Bottle (Courtesy of the East Hampton Historical Society)

last spring for their service in whaling this present season, who notwithstanding said contracts under hand and seal do now betake themselves to the service of other men, who do gladly except them, pretending some former engagement by which they intend to hold them, so that the Indians having received goods of one man in the spring upon account of whaling and now again of another to fit them for the sea, leave their masters to quarrel.

How often the Montauks were able to manipulate the negotiations and thereby "leave their masters to quarrel" is impossible to determine at the distance of three centuries. Like the slaves in the American South, the Indians apparently learned to maneuver within a restrictive framework that had been designed by another race. On one occasion in a neighboring town, the governor had to intervene when the Indians claimed "a Barrel of Oil out of every Whale which they shall take . . . requiring likewise payment for every stick of wood which they shall cut thereabout for their needful use in dressing, their diet or the like." This was a job action, a threat to a cozy labor system, and the governor understandably ordered the Native Americans to drop their illegal demands.

Names provide another insight into the character of race relations in East Hampton. During the 1650s the settlers had not been too sure that they could identify a local Indian simply by his appearance. One Indian looked pretty much like any other Indian. But the whaling industry brought the two peoples into regular contact, and although the English tried to deny the legitimacy of the Montauks' culture, the Indians refused to cooperate. The town records list many Indian whalers by names assigned to them by the white settlers: John, George, Harry, Major, Hector, Plato, Witness, Shine, and Cow. Just as frequently the contracts list the Indian whalers by their Algonquian names. These complex, unfamiliar words clearly challenged the clerk's ability to sound out syllable by syllable an alien language: Papasoquon; Unquonomomak; Quasequeg and his wife, Quasegues; Weompes; Wombanocum; Wampquat; and Tantoquin. Although a small point perhaps, the names that appear in the

East Hampton records testify to the ability of some Indians to preserve the integrity of their culture.

Just how much the Indian names had become a bone of contention in this community is revealed by the curious term *alias* that sometimes appeared in the whaling contracts. In these cases the Indians seem to have insisted on maintaining their otherness. They are not non-Indians, a category invented by their "owners or masters." They were not Nat, or John, or Will. Consider an agreement drawn up in December 1677. There is power, an indomitable spirit of cultural resistance, in this nearly incomprehensible passage:

> This agreement made between Thomas James, John Stretton, Senior, Thomas Diament, Senior, Thomas Chatfield, Senior, inhabitants upon East Hampton upon the East Riding of Yorkshire on Long Island one party: And Mousup, Sachem; Unquonimo Wunnanaugema, alias Antony; Jumpaus, alias Nat; Uncommouit Jeffry Quauquehide, alias Harry . . . Tantoquin, alias Will John Indian; Wompaquat, alias Haines . . . Quequecum, alias Hector; Maneeg, alias Will; Wumakauntakkum, alias Cowkeeper. . . .

The tragedy of race relations in East Hampton is not simply that the Europeans took advantage of the Indians' vulnerability. They also cut the Native Americans off from an opportunity to participate fully in the commercial processes that were altering the face of local society. The point is not that the Montauks wanted to become capitalists, but that they were never given a chance to respond creatively to the marketplace, and so instead of developing into a kind of local peasantry—say, on the model of Latin American societies—they were finally destroyed, the victims of the white man's uncompromising sense of cultural superiority.

By the end of the eighteenth century, long after East Hampton had ceased to be a major whaling port, the white inhabitants had all but forgotten how much the history of the Indians was actually their own history. The Montauks were something of a nuisance and an embarrassment, and their "friendliness" was an expression of desperation rather than of bargaining power. It was during this period that John Lyon Gardiner observed that the Indians had only themselves to blame for what had happened. In Gardiner's words, their "idle dispositions and savage manners prevent the most of them from living comfortable, altho' the soil is easily tilled & good. Rum has reduced them from a very powerful tribe to a few persons; they are continually disappearing. As they say, the pure old Indian blood does not run in all their veins; it is corrupted by the black and white men."

One wonders how Gardiner and his friends regarded a peculiar petition that the Montauks sent to the government of colonial New York on the eve of the American Revolution. The document observed that the "tribe" now consisted of only thirty families. These men and women were the descendants of the Indians who had granted land to the first settlers of East Hampton. Since that time, the petition explained, the Montauk people had had great difficulty maintaining their economic independence. To be sure, they "continued to reside in the Neighborhood; living principally by Planting, Fishing, & Fowling." They were "gradually wasting way," however, and "those who remain, now occupy a Tract upon Montauk Point."

The experience of living in such close proximity with the white colonists had apparently convinced some of the Indians of the superiority of certain aspects of European culture. They had long ago dropped their "Barbarian way of living, and are become, not only civilized, but christianized and are peaceable and orderly, and willing to behave as good subjects to his Majesty King George the third." But as the rulers of colonial New York surely understood, such a cultural transformation had not been easy. After all, "such a Change of Manners, as it exposes them to a Life of Labour, must introduce an Attachment to Property, without which they cannot subsist, perform the Duties nor enjoy the Rights of Subjects."

The Indians complained that their English teachers had not played fair. In fact, at that very moment they were busy crowding the Montauks out of their land on the pretended claim of old purchases. Confronted with an impossible situation in which they were told that they required property to exercise the "Rights of Subjects" while being denied land that was rightfully theirs, the Montauks appealed to the higher authorities. Their petition protested that "Inasmuch as the barbarous and unlettered State of the American Indians, rendered it impossible for them to keep Records . . . your Petitioners cannot ascertain what Lands have been, or remain still unsold." The Indians begged the representatives of the crown to help them establish what precisely they owned in East Hampton.

It is difficult to know what to make of this appeal. Perhaps it did not reflect the state of Indian culture but was prepared for the Montauks by someone who understood the kinds of liberal arguments likely to find a sympathetic audience in New York. On the other hand, the petition may have captured something of the spirit of an enterprising people who had once been the mint-masters of Long Island and had participated in the Whale Design, and who, when faced in the late colonial period with extermination, brilliantly turned the language of preindustrial capitalism against the very people who had destroyed their world.

IV

*W*hat about the black men? Their presence in seventeenth-century East Hampton is something of a mystery. We know almost nothing about the African-Americans whom Gardiner believed had corrupted the "pure old Indian blood" or how exactly they got to this community. If this were a study of the Carolinas or the Chesapeake, the discovery of black people in the seventeenth-century records would be no surprise. The slaves provided the labor that sustained the plantation system; they cultivated rice and tobacco. But what are we to make of slaves at the east end of Long Island? In a Puritan village? In a society that did not produce an agricultural staple?

My answer is that I do not know. East Hampton's colonial

blacks appear in the records like subatomic particles in a physics experiment. They have left traces of their existence in various government documents, but there is no direct evidence, nothing personal that would allow us to know them as individuals. All that we have are their names: Bess, Jack, Peter, Rose, Bristo, Betty, Hannah, and Simene. We will never know where they came from or who gave them these names.

We can at least speculate on how they came to find themselves in East Hampton. These African-Americans, or perhaps their parents, had been taken to New York City from West Africa or from a Caribbean island. New York had long been involved in the slave trade, and some of the first black slaves sold into Virginia were carried on Dutch ships operating out of what would become New York City. By the turn of the century its black population, including freemen as well as slaves, was as large as that of any English settlement north of the plantation colonies. It would have been easy for a Mulford or a Schellinger to bring an African-American back to East Hampton.

Whatever their backgrounds may have been, these men and women quickly became a part of everyday life in East Hampton. A crude local census taken in 1687 lists twenty-five "slaves": eleven males and fourteen females. By 1698 there were 558 blacks living in Suffolk County (558 out of a total population of 2,679), but it is impossible to tell how many of these people were inhabitants of East Hampton. Although no information is provided about the ages of these blacks or their masters, the census does make clear that in 1687 just under five percent of the town's population was African-American. And, of course, enslaved. The census lists people specifically in this category. But curiously, when the blacks turn up in the East Hampton probate inventories—really our only evidence other than the census—they are called "servants." The term is misleading, if not disingenuous, for there is no doubt about their status; they were chattel, a form of property. In John Stratton's will, we find listed among the table, blankets, and pewter plates two negroes and their child, valued at fifty pounds sterling. This was a very large investment. The men who inventoried the possessions of Abraham Schellinger estimated that "Bess and Jack" were worth eighteen pounds and forty pounds respectively. They were mentioned just after the farm animals (twenty-five pounds for one hundred sheep), and just before Schellinger's farm tools. John Mulford, Samuel's father, owned a male slave, but we do not know his price on the market.

During the eighteenth century the local minister—Nathaniel Huntting, who in 1698 had replaced Thomas James—seems to have worried a good deal about converting African-Americans to Christianity. He duly marked the baptism of the slaves, noting at the same time to whom they belonged. In 1724 a negro owned by Matthew Mulford received the sacrament; so too did Rose, a black woman who was then the property of a Captain Mulford. Huntting apparently doubted that these people could comprehend the confession of faith that was normally employed on such occasions, and in November 1723 he prepared a special service just for the blacks. The minister propounded to Peter, "negro sert. of Capt. Burnet," a statement:

> . . . agreeable to a short catechism in the book entitled the Servts. of Abraham, in the following manner: You believe that the Great God, who is the father, the son, & the H.G. made you and all the world—that the Ld. Jesus, who is God & man, saves them that look to him.
>
> That as for such as obey, God & the Ld. Jesus, your souls shall go to the heavenly paradise when the bodies die & your bodies shall be raised at the last day, to eternal life, but the wicked shall go into everlasting punishment.

Huntting may have been behind an order that appeared in the town records in 1732: ". . . the Negroes may sit in [the] hind seat in the second Gallery on [the] west side . . . if they are not voted down on Election day."

All one can really say with confidence is that black men and women were introduced into this community as slaves at about the same time that other changes of profound importance were taking place. East Hampton was not a slave society, certainly not in the sense that South Carolina and Jamaica were slave societies. The Indians served as a labor force, and the profits from oil and bone that flowed into late seventeenth-century East Hampton went to purchase consumer goods, among them black slaves. These African-Americans were at once a personal indulgence and a good investment for their owners. They may have devoted most of their time to domestic chores.

Whatever their employment, their presence in homes of the Gardiners, the Mulfords, the Schellingers, and other of East Hampton's more prosperous families was a conspicuous expression of material success. Since the colonial blacks did not have surnames—at least none that the town clerks bothered to record—we cannot trace the generations who followed Peter and Rose, Bess and Jack, Hannah and Bristo.

V

*T*o this point in the story, I have focused upon the local society. It is as if we have been examining the history of East Hampton through the lens of a powerful social microscope. From this perspective the core of the village—what I have called the "community"—dominates our sense of East Hampton as an historical entity. Surrounding this highly visible center we have encountered other groups: the Indians, the African-Americans, the poorer whites without adequate land, and the migrant laborers. We see them as separate, although dependent, bodies. Viewed in this way, colonial East Hampton becomes a fluid, complex set of human relationships that owes its very structure to the development of a market economy.

But, of course, this perspective is merely a convenient device for organizing bits and pieces of unwieldy evidence into narrative form. East Hampton was also part of a larger outside world. During the earliest years of settlement, these links had not seemed particularly important. East Hampton was essentially an independent commonwealth. Cut off from New England, the town came to view itself as separate, culturally self-sufficient, and capable of setting its own rules.

The Whale Design changed how the inhabitants of East Hampton imagined themselves in what may be called "political space." It is not that the town itself was no longer the center of their lives. Daily routines remained essentially the same; the ties of kinship were not at risk. It is just that as East Hampton became part of a wider political world with several distinct layers, the members of the community had to define themselves not simply as East Hampton, but as East Hampton in relation to competing sources of authority: the county, the colony, and the empire. In some American towns—the famous New England villages, for example—this process was retarded, largely because no one in the outside world cared much about what they were doing.

But East Hampton was ahead of the others. Indeed, the striking success of the various private whale companies drew attention to what had been up to that time an isolated village. Officials of colonial New York, especially a series of grasping governors, came to look upon East Hampton as a source of income, and they were forever demanding fees from the people who lived there: whale licenses, tariffs on imports, and taxes on the land. The challenge from the outside forced the leaders of East Hampton to defend their interests, to become lobbyists within an expanding commercial empire, and, as they did so, they were inevitably integrated into the very political structures that they were attempting so resolutely to resist.

The rhetoric of power—that is what politics is all about—contains contradictions that the people who employ it usually choose to overlook. The leaders of East Hampton were no exception. Although they did not want to share the profits of the Whale Design with the governors of New York, they could not very well state their case quite so bluntly. And so the men who represented the town did what others in their position have done for centuries. They couched their interests in terms of high principle, translating local needs into a more universal language of rights and liberties that other Englishmen could readily comprehend.

The irony is obvious. At the moment when the leaders of East Hampton were insisting upon their traditional rights and liberties as free-born Englishmen, sounding a good deal like the embattled patriots of 1776, they were reducing many people who happened to live there to social and economic dependence. The two processes went hand in hand. The men who spoke so eloquently about their own political independence were most likely to be the same persons who brought the Indians into debt, who enslaved the African-Americans, and who protested most loudly when the poorer whites requested land. Not surprisingly, at the center of this search for an effective political language was none other than Samuel Mulford.

There was no love lost between the towns on the end of Long Island and the government created by the Duke of York to rule his American province. The Duke was the future James II, a man whose religious and political opinions had been shaped by the violence of the English Civil War. The Puritans had executed his father in 1649, and when the Stuarts returned to the throne in 1660 after an unhappy exile, neither James nor his brother Charles expressed much affection for the independent-minded Puritans who had settled in the New World. What was even more worrisome, from the perspective of the American dissenters, James seemed especially fond of Catholics.

The governors whom the duke selected for New York reflected his own autocratic temperament. Their instructions made no provision for representative institutions of the type that seventeenth-century New Englanders had come to take for granted. The Long Islanders petitioned for political reform, and when the British reconquered the colony from the Dutch in 1674—the Dutch had held it for a single year—the people of East Hampton begged James to be returned to the government of Connecticut.

The duke dismissed what was in fact a hopeless request. His new governor, Edmund Andros, a soldier by training, labeled the leaders of the whaling communities "rebels" and in not too gentle terms told them that they had better swear allegiance to the government of New York or face arrest. John Mulford, Samuel's father, was one of the first inhabitants of East Hampton to accept the governor's invitation.

This story of the community's resistance is often regarded as a chapter—albeit a rather obscure one—in the long and glorious history of representative government in what would one day become the United States of America. And no doubt in some sense it was. It would be a mistake, however, to see the East Hampton whalers as American revolutionaries-in-the-making simply because they rejected the duke's high-flying notions about civil authority. Behind their protestations lurked the Whale Design and a network of commercial relations that was just beginning to transform East Hampton into a relatively prosperous community.

By the early 1670s the governors of New York were demanding the "king's share" of all drift whales found on the beaches of East Hampton. A share amounted to one-sixteenth of the oil and bone, and no one in the town bothered to pay it. When the duke sent a representative to the end of the island to investigate, he encountered the kind of group amnesia that sometimes greets Treasury agents looking for illegal stills in West Virginia. "The number of whales killed in those parts," reported a hapless investigator, "are never observed by any person, not the quality of bone or oil particularly taken notice of. . . . There is no share [that] cometh to your Royal Highness."

Relations between East Hampton and the duke's governors rapidly deteriorated. New York officials demanded the payment of rents to which James was technically entitled, but the major issue was free commerce. The men who ran the colonial government were no fools. They understood that the whalers of East Hampton wanted consumer goods, and in order to obtain what they regarded as the best selection on the best terms, they transported almost all of their oil and bone to Boston. The economic resources of a town in New York were helping to make Boston a major center of trade. Boston! A Puritan city.

It was more than James could endure. As Governor Thomas Dongan (1682–1688) explained to James, the people of East Hampton "refused to take our merchants' money or goods, and carried away their oil private[ly] to Boston and brought back goods from thence." Dongan punished the independent-minded traders by slapping an import tax of ten percent on all goods imported into East Hampton from any port outside the colony of New York.

This order, coupled with the other issues, seems to have converted the leaders of East Hampton into passionate students of English constitutional history. They expressed their local grievances in terms of general principles that they hoped would find sympathetic resonance in the mother country. Alas for them, the political language that they adopted must have sounded to James like a distant and unpleasant echo of the rhetoric that the Parliamentarians had employed against his father during the English Civil War.

In a "Humble Address," a document signed by John Mulford, the citizens of East Hampton claimed to have been deprived of "our Birthright freedomes & Privelledges." Indeed, they feared that "our freedome should be turned into bondage & our Antient priveledges so infringed that they will never arrive at our posteritie." Surely the king—by that time the Duke of York had become James II—did not want to rule "over bond men oppressed by Arbitrary Impositions & executions." Such appeals fell upon deaf ears.

Fortunately for East Hampton, James had his hands full with other, more pressing, problems in the mother country. In 1688 the Protestants of England ran the Stuart monarch out of the kingdom and invited William and Mary to rule in his place, a victory allegedly for constitutional government that came in time to be known as the Glorious Revolution.

Even without James the political waters of colonial New York were treacherous for the people of East Hampton. They were feeling their way in an increasingly complex imperial system, and finding that events largely beyond their immediate control were forcing them to become what we might describe today as "lobbyists." The same process was occurring in other parts of colonial America. Different groups with different economic interests clamored to be heard. The sugar planters made demands; the tobacco planters petitioned on their own behalf. They all employed the language of rights and liberties. And the whalers joined the chorus, learning the melody and libretto as they went along.

Samuel Mulford rose to prominence in this uncertain political situation. It is not difficult to understand why he became something of a symbol of the community itself. Mulford was a product of this changing society. As we have seen, he was one of the more energetic supporters of the Whale Design. In fact, like many of his entrepreneurial neighbors, Mulford had responded creatively to a commercial world that opened up at the end of the seventeenth century. His father had left England, a voyager in the great Puritan exodus known as the "great migration," and now, as East Hampton residents found themselves involved politically and economically in a wider outside world, the son reestablished the contacts that the founding generation had severed.

Samuel seems to have spent much of his early adult life attending to his business affairs. In fact, it was not until the death of his father, a powerful figure in the life of the community, that the son was given major civic responsibilities. The late 1680s marked the turning point in his public life. He was elected a selectman of the village, made captain of the local militia, and chosen to represent East Hampton in various dealings with the colonial government.

Although his name appears with increasing frequency in the town records, Mulford remains a peculiarly elusive figure. No picture of him has survived; I suspect that he never bothered to have one made. We know nothing, therefore, about his physical features or the shape of his face or, most lamentably, about how he presented himself when he was conscious that others were looking.

This is perhaps not as serious a problem as it might appear. His contemporaries—many of them political enemies—have left a good many clues to Mulford's character. They allow us to imagine a person who was extraordinarily ambitious. They suggest other adjectives as well: tough, clever, articulate, blunt, and obstinate.

Most especially obstinate. The inhabitants of East Hampton may have viewed Mulford's stubborn streak as a sign of strength, but outsiders clearly found it annoying. Moreover, I suspect that his religious beliefs put some people off. There is no doubt that Mulford was a Puritan, and in social circles that were beginning to lose touch with the teachings of John Calvin, he probably seemed a bit out of place, a throwback to an earlier age. One urbane governor of colonial New York wrote a farce in which Mulford appeared as "Mulligrub," a long-winded self-righteous bore.

Whatever his faults, Mulford knew what he wanted. In political affairs he was a tenacious fighter. He never conceded a point, and when he lost a contest on one level of government, he immediately appealed to a higher one, pursuing his interests so doggedly that he eventually exhausted almost everyone with whom he came into contact. And although he could be charming, Mulford did not mince words with people he disliked. In his eighteenth-century history of East Hampton, John Lyon Gardiner says of Mulford:

> He was a man of an original genius, of good judgement but of an odd turn. He was a native of East Hampton and is the same person who is said to have been expelled [from] the house [the New York Assembly] for saying it was governed by the Devil, but readmitted on explaining his meaning which was that the house was directed by the Albany members, they by Colonel Schuyler, he by the Mohawk Indians, and they by the Devil.

In 1840 David Gardiner sketched a similar picture of the early town leader:

> Samuel Mulford was in his speech rapid, and possessed of a temper at times rather hasty; he expressed himself occasionally with more instability and less guardedness than

a due respect to prudence would seem to demand. But such was the structure of his mind, that he could hold no toleration with what he was convinced was wrong, and he could yield nothing in combating for principle. In his feelings, his habits, his associations, his religion, and his great simplicity of manners, he was essentially a republican.

One bit of East Hampton folklore involves Mulford's curious nickname, Fishhook. According to this oft-told tale, Mulford traveled to London early in the eighteenth century in an attempt to gain an audience with the king. The great metropolis proved a little too fast-moving for this country fisherman, however, and one day while he was waiting outside the royal palace, a pickpocket snatched Mulford's money. He responded by sewing fishhooks inside the pockets of his coat. According to the story, the whaler's ingenuity impressed everyone, even the king.

Most likely the entire story is a fabrication. There is certainly no evidence that Mulford ever lined his pockets with fishhooks. The tale probably has what may be called a structural truth, for if one pushes the interpretation beyond a device for catching pickpockets, one sees that this is just another story that East Hampton has told itself about itself. Mulford obviously represents the community, virtuous and independent, a resilient individual who finds himself temporarily overwhelmed by the demands of the larger world. In that sense, Trevor Kelsall was correct; it required a certain "wryness" to survive in East Hampton. For those who searched for deeper meanings, the Fishhook legend must also have suggested that the town that failed to defend its own economic interests would soon discover that political "pickpockets" had stolen its treasure.

During the early years of the eighteenth century, the whalers of East Hampton matched wits with a clever, though somewhat bizarre opponent, the governor, Lord Cornbury. Like so many British officials entrusted with important positions in the American colonies, Cornbury felt that he was grossly underpaid. Indeed, royal appointees had constantly to search out new sources of revenue in a type of beggaring operation that made some of them appear more grasping and corrupt than in fact they probably were. Cornbury's aggressive self-interest certainly alienated a good many members of the New York Assembly, and one of them, Lewis Morris, has left an extraordinary description of the governor: ". . . of my Lord Cornbury; of whom I must say something which perhaps no body will think worth their while to tell, and that is, his dressing in woman's clothes everyday." Lewis may have exaggerated the frequency of such displays, but one portrait that has survived from this period shows Lord Cornbury dressed like Queen Anne. He apparently liked to celebrate her birthdays in this manner.

Not surprisingly, the governor does not appear to have cared much for Samuel Mulford. They were very different kinds of men. But the whales—more precisely, the increasingly visible prosperity of East Hampton—made the community a tempting target for an impecunious official. As Mulford and his neighbors discovered, it was becoming difficult to resist external interference from the likes of Cornbury. Loss of political independence was an aspect of belonging to a commercial empire that they had not anticipated. The appointed royal governors sent to New York during the early decades of the eighteenth century had powerful prerogatives; they were certainly ready to influence the course of law when that suited their own purposes. If they had any political sense whatsoever, they found ways to make good friends in the colonial legislature.

Cornbury worked the system well. No sooner had he arrived in the New World than he announced that the whale was a "royal fish." Like other valuable resources—sturgeon, for example—these mammals had traditionally belonged to the crown. By extension, therefore, something that belonged to the monarch must belong to the monarch's personal representative. The logic was tortured, even under eighteenth-century law, but Cornbury pushed ahead. Henceforth, the whalers of Long Island would deliver the crown's share of every whale they caught directly to the royal governor in New York City. Moreover, he expected them to purchase licenses if they intended to pursue offshore whaling, and, to no one's surprise, all the fees that were collected seemed to end up in the governor's own pocket.

There is no need to recount the details of this particular battle. In the end, Cornbury's bark proved worse than his bite. On one occasion, he dispatched agents to East Hampton to find out why no one bothered to treat right whales like "royal fish." The answer was predictable enough. However angry Cornbury may have been, he did not have the bureaucracy that would have been necessary to enforce his will on the recalcitrant whalers of Long Island. They continued to send their whales, and almost everything else that they produced, to New England. As the governor fully understood, these stubborn East Hamptoners wanted to have their cake and eat it too. Stated somewhat differently, they wanted the benefits of participation in an economic system, but stoutly resisted the political encroachment that inevitably accompanied it. In 1703, Cornbury informed his superiors in London:

> There has for some time been no Trade between the City of New York and the East-end of Long Island, from whence the greatest quantity of whale oil comes. And indeed, the people of the East End of Long Island are not very willing to be persuaded to believe that they belong to this province. They are full of New England principles. They choose rather to trade with the people of Boston, Connecticut, and Rhode Island, than with the people of New York.

It was during this crisis that Mulford first journeyed to London. Like other colonists throughout America, he was learning some political tricks of his own. If the governor threatened to tax the source of local prosperity, and if the members of the colonial legislature failed to bring relief, then one could plead the case in Britain itself. In other words, events in New York were forcing Mulford to become a lobbyist on an even grander scale. In that sense he was not unlike modern farmers who travel to Washington in search of protection from various state authorities.

Governor Robert Hunter was another royal appointee who

had a fortune to make in this world. And, like Cornbury, whom
he replaced in 1710, he saw in East Hampton an opportunity
to feather his own financial nest. Once again, the offshore whalers were ordered to purchase licenses. Once again, they were
told to deliver to the governor his share of the "royal fish."
And once again, the people at the end of the island were threatened with heavy penalties, such as a tax of ten percent on all
European goods imported into New York from another colony,
if they continued to trade with the merchants of Boston.

Mulford took up the challenge. In this controversy he spoke
not only for his own interests, but also for those of the community. Indeed, that was the source of Mulford's strength. At
a critical moment in the history of East Hampton, this man
managed to bridge the political space that separated his neighbors from the various levels of officialdom that now governed
a commercial empire. In that sense, Mulford was a broker, a
mediator who had somehow learned to translate the hopes and
fears of a small whaling community into language that outsiders
could comprehend. Put another way, Mulford's genius was his
ability to help the people of East Hampton—those who regularly sent him to the New York Assembly—to imagine themselves in time. He knew how the village had got to be the way
he found it. After all, the history of East Hampton was his
history, and the history of two generations of Mulfords working
to be something more than they might have been had they
remained in Kent. To the colonial governor or to the members
of the New York legislature or to the gentlemen in London
who tried to kept track of it all—different audiences making
different demands—Mulford told a story of whaling companies
and local warehouses filled with consumer goods, of people
eager to make deals in distant markets and yet who, even at the
instant that they were being swept up in a larger market economy, remained apprehensive that their success might somehow
compromise the independence that their fathers had dreamed
so long ago.

Mulford developed most of these themes in a famous
speech delivered before the New York Assembly on April 2,

1714. It got Mulford expelled from the legislature. His colleagues explained that the representative from East Hampton could say whatever he liked about Governor Hunter's commercial regulations so long as he said it in the Assembly. But Mulford broadcast his views. He paid to have his speech published. He wanted everyone to know that the tariff denied the people of New York what he called their "Birth-Right Privilege."

Mulford insisted that the governor was using the law to strangle trade, the lifeblood of communities like East Hampton. For the honest citizen, doing business in New York had become a nightmare:

> . . . there was so many Officers and Subtil Fellows to Inspect into every nice Point in the Law, and if they were not fulfilled and observed in ever particular, their Vessels were Seized: So that not any man was fit for Master of a Vessel to go to *New-York,* except he were a Lawyer; and then they should not escape, except it was by Favour.

Behind these words lie many conversations with Schellinger and other local merchants who had been forced to accept a set of seemingly arbitrary regulations that undermined East Hampton's prosperity. And that was the real pity of it all. Governor Hunter's actions severed the commercial links that had made it possible for little towns like East Hampton to escape the agricultural backwater and to enter the main channels of imperial trade. "Our Vessels being thus carried and drove away, we had not Vessels to carry the Growth of the Countrey to a Market; nor bring us such Goods as we wanted." This was the experience of the warehouses being turned into general economic principle, something that Adam Smith and his Scottish friends would do far more effectively for another, more receptive, audience. For the people of East Hampton, and therefore for Samuel Mulford, traditional English freedom and liberty had come to depened in some important way upon the open exchange of goods "For where Trade is so Clogg'd, Navigation Discourag'd, Strangers Deter'd to come, [it] causeth Goods Imported to be Scarce and

Dear, and the Growth of the Countrey Low; which was the Misery of many in this Colony."

What is so striking about Mulford's performance is his mastery of the language of contemporary British politics. The visit to London in 1704 had not been wasted on this man. In fact, the purpose of publishing his speech before the New York Assembly was not to persuade his own Long Island constituents, who had heard it all before. Nor was he aiming to convince the royal governor and his followers of the logic of his argument. The intended audience lived in the mother country. Mulford tried audaciously to preserve the independence of his own community by appealing over the heads of the colonial appointees, and, in this effort, the old whaler realized that it would not be enough to describe East Hampton's problems in purely economic terms. He had to catch the idiom of the Glorious Revolution.

> We have an Undoubted Right and Property by the Law of God and Nature, settled upon the Subject by Act of Parliament; which is not to be taken from them by the Supreme Power, without due Course of Law. The End of Law is to secure Persons and Estates; the End of Government to put the same in Execution, to the purpose that Justice be done.

The people of East Hampton were transformed in Mulford's brilliantly effective discourse into true Englishmen, authentic defenders of ancient rights and liberties, and virtuous patriots holding out against a gang of corrupt hirelings who would have been more at home in the reign of James II. "And I am of the Opinion," he declared with a marvelous sense of historical irony, "that there is some amongst us that would have made Notable Counsellors in King *James* the Second's time."

The point is not that Mulford and his neighbors were hypocrites who cynically appealed to abstract principle simply to gain narrow and selfish ends. Rather, the tariffs on consumer goods and the restrictions on whaling provided them with a context in which a more general political language of rights and liberties found meaning. By phrasing his protest in terms of traditional rights and liberties, Mulford situated East Hampton in an imagined empire administered by men who may not have known the first thing about whales, but who responded almost instinctively to claims based upon "The Law of God and Nature, Settled upon the Subject by Act of Parliament."

The tempest over whale licenses eventually degenerated into nothing more than a fight between two strong-willed men. Hunter offered the troublesome whaler a deal. If he would publicly apologize for his behavior, the governor would drop all legal proceedings. But Fishhook refused to surrender, and, jumping bail in 1716, this proud, embattled, seventy-one-year-old man traveled once again to London, where he launched a fresh campaign to embarrass the colonial adminstration.

To Hunter's immense surprise Mulford almost succeeded. In 1718 the Council of Trade and Plantations sent Hunter a letter that reveals among other things just how adept Mulford had become at working the political levers of empire:

> They cannot find in his [Hunter's] Commission that the whale-fishery is reserved to him, as he intimates in his letter. . . . [They, therefore] request him to explain and to send a full answer to Mulford's petition, together with a return of the whale-fishery and dues paid thereon.

Hunter could not believe what was happening. Did the colonial administrators in London not see that they were dealing with "an enemy to the Publick"? To be sure, Mulford had circulated a "paper" among his constituents on the end of Long Island, but who, the governor asked in disgust, had signed it? Only a woman, a madman, and a boy! "If the voice of a whole Province," Hunter blustered, "is not judged of force sufficient to disprove the simple allegations of one crazed old man, it will be in vain for me to endeavour any more at being pronounced innocent."

And that was the end of it. There is no record of how the controversy over the whale licenses was finally resolved. Sadly, it no longer mattered. Mulford returned from the mother country to find himself the hero of a town in retreat. East Hampton had already begun to sink into a torpor, a long sleep that later generations would assume was the true history of their community.

VI

*I*t was the environment that finally betrayed the people of East Hampton, or perhaps it was the other way around. The colonists had asked a great deal of the land and the sea. The annual harvest provided the entrance fee to the wonders of a consumer economy, and, with each passing year, the inhabitants pushed a little harder, to breed a few more sheep, harvest a few more right whales, ship more local commodities to distant markets. No one thought specifically in terms of maximizing production. It was just that each family took advantage of opportunities as they presented themselves. For them an extra barrel of oil translated directly into various material comforts: yards of printed cloth, a pewter plate, a large looking glass, and, as the population of the village grew, more and more people made ever greater demands upon the town's finite resources.

Indeed, like the great tobacco planters of the Chesapeake and the mighty sugar barons of the Caribbean, Mulford's generation inscribed a commercial vision onto the very landscape of the New World. The results may not have been as dramatic in East Hampton as they were in other parts of the empire, but the process on the eastern end of Long Island was basically the same. In this healthy, temperate environment the town herd grew, and then grew some more, from fewer than a thousand sheep in 1678 to over 15,000 head a decade later. And there were cattle and pigs as well. This huge, hungry animal population provided the hides and meat that merchants like Schellinger carried to Boston, New York, and the West Indies.

The colonists cut down the trees to make way for the animals. Of course, that decision possessed its own economic logic. The trees were turned into lumber and shingles, and the open land where they had grown became pasture. More pasture meant more animals. Thousands of separate decisions were changing the face of East Hampton.

The first thing that people seem to have noticed was that the trees were gone. Trees are a renewable resource, but all those munching animals retarded new growth. By the early decades of the eighteenth century, local farmers began to complain that they did not have enough wood to build fences, and there is no question that the overcutting forced town leaders to take "into consideration the great damage done to the freeholders by reason of sheep and swine running or grazing on our commons by reason of our fencing stuff being so scarce we can't fence against them." Laws were passed to protect trees growing on common land, and informers were encouraged to come forward with information about anyone illegally felling a tree. The situation at Montauk became so critical that the town meeting accepted a new definition of a fence, one that did not require wood at all. It was decided that ditches "four feet from the top of the land to the bottom of the ditch shall be esteemed a sufficient fence throughout our Township Westward of Montauk."

The deforestation of East Hampton almost certainly depleted the supply of fur-bearing animals, like otter, fox, and wildcat, and it is possible that the cutting of so many trees contributed to the great fires that repeatedly swept the township during the eighteenth century. The destruction of forest inevitably alters drainage patterns, and, as in the pine barrens of New Jersey, the plant life that survives under these conditions is often drier in character than the lush trees that it replaces. A bolt of lightning can set off a huge blaze. Whether this process actually occurred in East Hampton is difficult to say, but whatever the cause, the town found itself confronted almost every year with the problem of paying the men who had been sent out to fight the range fires.

I wondered as I read the records of these events whether Mulford's contemporaries recognized that they had created an unnatural landscape. Did they—like Helen Rattray today—resent the changes that had occurred? Perhaps they did not see the changes in the land or, if they did, did not think them important enough to discuss. Maybe they came to like them, saw them as signs of progress and enterprise. These are truths lost to historians, the private thoughts and idle conversations, evanescent reflections on what must remain an irretrievable past.

The decline of the Whale Design could not so easily be ignored. At stake was the future of East Hampton itself. Sometime at the end of the first decade of the eighteenth century, the number of whales taken offshore began to drop. Figures for the production of oil reflected that. In 1707 the local companies sent about 4,000 barrels to market, but that was the last really good year that the local whalers had. During the entire whaling season of 1711 only four animals were killed off East Hampton, and, as the income generated by the trade fell, people began to complain. In 1718, for example, Mulford informed a colonial committee in London that "their [sic] is very little [whale oil] gott to go any where: and the people are become miserable poor." One would be tempted to dismiss such statements as self-serving hyperbole were it not for reports of a similar character that came from other sources. William Smith, author of a colonial history of New York, claimed that "the whale fishery, on the south side of the island, has declined of late years, through the scarcity of whales, and is now almost entirely neglected."

The parallels with the decline of the striped bass in modern East Hampton are striking. Then, as now, people tried to make sense out of what was happening to their lives. Everyone seemed to have an explanation for the disappearance of the right whales. The one that the local whalemen found most difficult to accept was the one that raised questions about their own culpability. In point of fact, the evidence indicates that the problem most certainly resulted from massive overfishing, not only in the waters off Montauk, but also in other whaling areas of colonial America. The *Boston News Letter* noted in 1727 that "We hear from towns on the Cape that the whale fishery among them has failed much this winter, as it has done for several winters past." Another observer reported—with remarkable common sense—that "whalebone and whale oil [in the Middle colonies] . . . will soon grow less plentiful as the people increase." The inhabitants found themselves participants in what may well have been the region's first major ecological disaster.

Governor Hunter offered another, even less agreeable, explanation for the precipitous decline of the Whale Design. The disappearance of the right whales was all an invention, a trick that Mulford and his friends had cooked up to avoid paying taxes. The strength of his case seems to have depended more on vitriol than on logic. Hunter, the outsider pretending to possess an insider's expertise, insisted that the number of whales was not really the issue. Rather, the whaling companies of Long Island were just not very good at catching them. In recent years, he declared, the trade had drawn too many fishermen who were eager to make large profits but who had not bothered to learn the mysteries of the profession. In fact, the governor had it on good authority that these incompetents managed only to wound the whales. These animals then communicated the danger to the other whales, and the whole pod swam to safety. In any event, the governor continued, the production figures submitted by the East Hampton whalers were disingenuous. "The truth of the matter," Hunter assured his superiors in London, "is that the town of Boston is the port of trade of the people inhabiting that end of Long Island of late years, so that the exportation from hence of that commodity must in the books be less than formerly."

Mulford dismissed all of this as nonsense. The problem was not the incompetence of the local fishermen or even the number of whales swimming offshore. The crisis had been caused by meddling fools like Hunter. There would be plenty of whales if the colonial government would just get off the whalers' backs and let them go about their business without having to worry about licenses and regulations. "The imports of whale oil and bone from New York have greatly decreased,"

Mulford protested, "owing to disputes with the Governor as to a duty for whales catched there. We propose that the inhabitants have free liberty to kill whales." Here was the voice of the true Bayman. Give the people of East Hampton their "free liberty," and one way or another, they will take care of themselves. "I say," argued Fishhook, "that there was more people went a whale fishing on Long Island twenty or thirty years ago when they were undisturbed [by government regulations], than hath done of late, which if they had not been discouraged might have been now double that number."

But in this case Mulford was wrong. The offshore whales were scarce. Some East Hampton whalers—or more likely their sons—joined the deep-water fleet that began to sail out of Sag Harbor sometime in the mid-eighteenth century. The large vessels used to hunt the sperm whales could not put into the shallow waters of Northwest Harbor, and the warehouses that Mulford, Schellinger, and others had built during the peak of the offshore whaling boom were dismantled for other purposes or simply allowed to decay.

The sons of Samuel Mulford listed themselves as "yeomen" rather than as "merchants." Unlike some ambitious colonists who moved to the expanding commercial ports of Philadelphia, New York, and Boston to take advantage of new opportunities, the Mulford boys adjusted to the diminished world of East Hampton. The pattern of their lives was more like that of their grandfather, John, than that of their father. For me, a tragic accident symbolizes the end of an era. On February 24, 1719, Reverend Nathaniel Huntting noted in his journal:

> This day a whale boat being alone, the men struck a whale
> & she coming under the boat in part staved it, and though
> the men were not hurt with the whale, yet before any help
> came to them, four men were tired & chilled & fell off the
> boat & oars to which they hung & were drowned, viz.
>   Henry Parsons
>   William Schellinger, Junior
>   Lewis Mulford
>   Jeremiah Conkling, Junior.

It is perhaps not surprising to discover that during this period of economic adjustment the inhabitants of East Hampton seem to have returned to the religion of the founders. Under Huntting, the town's second minister, the local church had not exactly flourished. To be sure, mothers and fathers still brought their children forward for baptism, but the congregation during the decades of prosperity remained small. But when Huntting retired, the town turned to Samuel Buell, a recent Yale College graduate who had become a powerful voice in the religious revivals known as the Great Awakening. The famous evangelist, Jonathan Edwards, came to East Hampton in 1746 to deliver Buell's ordination sermon, and for half a century Buell preached the message of the New Birth to the inhabitants of a community that had turned in on itself. "Thus," he proclaimed in 1792, "have we seen and known since I have been your pastor . . . four harvest times and seasons of the plentiful out pouring of the Holy Spirit, and times of the flocking of souls to Christ."

It was during Buell's long ministry that people first began to write about the history of East Hampton. As we have seen, they described a community that did not appear to have changed much since its founding. John Gardiner concluded that "nothing more than usual for all country towns has taken place in East Hampton for this century past. Remote from their Capitol, they have lived plain Agricultural lives & generally happy." These pious "graziers" had somehow escaped the changes that had so profoundly altered the rest of America. And Timothy Dwight described East Hampton almost as if it were a living museum: "A general air of equality, simplicity, and quiet is visible here in a degree perhaps singular. Sequestered in a great measure from the world, they exhibit scarcely a trace of that activity which everywhere meets the eye in New England."

But, as I have suggested, the fathers and grandfathers of the complacent graziers who greeted Dwight had been entrepreneurs, and, in their effort to transform a sparse habitat into a land of commercial plenty, they may have doomed East Hampton to a future of quiet marginality, to a long century of torpor. This is not a case in which we should seek to assign blame. The people who inhabited Samuel Mulford's world did not appreciate—any more than do some of the modern Baymen—that the sea could not indefinitely sustain their dreams. For them the disappearance of the right whale must have been as unsettling as the decline of the striped bass is for us. One thinks of the disconsolate fisherman who told a *New York Times* reporter, "I'd be out catching bass if I could. That's what I want to do. That's what I know how to do." He would have understood that earlier crisis. And if he really thought about it, he just might conclude that Mulford's sons had not wanted to become "yeomen" at all.

And so, how might a community such as this in the late twentieth century imagine itself in time? It is not obvious—at least, not to an outsider whose memories are of other places—that a genealogical story celebrating the accomplishments of the founding families provides an adequate perspective. To be sure, the "winners" in the past should be given their due. It would be foolish to attempt to write them out of history. Their achievements were, in fact, impressive. The Whale Design was a boldly creative response to opportunities presented by a developing market economy. Loper taught his neighbors how to organize the human and natural resources of East Hampton in new ways. And for a moment the town had held its own in a commercial empire.

But surely that is not enough. There is more to the story that a troubled, twentieth-century East Hampton could tell itself about itself. It might want to consider closely the historical costs of development. The independent whaling companies were a triumph of ingenuity for some families, the ones that are featured in the local histories, but the world of Samuel Mulford was not a particularly attractive place for the indebted Indians, the enslaved African-Americans, the migrant laborers, or the land-poor inhabitants: in other words, precisely the men and women who once lived in East Hampton but who were never truly of it. This is not an imagined past for which many modern Americans can have much nostalgia. So they may feel a little angry, perhaps even cheated, because they wanted a story about a simpler time when self-sufficient farmers pulled together for the common good.

Perhaps these incomplete records, a chronicle of special pleading and embarrassed silences, can be woven into a different kind of story altogether. What we have encountered in this particular past is human agency, generations of people making decisions about the shape of their lives, doing the best that they could, and taking actions that they may have secretly regretted. Within this interpretation, East Hampton becomes a fluid field of choice.

What we really have is a narrative of separate, seemingly unrelated decisions stretching from the little villages of Kent and Devon, to the "stinted" pastures of Lynn and Salem in the Massachusetts Bay Colony, through the sorting out of a founding generation that was too equal to be at peace with itself, and, eventually, to flush times, to prosperity that fizzled, leaving East Hampton a sleepy country town. It is not a particularly ennobling history. It certainly does not lead to anything like the flowering of American democracy. But it might be a story that could help a modern population anxious about the effects of unfettered development to imagine itself in radically different ways than it has for a very long time.

CHAPTER FOUR

Bank Where The Whale Was Tried

I don't think there is a local name in this Town that hasn't been touched in one way or another by the whaling industry or the international trade which was conducted from this shore. . . . Whale products and furs were shipped from [Northwest Harbor] . . . and essential commodities such as spices, molasses, and timber were brought back from Connecticut and the West Indies. The Trustees granted permission for the earliest pier and wharf on this shore . . . [and we now have] a chance to preserve a perpetual peace for the restless spirits wandering in dissatisfaction of past mistakes for not recognizing the future value of preservation.

Cathy Lester,
Letter to the Editor,
East Hampton Star, June 16, 1985

For more than three centuries the Mulford family has owned land on what eventually became known as Buell Lane. The street took its name from the Reverend Samuel Buell, the revivalist who settled here in the mid-eighteenth century. The lane—really a busy highway—runs west from the historic district. It is lined today by houses of weathered cedar shingle, soft brown structures set back from the road on neat green lawns, the sort of homes that casual visitors associate with colonial East Hampton but that in fact were probably built in the late nineteenth century. The earliest settlers employed this road to reach their outlying fields and perhaps even on occasion to travel to the town landing at Northwest Harbor, where Samuel Mulford and his neighbors, William Schellinger, had constructed warehouses.

It was in his house on Buell Lane that I met the Reverend David Mulford. He is certainly not the sole surviving member of the Mulford family who still lives in East Hampton. A huge local clan traces its origins back to those founding brothers, John and William. What distinguishes David, who is descended from William, from most other Mulfords in the area is his special interest in genealogy. He began his research into the history of the family as a college student, tracing the generations of Mulfords who have lived in this place, Revolutionary soldiers and sea captains, prosperous yeomen and struggling fishermen, successes and failures, a chain connecting the earliest Mulfords to their descendants of the twentieth century.

I had come to see David—at least originally—in the hope that he might be able to add something to what I had found in the colonial town records. Perhaps while conducting his own research he had heard stories about Samuel Mulford, family anecdotes passed from generation to generation, which, whether true or not, might give some insight into how the people who shaped the history of East Hampton imagined themselves within that story. I thought of this man not as the genealogist in the strict sense of that term, but as a keeper of a leading family's own folk memory. At a minimum, I reasoned, the discovery that someone else shared his interest in the early Mulfords might remind him of half-forgotten letters or documents from the seventeenth century now stored in some corner of the attic.

The house itself was quite modest, occupying a large piece of land, and, as I parked my car in David's driveway, I noticed that the property included a sizable old barn. Not too long in the past Mulfords must have earned their living from the soil. They certainly kept animals. I could see the remains of what I took to be horse stalls. What aroused my curiosity was not so much the barn's apparent antiquity but rather mysterious signs of heavy construction. I could not quite make out what was happening. There were no workmen on the site. Someone had excavated large amounts of soil and rock from underneath the structure. Beams and other parts of the frame had been jacked up. I dug into a pile of debris with the toe of my shoe, half expecting to unearth the kind of treasure that Trevor Kelsall reported having discovered in other old barns. I found nothing of interest, however, and after exploring the building for a few minutes, I concluded that it must be undergoing restoration.

I was mistaken. When I actually met David—a Presbyterian minister, then working in New Jersey, who had been born in East Hampton—he explained that someone had purchased the barn and was moving it to another location on the South Fork. David did not pursue the topic. His tone seemed matter-of-fact, as if the metamorphosis of a Mulford barn into an artist's studio or summer cottage represented nothing particularly unusual or disturbing. He led me into the house, apologizing for the boxes piled in almost every room. The significance of these cartons did not sink in until our conversation was almost over.

During those first minutes, we turned our attention to the Mulfords of the early colonial period. It was soon apparent that I was doing most of the talking. I should have remained silent,

asked more questions, but almost despite my own best inten-
tions, I found myself telling him all that I knew about Samuel
Mulford, the warehouses, and the whales. Though I suspect
that David had heard much of this before, he listened patiently
to what I had to say. It was he who asked the questions. The
contours of my story were familiar enough. It was a tale of
Mulfords, but, as he was quick to appreciate, I brought new
meanings to those ambiguous records that he had studied so
long ago.

In his turn David recounted his memories of the celebration
of East Hampton's three-hundredth anniversary of 1948, of the
two aging, eccentric farmers who until the early 1940s had
occupied the Mulford Farm, and of his father's outspoken belief
that the automobile had ruined the village. As this earnest, genial
man spoke about the history of this community, I studied the
details of his face. I noted his manner, the way he moved, the
rhythms of his conversation, for in the absence of a contemporary picture of Samuel Mulford, I had half convinced myself
that David represented a direct link with East Hampton's distant
past.

Without quite admitting it even to myself, I had come to
Buell Lane to visit Old Fishhook. Even now, months after this
conversation took place, I still wonder how much of Samuel I
saw in David. Ordinary experience would suggest that there
might have been some connection. Anyone who has closely
examined old family photographs immediately notes how similar people who lived a century or more ago are to those we
know today. We identify subtle continuities, features that echo
in the children and their children's children. These common
elements strike our eye even though the dress and hairstyles of
other periods remain foreign. I remember once having seen
photographs of President John Quincy Adams and a modern
descendant who happened to bear the same surname. Both men
were very old at the time of the sittings, and, though separated
by more than a hundred years, the two Adamses looked as if
they might have been brothers. They gazed into the camera

The Reverend David Mulford and T.H.B.

with identical intensity, challenging, confident, inquisitive, an
imperious look that I imagined might have been peculiar to the
Adams family.

However unsound my speculation may have been, it compelled me to admit that I had somehow constructed a mental
image of Samuel Mulford. I suspect that most historians do just
what I had done. Names that appear on ancient documents do
not long remain abstractions. They are translated in our imaginations into real people. Words in old records that seemingly
have nothing at all to do with a person's appearance suggest for
reasons that I do not fully understand an actual physical being.

We know the men and women we study just as surely as if we possessed a photograph. We conjure them up out of ourselves.

The problem was that David Mulford did not seem at all like the Samuel Mulford that I had invented during many months of research. David is a handsome man. He has an open, friendly face, one that expresses contentment rather than complacency. One senses that he has come without resentment to understand his own limitations. He is a listener, sensitive during our conversation to the nuances of language and tone.

My imagined Samuel Mulford, however, would have been a shorter, more powerfully built man. Though not exactly dour, he would have been slow to laughter, and, had anyone painted his picture, the artist would have portrayed him as a serious man. A flicker of impatience might have played across his face. I am not at all certain that I would have felt comfortable in his presence. Even during ordinary conversation, he would have given some hint of an explosive restlessness, a volcanic dissatisfaction that took extraordinary self-discipline to control. If he had been in David's place, Samuel would have shifted his weight nervously in his chair or tapped his foot on the floor, suggesting to a stranger that there were chores to be done, deals to be negotiated. I suspect that he would have found it difficult to mask his own ambition. His eyes would have betrayed his drive, and though, like David, he would have been capable of considerable charm, he would have impressed his visitor as rigid, even stubborn in his judgment, a stern disciplinarian who seldom doubted the moral righteousness of his own actions.

But then perhaps I had got it all wrong. Perhaps I had projected onto the records of early East Hampton a physical presence that had never existed at all. Samuel may have been more like David than I can possibly comprehend. I had told myself a story about a seventeenth-century community in which the lead actor had been a creatively restive entrepreneur, and in this invented world I found it difficult to imagine a person who might have been genial, reflective, sensitive, at peace with himself. David was unwittingly subverting my interpretation. But then, I probably in some measure subverted his.

To my surprise there was a seventeenth-century document in the attic. David produced a deed of sale recorded in East Hampton on June 6, 1692. It described property in Boston that Samuel Mulford had purchased for eighty pounds sterling from one Jonathan Osborne, "West Jersey shoemaker." Neither Mulford nor Osborne seems to have been too sure exactly what the sale involved. I suspect that Osborne had recently inherited the property from his father, and that, at the time of the sale, neither man had actually viewed the house and land. The deed noted simply that the property was located "in the towne of Boston in New England, near that mill pond as may appear in the Boston Records or some writing there." Apparently, Samuel contemplated moving to Massachusetts. Perhaps he dreamed of becoming a major merchant. His father had just died, leaving him free for the first time in his life to do as he pleased. Or perhaps Samuel had had his fill of the autocratic men who governed colonial New York.

David and I examined the deed on his dining room table. While we were struggling to transcribe the seventeenth-century hand, he informed me that the document would soon be deposited in the Long Island Collection. He would not even have found the Boston deed, he observed, had he not been preparing to transport most of his belongings to Florida, where he had just accepted a new position. This decision explained all the boxes; he was moving. The house and land on Buell Lane, David explained, would remain in the family, a rental property during the summer months, but he doubted that he would be able to spend as much time in East Hampton as he has done in the past.

The news startled me. I hardly knew this man, and yet I found myself slightly annoyed by his decision. His departure from the village somehow threatened my own ability to imagine a local past. I was vexed by East Hampton's refusal to stay put. The strands of interpretation were elusive, fluid, always mocking my attempts to bring stability to the narrative.

I

I am in a place with a delightful name: the Paradise Cafe. It strikes me as an ordinary coffee shop—the kind that one would expect to find in any small American town—where people come in the morning to talk of business and automobiles. For David Swickard, the man at the East Hampton Historical Society who hired me, the major virtue of the Paradise Cafe is that it is located in Sag Harbor: in other words, happily removed from the telephones and visitors and volunteers who inevitably transform his office into a noisy local bazaar. He is accompanied today by an assistant, Jay Graybeal, the Historical Society's curator, who has been assigned the task of translating my research—the reports of a Resident Humanist—into actual exhibits.

Graybeal really has a challenge. After all, it will be he—and not I—who must eventually communicate an imagined past to the people who will visit Mulford Farm. I speak of abstractions, imagined pasts that I have glimpsed in the archives, but the vision will be lost unless he can capture a set of meanings—a story that East Hampton can tell itself about itself—in evocative displays of artifacts. Together we shall create symbols out of everyday objects, investing bits of glass and ceramic, scarred furniture and faded cloth, with special properties of interpretation. Jay has an intuitive sense that exhibitions of this kind are not neutral or objective statements. To pretend that they are is intellectually dishonest. Like written documents, the things of material culture, by their very arrangement, their exclusion or juxtaposition, become highly charged texts that must be read and then contested.

Graybeal is a Southerner. He cannot quite explain how be came to be in East Hampton. He would certainly rather be in Maryland or Virginia, interpreting the battlefields of the Amercian Civil War. But, for the moment, this is where he works, and it is clear to me at least that he is very good at what he does. Unfortunately, there are people in East Hampton who do not quite understand what it means to be a professional curator.

They look at the society's collections as assembled curiosities or as objects out of a private past that remind them of an uncle or grandfather. They do not like being told that they cannot fondle a particular item that may in fact have come down through their own families.

Jay once told me that soon after he arrived in East Hampton he discovered that over the years the Historical Society had been given a number of toolboxes. Some of these had belonged to early nineteenth-century craftsmen and artisans who he now believes may have produced important pieces of furniture. Although their chairs and chests of drawers seem by metropolitan standards a little crude, their work reflected regional styles and local idioms. Other toolchests probably belonged to ordinary carpenters. In any event, someone had carefully rearranged the various implements so that the planes were all in one place, the hammers in another, the awls and chisels somewhere else. Order had been produced out of chaos. And of course, the disassembled tools—looking like items destined to become decorations in franchise steakhouses—had been wrenched out of their proper historical context. There was no way of telling which set of tools had actually belonged to a certain craftsman. The planes were now just planes.

David wanted to know what I had discovered in the town records. It was time to give an account of myself. And there, on the back of a place mat in the Paradise Cafe, I brought all the scattered pieces of interpretation together. As they looked on, I drew arrows and boxes, constructed columns of figures, and scribbled names of long-forgotten participants in the Whale Design.

David asked me later whether I had planned this presentation. But I had not. The elements of a history of East Hampton poured forth with an energy and conviction that even I found a little surprising.

"The key is commerce," I explained, probably sounding more like a history professor that I would have liked. I had to tell a story that was believable as well as accurate. Like a traveler who has visited an exotic place, I wanted to give my audience a sense of "being there," even if being there meant taking them on a journey through the local archives.

"The problem with the Mulford Farm," I continued, "is that it has come to symbolize a lost Golden Age, a time when self-sufficient yeomen farmers formed a genuine community. But this is a romantic vision of the past. The people who lived in this house were never self-sufficient. They had no desire to seal themselves off from the outside world. What we have failed to appreciate is how much the early settlers of East Hampton were participants in a complex process, one that involved from a very early period of their history the consumption of distant manufactures—the things that Schellinger and Mulford displayed in their warehouses at Northwest Harbor—as well as the export of locally produced goods."

I addressed David and Jay as co-conspirators. The "I" behind the interpretation became a "we." "*We* are not concerned with a particular set of buildings," I insisted, "but rather, with a process that affected the lives of all the people who lived in this village. In that sense we are not focusing our attention on a particular house in which Samuel Mulford happened briefly to have resided. The Mulford Farm in itself has no special historical interest. To be sure, it is charming. But there are other houses in this region that are better preserved, architecturally more significant.

"What we are after is the world of Samuel Mulford, a set of social and economic relationships that bound peoples of different race and status together in ways that seem remarkably modern, for in their effort to participate in a vast colonial marketplace these men and women exploited not only each other, but also a fragile environment. They demanded more of nature than it could provide, and so, even in the earliest decades of East Hampton history, we encounter people having to deal with the unintended consequences of largely economic decisions. It was no accident that the whales were killed off, or that the farmers did not have enough wood for their fences. The forces that changed the physical face of East Hampton also brought black slaves to the community and radically affected the lives of the Montauk Indians. No doubt, such changes occurred in other towns, but because of the whales, the process was accelerated in East Hampton.

"So long as we insist on treating the colonial past as preindustrial, or premodern, or pre–summer people, or preautomobile," I argued, "we are bound to miss the continuities that in fact run through the entire history of this community. The problems that concern everyone so much today—the disappearance of the striped bass or the destruction of the environment—are not new. In fact, one could argue that the ecological disruptions of the colonial period were as severe as those that agitate residents today.

"In any case, we have an opportunity to develop a new interpretation of East Hampton's history, one that includes the blacks as well as the Indians, that reminds us of the strong-willed women who helped the early society to sort itself out, that reveals the creative as well as the destructive aspects of commerce, and that reminds visitors that persistence is as much a factor in the story of this community as change."

I pause. David and Jay are studying my drawing on the place mat. It looks more like a plan of battle than the outline of a historical interpretation. Lines now run from Indians to whales, from Samuel Mulford to London. The pieces all fit, but, depicted in this way, a whole set of human relationships has been transformed into a labyrinth, a visual complexity that does in fact reflect an imagined society at the time of the Whale Design.

"What I would hope," I conclude, "is that visitors would come away from your exhibitions with a fuller appreciation of a commercial process. They might, for example, start with Mulford Farm. The house was a center not only of production—hides and meats, for example—but also of consumption. The two aspects of the colonial economy were in balance. You could point out the type of imported manufactures that someone like Samuel Mulford might have owned. And the people at the Marine Museum could explain something about the ships—the ketches, pinks, and snows—that connected seventeenth-century

East Hampton with Boston and New York, with London and
the West Indies. You would surely want to emphasize the importance of offshore whaling. The point, of course, is that your
two major properties would become expressions of an integrated interpretation of local history. To understand the world
of Samuel Mulford one would have to visit the Marine Museum
as well as the Mulford Farm. In a sense, the visitor's movement
through East Hampton would replicate the circulation of late
seventeenth-century commerce."

That, as I remember, was the core of my report, the reflections of a Resident Humanist. Of course, I told Jay and David
about specific documents, about particular men and women
who except for the relentless trackings of the genealogists had
up to now been largely anonymous persons, but who in this
restructured narrative had acquired significance. They had taken
on historical personality. David reacted with enthusiasm.
Though he seemed surprised by the emphasis on the community's commercial foundations, he expressed special interest in
what he saw as recurrent patterns. It was not that he thought
that my research would address current ecological problems.
Rather he spoke in the Paradise Cafe of continuities. For him
a reinterpretation of history raised philosophical issues. East
Hampton had been from the very beginning a place where
people made deals, viewed the natural environment as a field
of commercial opportunity, and had suffered the consequences
of their own decisions. Though the technologies had changed
over the centuries, the cultural underpinning of this society had
shown remarkable persistence. There was indeed much of the
past in East Hampton's present.

Jay immediately accepted the new interpretation. In fact,
long before I arrived in East Hampton, he had begun to question
the elements of the local myth. Town historians spoke of self-
sufficient yeomen, but, as Jay quickly discovered, the artifacts
refused to cooperate with this interpretation. He found himself
confronted with goods that had clearly orginated in Boston and
New York, in distant ports, and it seemed incongruous to the
society's new curator that the East Hampton farmers would

have owned so many things that they could not possibly have produced. My research corroborated his suspicions. Even as we sat in this Sag Harbor cafe, Jay announced that future exhibitions would depict the workings of the marketplace, tracing links not only among the families of early East Hampton—the traditional approach to "micro" history—but also among communities in an expanding Atlantic economy, the perennial concern of "macro" history.

But looking at my own place mat interpretation of East Hampton history, I felt a little uneasy. It was not that I had created a past that had not existed. The documents had spoken of whale companies and dependent Montauks, black slaves and consumer demand. My disquiet was more philosophical in origin. The lines and boxes that now appeared so plausible—a graphic depiction of a past society—were taking on a solidity that seemed to be closing off imaginative possibilities. The founders were being forced into yet another analytic system, one that had the unfortunate effect of making them sound a little too much like modern entrepreneurs. Commerce was obviously an important aspect of their lives, one that I could document from the town records. It had shaped this society and the way that people of different races and backgrounds had seen themselves within it.

But I was also painfully aware that this was a partial truth. It was a story told from records that just happened to have survived, that contained errors and omissions, that reflected the biases and special pleadings of those who had been entrusted to keep the village chronicles, that was silent about the founders' religious values, about their lives as fathers and mothers, as lovers, as people who for one reason or another had passed through East Hampton. I wondered about the man who had gone off to New Jersey to become a shoemaker. I had expanded the story of this community to include more than just the patriarchs of the leading families, but somehow I had not found a place for this particular immigrant who had sold his land to Samuel Mulford. He would have to wait, I decided, becoming

Jay Graybeal

at some future time part of someone else'e imagined history of East Hampton.

"Now," I declared, "we have got to find the warehouse at Northwest Harbor."

Somehow this step in interpreting the local past seemed so logical, so inevitable, that none of us gave much thought to what finding a late seventeenth-century warehouse might involve. From our new historical perspective, however, Samuel Mulford's warehouse appeared even more significant than the Mulford Farm, the buildings I had originally been hired to interpret. No one at the table seriously thought that the warehouse would replace the house and barn in the center of the town's historic district. But it was possible to imagine a presentation of East Hampton's history that would take visitors to this community not only to the farm and the Marine Museum, but also to a site somewhere on Northwest Harbor where men exchanged the dreams of a commercial society.

David said that Jay could assist in the search. Jay did not require much encouragement. Even if we had been treasure hunters, I doubt that the anticipation of discovery could have raised the level of excitement much higher than it was at that moment in the Paradise Cafe.

II

*N*orthwest Harbor is appropriately located several miles to the northwest of the Village of East Hampton. There are many ways to travel there by automobile. In colonial times the settlers may have had even more choices, for as we know from the early records dozens of public roads large enough to carry cart traffic crisscrossed the woodlots and pasture lands. Over the centuries many of these paths have fallen into disuse. A few local residents still know where many of these roads can be found, but without a knowledgeable guide or an old map, the visitor could not possibly spot them among the undergrowth. The names of the modern highways—Merchant's

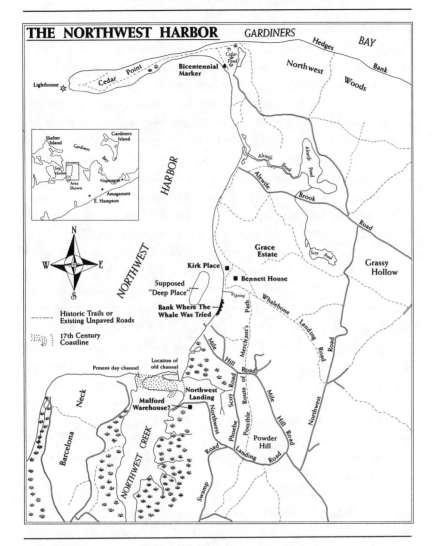

Map of Northwest Harbor (by Janice Harper)

Path, Swamp Road, Bull Path—are all that survive from that earlier history.

At the end of Northwest Landing Road, there is a decaying parking lot. For a small fee payable to the town of East Hampton, one can launch a small boat here. Much of the ground around the landing area is marshy, drained by an ill-defined tidal creek. To the west, across Northwest Creek, perhaps a quarter of a mile away, rises Barcelona Point, an impressively wooded headland, and beyond that promontory, on a clear day one can just make out Sag Harbor low on the horizon.

I walk out among several large sand dunes to a place where I hope I can gain a better view of Northwest Harbor itself. A path runs along a snow fence down to a beach. A sign—newly posted, I would guess, since the paint has not faded even in the direct sun—catches my eye. It carries an urgent message from the "Long Island Colonial Water Bird Association," admonishing people like me to take extreme care not to disturb the birds that construct their nests in the sand grass. Why these birds are described as "colonial" remains a mystery; perhaps they nest in colonies. Several species—the piping plover, least terns, roseate terns, and black skimmers—are particularly vulnerable and threatened with extinction. "These birds," the sign explains, "return in spring to nest on the few suitable sites left on Long Island. Their camouflaged eggs are laid in nests on the ground. Frightened adults fly away when disturbed, exposing eggs and young to life-threatening temperatures and predation. The development of shore areas and recreational use of beaches leaves these birds with few vital breeding sites. Without your help, the beauty they bring to our shores will vanish. This is one of the last places they can use. Help them—please do not enter nesting area."

It would take courage to climb over this particular snow fence. A second, newer, and much more menacing sign announces: "TICK INFESTED AREA." These "eight-legged, wingless, parasitic arachnids," the signs warns, carry among other diseases Lyme fever, babesiosis, and tularemia. I do not know exactly what these illnesses involve, but a grossly enlarged drawing of a tick would make anyone uneasy. Overcome suddenly by the sensation that these ugly parasites are even now crawling up my leg, I stick to the main path, following the tracks of a large four-wheel-drive vehicle that not too long ago must have startled every water bird in the area.

From the beach at the Town Landing, I enjoy an unob-

Tick Warning

structed view across Northwest Harbor, a gentle crescent, perhaps a mile or so from tip to tip. I stand on the most southerly
point of this great arc. A little to the north, just beyond what
appears to be an impassable swampy area, an abandoned stone
wharf or breakwater juts out into the bay. I later learn that this
is all that remains of a marina that has gone out of business.
Today, there are no signs of life, no pleasure boats, no sounds
of motors. Only a hundred yards beyond the marina, Mile Hill
Road runs down to the water's edge. A summer camp operated
near this site within recent memory, but it too has been deserted.
Several grassy fields indicate where the children must have
played.

Beyond the camp, about halfway along the crescent, a heavily wooded section begins. Indeed, from my vantage point on the beach I cannot make out any further signs of human development, not a single summer cottage, nothing but dense greenery. The woods continue all the way to Alewife Brook Landing, and from there on into Cedar Point Park, a state camping ground, which during the summer months draws thousands of people from all parts of Long Island. At the tip of Cedar Point, directly opposite the mouth of Northwest Creek, is a large lighthouse, which from this distance looks like a medieval castle silhouetted against the openness of Gardiner's Bay.

The local fishermen love to work the quiet waters of Northwest Harbor. It has long been recognized as one of the best sources of bay scallops to be found in the entire state of New York, and even from where I am standing on the beach, I can spot what I take to be an occasional young scallop swimming near the surface of the water. They are in search of suspended food particles. The little scallops propel themselves by clapping the two halves of their shells together and expelling jets of water. If they are not harvested or eaten by gulls or starfish, scallops can live for several years, growing ever larger until they die. The older scallops are less active, but on this bright day, they too are visible on the sandy bottom. I have been told that private companies have seeded oyster beds near here. An abundance of shells scattered along the beach offers further demonstration of the rich sea life to be found at Northwest. Though the water is generally too shallow to allow navigation by large vessels, it is deep enough at high tide for the Baymen. And because it runs south to north, the harbor provides excellent natural shelter from the severe winter storms that blow in from the east.

But, like the nesting birds, the bay itself is part of a fragile environment. Though the water looks clean enough to me, I know from talking to local people that conditions have deteriorated rapidly in recent years and that additional shoreline development could transform Northwest Harbor into a kind of dead sea. Recent studies have discovered that the flushing time of this little bay is remarkably slow, about twenty-two days. Pollutants that enter the harbor—floating rubbish and invisible chemicals, which have the potential to destroy the scallops and other sea life—move back and forth with the tides. The slow-moving tributaries such as Northwest Creek clean out these waste products even less efficiently than does the harbor. Some ecologists suggest that pollution of this sort is responsible for the "brown tide," algae that choke out the protoplankton on which the scallops feed.

Sand and shingle beaches gird the crescent. Most of the rocks along the shore are small, rounded by the constant movement of the sea into smooth shapes that I find perfect for skipping across the choppy waves. A few massive boulders stand at water's edge near Alewife Creek. These giant rocks have a mysterious character; it is hard to imagine how they could possibly have gotten here. They seem like the great sculptured slabs of Salisbury Plain or Easter Island, products of human agency. The creator, however, is not Stone Age man or more recent wharf-builders like Samuel Mulford. It is ice. The glaciers that formed Long Island some twenty thousand years ago left behind these strange boulderes, which are called erratics.

The beaches on which they are found are generally narrow, running back from the high tidal mark only a few yards before rising sharply into bluffs, some ten to fifteen feet above the water level. In this slender buffer zone between land and sea, an occasional great tree has somehow managed to root itself. A few are dead, bleached trunks outlined against the sky. Here the osprey construct their huge nests.

People who knew this area are not certain how much the beach has moved over the last several centuries. One man swears that the beach once extended at least three hundred feet out into the water. According to this theory, storms and currents eroded Northwest Harbor into its current shape. Other locals are equally certain that the beach had grown, so they advise some one who wants to find a seventeeth-century warehouse to look in the heavily wooded area well away from the water. I examine several old maps—the oldest dating from the early decades of the nineteenth century—but I can see no significant changes. Northwest Harbor looked then pretty much as it does today.

The wooded land behind the bluffs is for the most part flat. The sandy ground drains quickly, and, unless there is a working spring in the immediate vicinity, the soil becomes dry, friable to the touch. In fact, even where the vegetation is thickest, the mold seldom runs to more than six to eight inches; below that, one inevitably runs into sand. Because of the many oaks that grow here, the topsoil has become highly acid; even during the nineteenth century farmers found that they had to "sweeten" the soil regularly, usually with cheap varieties of fish—generally alewives or menhaden—which they spread on the fields as fertilizer. Today, the upland sections of Northwest Harbor support a surprisingly large variety of plants and animals, some of which appear on the state list of endangered species.

These woods also contain the visible ruins of a small nineteenth-century settlement. A score of farm families lived at Northwest Harbor, and, though they do not seem to have been a particularly prosperous community, they did manage to build a small school. Anyone who walks the woods encounters the remains of their residence, small family cemeteries, house foundations, and shallow wells. Someone told me that the local black families once buried their dead in this area, but in all my explorations, I never saw such a site.

The more often I went there, the more certain I became that I had stumbled upon the location of some lost structure, perhaps even the warehouse itself. A strange depression in the ground could spark the imagination, but, in point of fact, all my discoveries turned out to be "kettle holes," small pits formed by the melting ice of retreating glaciers.

To this day there are people in East Hampton who describe these ruins as the "old Bennett house" or the "Ranger farm." The locals refer regularly to Scoy Pond. It is as if these nineteenth-

century families still lived at Northwest Harbor, still had a claim
on the land. The survival of the old names helps to mask
change. Several modern residents of East Hampton told me
the story of Josiah Kirk, a man who during the nineteenth
century built a group of farm buildings on a high bluff facing
Sag Harbor. It was a beautiful location. About all that remains
is a trash pit and several stately linden trees. The trees stand
out. There are no other lindens in the area. I like to imagine
that they brought the man who planted them a certain amount
of pleasure, but Kirk does not appear to have known contentment. He was driven nearly to distraction by neighbors who
gathered seaweed on the beach immediately in front of his
house. They insisted that they had as much right to the seaweed
as did Kirk, and when they persisted, he sued them all for
trespass. Though Kirk eventually won the case, court costs
wiped out his entire savings, and, according to local tradition,
he died in poverty.

Kirk and his neighbors force us to think of Northwest
Harbor as a constantly changing landscape. It is really an unstable canvas on which each generation for as far back as there
are records—archeological as well as legal—has made a temporary mark. We confront at Northwest Harbor cycles of land
use, some more destructive than others. What remains constant
is the exploitation of nature. The ground on which I walk contains piles of shells, testimony to ancient Indian camps. Then
came the whalers, the farmers, a shipbuilder. Some cut the trees;
some let them grow. The landscape reflected their needs.

In time someone constructed a "fish factory" near Alewife
Creek where the menhaden were ground into fertilizer. Others
experimented with a small oyster industry, but they failed. The
supply of oysters and menhaden was soon exhausted. The farmers did little better. When Kirk and his neighbors found that
they could not make a decent living raising crops, they sold the
land to other people with other dreams. One of the Gardiners
raised buffalo here. Another man, W. R. Grace, bought up so
much land that it came to be known as the Grace Estate. Again

the trees returned. A marina. A summer camp. More failures. The Baymen came to Northwest Harbor to harvest the scallops: another natural resource, perhaps another disappointment. Now the land itself is the only commodity worth exploiting. Subdivisions—the product of what local planning reports now call "instantaneous development"—will soon dominate a landscape where history seems to have been forgotten.

But the odds are that Northwest Harbor will again disappoint those who try to possess it. That is certainly the impression I got from Larry Penny, the ecologist for the Town of East Hampton. He and I hiked over the Grace Estate one afternoon, and, as he pointed out various endangered plants that grew along the trails, he observed that he has known many people who have purchased property in this area. They seem inevitably to go through a cycle of shifting moods. When they first arrive, they imagine themselves to be pioneers. They build their homes in the heavy woods. They praise the beauty and privacy of the place. But with these benefits come the insects, and within a short time the modern pioneers are complaining of the mosquitoes and the ticks. They hate the poison ivy. To combat these annoyances they push the forest back, away from their cottages. Landscapers are called in to lay down lawns, to open up the woods, to provide the newcomers with the "farm feeling" on their own terms. In the process of ordering the environment, of course, many of the attributes that drew these people to East Hampton in the first place are lost.

Penny and I talked about the future of East Hampton under the linden trees at the Kirk site. From this elevated situation we could see much of Northwest Harbor. I could imagine another time when Samuel Mulford traveled the same trails that we had walked. Perhaps he had even helped to lay them out. Indeed, Penny and I agreed that Mulford might well have constructed his warehouse quite near to the place where we were standing. But we did not know for sure. The search for that past had just begun.

III

"*Y*ou don't really need an archeologist," someone at the Village library counseled. "I know exactly where you can locate the Mulford warehouse. And Schellinger's too. They're both in the state park."

"You're joking," I responded incredulously.

But he was quite serious. This man, whose name I have now forgotten, handed me a small pamphlet that the Town of East Hampton had published during the bicentennial celebration of the American Revolution. It contained not only a map showing the exact location of the two colonial warehouses, but also a description of the marker that a local committee placed at the site.

According to the pamphlet, all I had to do was drive out to the state park at Cedar Point. It sounded so simple. Indeed, the discovery of the pamphlet left me feeling a little embarrassed. I wondered how I could possibly have missed the documents that the members of this committee must obviously have had in their possession. The news of the warehouses surprised Jay Graybeal as much as me. Both of us had assumed that the colonial vessels that carried the whale products and consumer goods would have required deeper water than could be found anywhere near Cedar Point. We were also puzzled by the absence of major seventeenth-century roads in this particular area. One would think that the early settlers would have established cart paths. Still, there was no disputing the evidence before us. The pieces of a new commercial interpretation of East Hampton's early history were now in place.

Tony Kelly and I decided to get a photograph of the marker. What should have been a relatively easy task turned into a major ordeal. The problem was the ticks. Throughout the summer, the infestation had grown steadily worse, and though the tourists seemed blissfully unaware of the danger, the permanent residents told us frightening stories about people who had suddenly taken ill. A tick had bitten David's wife— no one knew where or when the incident had occurred—but she too was now very ill. The concern threatened to become panic. It was the obsession of social gatherings. Everyone started examing their pets thoroughly before allowing them in the house. Socks had to be checked, children warned. Walks in the woods were out of the question.

No one thought it was wise for Kelly and me to venture even the short distance from the car park at Cedar Point to the spot where the warehouses had been located. I was informed that commercial insect repellents offered no protection. These were apparently very tough ticks. They leapt onto clothing from low bushes; they dropped down onto people's heads from tree branches. It only required the warmth of a passing human being to activate these deadly creatures. The fear spread.

Tony and I were not easily deterred. After all, we had survived whale poison. If we dressed properly, we concluded, we would certainly reduce the risk. The challenge was in spotting the tick before it reached an exposed area of skin. For this, white pants were essential. So too were long white socks, substantial ankle-top boots, a heavy, long-sleeved shirt that could be buttoned tightly at the wrists and neck, and a hat that covered the entire head. Unfortunately, between us we had only enough money to purchase one complete "antitick" outfit, and since Tony was actually going to take the picture, he spent the better part of an afternoon searching the smart stores of Main Street for items that salespeople clearly regarded as unfashionable.

We drove out to Cedar Point on one of the hottest days of summer. Despite the tick alert, the park grounds were full of campers. These were definitely not the sort of people one normally encounters in a historic district. Soon after passing the main gate we spotted a large muscular man walking a pit bull on a heavy chain. The dog's owner wore thick leather wristbands. Families with hordes of small children seemed to take little notice of either him or us. We tried to park as close to the warehouse marker as possible. On our chart, we calculated that Tony would have to walk only about two hundred yards through a tick-infested area.

Tony emerged from the car looking like a bee-keeper. We checked his clothing one last time. The temperature must have been in the mid-nineties. Sweat poured down Tony's face. White pants. Socks tucked in. Neck buttoned. Camera and film. And then he resolutely set off down a little well-worn path that led to the beach. He was followed by two young women dressed only in skimpy bikinis. Their insouciance amazed me. They did not give the slightest indication that they regarded the man in the "tick" outfit as the least bit strange.

After fifteen or twenty minutes, Tony trudged back to the parking lot. He had encountered not a single tick. Relaxing in the car, he explained that he had found the marker exactly where the bicentennial map told us that it would be. His tone betrayed disappointment. The site itself was almost completely overgrown with poison ivy. Unless someone cleared the vines, he thought, it would soon be impossible even to see the marker.

"You know," Tony mused, "I have a theory about the ticks."

"What's that?" I responded, feeling somewhat guilty that I had not taken the picture myself.

"They may be the town's best defense against the developers. Think about it. Who will want to spend all that money just to worry about the ticks? It's crazy."

As he peeled off various layers of protection, he seemed to speak of the ticks with a certain fondness.

Later that day we saw Carleton Kelsey, the town's official historian and a member of the original bicentennial committee that had placed the marker at Cedar Point. I asked him how he had known that the warehouses had been located there and not near the Kirk place or at the town landing at Northwest Creek.

"We didn't," he shot back.

"But we saw the marker," I insisted.

Kelsey explained that he and his colleagues did not have the slightest idea where Mulford and Schellinger had constructed their warehouses. The major concern during the bi-

Bicentennial Marker for Warehouses at Cedar Point

centennial celebration was locating a place where the marker would be safe. It seemed unlikely that anyone would steal it off the beach. Moreover, the state government apparently cooperated with the committee's plans.

I must have looked a little like a child who has just learned the truth about Santa Claus. Pragmatism had defeated historical accuracy. If one could not trust a bicentennial committee, whom could one trust? But Kelsey did not seem the least apologetic about the committee's course of action.

He assured us that we will never find the Mulford warehouse. No one can. It's under the water. Three hundred feet into Northwest Harbor. According to Kelsy, it's "long gone."

Kelsey insisted that the beach has changed dramatically over the centuries. But though his account of local geology sounded plausible, I was skeptical. The early nineteenth-century maps—at least, the ones that I had seen—did not suggest much beach erosion at Northwest Harbor. Some, perhaps, but not a hundred yards.

"So, where is it?" Kelly asked later.

"Mulford's warehouse? Somewhere between Alewife Brook and Northwest Creek," I responded sharply. "Who knows?"

IV

*E*ach year the members of the Ladies Village Improvement Society sponsor a fund-raising event on the spacious grounds of the Mulford Farm. The equipment for this popular fair is stored in a shed that sits on a gentle slope about a hundred feet behind the house where Samuel Mulford once lived. Near the shed stands a large weathered barn, allegedly built in 1721, and, although it may possess considerable historical significance, it too is used largely for storage.

I came here on another sweltering summer afternoon to talk with Jay Graybeal about the location of the elusive Mulford warehouse. He placed a couple of well-worn chairs in front of the open barn doors. Jay looked more at ease in this setting than he did in the offices of the Historical Society. Sitting in the shade with our feet propped up, we could imagine ourselves far from here, in North Carolina or Virginia perhaps, in country places that we have both come to love. In fact, we chatted for a long time of hunting dogs and red-clay farms.

Not many people visit the Mulford Farm on a day like this. The locals joke defensively that the museum is good for filling a rainy afternoon. But in fact not many of them appear on those days, either. The heat did not discourage one middle-aged couple, however, and they resolutely walked up from the main house to where Jay and I were lounging.

"Anything else to see?" the man inquired. It was clear from the tone of his voice that he was not entirely pleased with what he had just seen in the Mulford House.

"Take a look for yourself," Jay responded pleasantly, pointing through the open barn door to a jumbled collection of unsold yard-sale items and exhibit props. The couple spent several minutes in the barn and then quietly slipped away. I wondered silently what these strangers have made of what they have seen. How they had interpreted Jay's attempt to interpret the history of early East Hampton?

"What do we really know about the warehouse?" I finally asked. It was a rhetorical question. Jay knew the records of colonial East Hampton as well as I did.

"I sometimes have nightmares about the warehouse," I confessed. "I wake up in the darkness wondering whether we have imagined the warehouse, created it out of thin air."

But it was not the warehouse that I had created. It was the interpretation that I pinned to that warehouse that was the source of anxiety. In the past—my past—interpretations led largely passive lives. They sat docilely in scholarly monographs waiting to be accepted or rejected. Here, however, theory insisted on application. It was taking on an existence of its own.

Jay listened patiently.

"All right," I asked, "just what is the evidence?"

As we went over it together, we were well aware that the central document described a grant that the townspeople of East Hampton made to Samuel Mulford on April 7, 1702. The wording was curious. At the time of the grant Mulford had apparently already built a substantial structure at the town landing at Northwest Harbor. For some reason, however, he was not very happy with the arrangement. Perhaps his business was expanding. Or perhaps he was a squatter who did not want to be evicted. Whatever the explanation, he certainly wanted his neighbors to help support the endeavor. Even more interesting, he appeared to have regarded the warehouse as a kind of public structure, a place designed to promote the general welfare of the community. The local voters seem to have accepted what sounds like a surprisingly modern argument, for at their "legal Town Meeting," they decided

> . . . by a major vote that, whereas, Captain Samuel Mulford having erected or built a warehouse at Northwest landing place, and for his encouragement to maintain the same, that he should freely have the full enjoyment of the land it stands on with sufficient addition of the land to the same, to set reasonable enlargement of the said warehouse upon, and also a convenient way to pass to and from the same, by cart or travelling, so long he and his heirs shall continue said warehouse.

Jay and I concluded that the convoluted syntax of this document provided an important clue in our search for the warehouse. The local voters were reacting to economic success. In other words, the grant to Mulford was not part of an effort to promote future trade. The volume of commerce passing through Northwest Harbor was already substantial by the turn of the century. Indeed, only two years earlier the town had decided that "Mr. Abraham Schellinger should have Liberty to erect and build a wharf at the North west Harbour: at such a Convenient place: as he with the advice of the trustees of their order shall think Meete." The records made no mention of a Gardiner warehouse, but it may have been located near the other two. The men who worked in these buildings—during certain seasons of the year, perhaps as many as thirty—almost certainly did not live at Northwest Harbor. Most likely they commuted to the landing each day, often carrying heavy items that would have required good roads.

We had no doubt, therefore, that we were looking for a major commercial site. The difficulty was interpreting the cryptic references to location. What exactly had the town leaders had in mind when they granted Schellinger a "convenient place" or authorized Mulford to lay out "a convenient way"? The warehouse builders were probably given some discretion in actually selecting a suitable piece of land, but surely the trustees had a general idea where the construction would take place.

In fact, everyone did. The people who voted at these "legal town meetings" did not have to be informed exactly where to find the Northwest landing place. They knew the topography of this area, the maze of woodland roads, and the character of the tidal creeks. It is the knowledge that they took for granted that causes us so much trouble today.

But however incomplete they appear, the town records must be read very carefully. I could have saved myself a lot of research time had I followed this advice. I developed a theory that if we could just find an inventory of Samuel Mulford's possessions at the time of his death, we could discover the exact location of his warehouse. Would he not have transferred ownership of the buildings to his son? And would legal procedure not have required him to provide a reliable description of the location of the property? Over a period of several weeks we hounded archivists throughout the state of New York. Each trail led to a dead end. Some records, we learned, had been destroyed in a fire in Albany during the late nineteenth century; others that we thought were stored in New York City seem to have been lost. Each disappointment only increased our certainty that we were on the right track.

And then Jay destroyed the entire theory. The original town grant, he noted, had *not* given Mulford ownership of the property at Northwest Harbor. He possessed only the right to *use* the land, and so it seemed quite unlikely that he would have included what he did not own in a final testament.

When a copy of a 1724 deed transferring ownership of Mulford's home to his son Matthew turned up, it seemed to support Jay's hypothesis. It contained no mention of the land where his wharf had been located. There was one peculiar reference in this document, however, which at the time neither of us could understand. Samuel gave his son Matthew what one transcriber read as a "winehouse." Jay thought that the word was actually "wairehouse." This clue—if indeed, it was a clue— did not give us much help in finding the structure that Fishhook had built during the 1690s. It seemed highly improbable that this curious "wairehouse" could have been the Northwest Harbor warehouse, and also unlikely that Matthew, who was not a merchant, would have moved a structure of such size off the land that was still owned by the town.

The land records of colonial East Hampton offered almost no assistance in solving the mystery of the lost warehouse. To be sure, over the years the town granted specific persons specific parcels of land. All of these real estate transfers were carefully listed, often alphabetically, and a few descriptions even mentioned a "harbor."

But try as we would, we could not crack the code. The records possessed an arcane logic of their own. The clerks defined each piece of land in relation to various other pieces, and those in relation to still other pieces, and since the seventeenth-century listings rarely contained references to precise locations—the sorts of coordinates that a modern surveyor might provide—we could never untangle the crazy-quilt boundaries of Northwest Harbor. An example taken from John Mulford's holdings graphically reveals the problem that we confronted. On page 5 of Book A of the East Hampton records, we discover that Samuel's father received

> . . . three acres at the Nor[th]west meadow be it more or less, bounded with Richard Brooke on the South and John Stretton's meadow on the North, the creek East and the woods West.
>
> Also one parcel more at the Nor[th]west containing two acres more or less, bounded by Benjamin Conkling's meadow on the West and the creek on the North and Thomas Diaments on the East and the woods on the South.
>
> And also three acres of meadow at the harbor, be it more or less, bounded by Benjamin Conkling's on the Westward and the creek on the Nor[th]west, Thomas Diaments on the Northeast and the woods on the Southeast.

In other eighteenth-century land records the warehouse appeared like a mirage. It was a distant landmark known only to a distant people, and whenever Jay and I tried to reach it in a specific location, it disappeared. In 1710 the town of East Hampton gave Captain Josiah Hobart a section of land situated "near Captain Mulford's warehouse in swamp and upland that joins to the Northside of the highway that goes thereto." Other contemporary grants mentioned a familiar "highway that leads to Captain Mulford's warehouse." These were important hints, of that we were sure, but since much of the land that encircles Northwest Harbor could fairly be classified as either "swamp" or "upland," these clues did not give much guidance. Indeed, a number of ancient cartways seemed to fit what was in fact a very general description.

Perhaps the most baffling piece of evidence was a reference in the town records to a road apparently laid out sometime during the early decades of the eighteenth century. Local officials permitted construction of "one highway to begin at the highway that runs down to [the] Northwest landing place, to turn out at the Mile Hill and so to run northly by and to the corner of William Barnes, his meadow, to the bank where the whale was tried by Northwest Bay."

What whale? Was there someting so very unusual about this particular whale—after all, almost all right whales were taken off the Atlantic shore—that the place was incorporated into local legend? The reference to the Barnes land and to the "bank" indicated that the road had once run along the sandy bluff near the Kirk site. It seemed possible that Mulford and his workers could have boiled down the malodorous blubber at this location. They could easily have then loaded the oil and bone onto ships moored in the protected harbor.

This theory took on additional plausibility when we discovered that another old road had run all they way from Amagansett on the Atlantic beach to the "bank where the whale was tried" and was known as "Whalebone Landing Road." When, precisely, people began calling this deserted cartway by this name was not clear either from the old maps or colonial records. But its very name—coupled with the possible construction in colonial times of a trying works—suggested that it was here, and not at the Northwest Landing, that we should look for Mulford's warehouse. Of course, there was always a chance that Mulford owned two separate buildings, one for trying oil and another for merchandizing goods.

Jay and I were not particularly discouraged by all these amibiguous texts. If nothing else, the frequent references to the Mulford warehouse seemed to strengthen my own commercial interpretation of East Hampton's early development. The building seemed to have figured centrally in the visual imagination of these colonists. It had been a place where deals were made— some of questionable character—and goods sold. In 1702 a sloop called the *Mary* went aground in suspicious circumstances, and when colonial authorities launched an investigation into what had happened to the ship's cargo, they learned that they had been taken to "Captain Mulford's warehouse." These were years when pirates such as the infamous Captain Kidd visited East Hampton—indeed, he is said to have buried a treasure on Gardiner's Island in 1699—and perhaps such shady figures occasionally appeared at Northwest Harbor.

Most of the business transacted at the warehouse seems to have been quite unexceptional. Legitimate merchants from New England rented space in the Mulford warehouse to store popular consumer articles. Joshua Hemstead, a successful farmer-merchant who lived in New London, Connecticut, carried sizable quantities of rum to Northwest Harbor on consignment. His customers seem to have purchased small amounts of liquor—a quart or two—from Mulford, and when the barrels were empty, Hemstead sailed over from the mainland with a new supply. An entry in the Hemstead diary for April 20, 1718, indicates that the warehouse must have been a fairly large structure, large enough in any case to keep the stock of other merchants. "I brought over the goods that John Davis brought from New York in July last," Hemstead noted, "which hath been ever Since in Mr. Mulford's warehouse. I paid the Storage 3 shillings 10 pence . . . in New York money."

"So, we know that the warehouse really existed," Jay stated. "And we know it could have been located anywhere between the Kirk place and the town landing."

"That represents progress," I responded a little defensively. "At least we know that Mulford did not build his warehouse at Cedar Point Park or at Alewife Creek. The problem is Northwest Creek."

What do you mean?"

"How could there have been a major seventeenth-century harbor near the present town landing?" I asked rhetorically. "It's too shallow." As we talked, I was thinking of the place where I had first gone to view Northwest Harbor. I had walked at least a hundred yards out into the water at low tide. This was not a location where one could conveniently load barrels of whale oil onto a sailing vessel.

"And in any case, the Northwest Creek flows into the bay over against Russell's Neck, on the Barcelona Point side of the inlet, and so it seems impossible the swamps and upland associated in the old records with the Mulford warehouse could be located anywhere near the modern Northwest Landing Road. My guess is that we'll eventually find these buildings somewhere to the north of the landing, probably in the area of the bank where the whale was tried."

"I wish we had a smoking gun," I continued. "It would make our work a whole lot easier."

"You mean because of the money?" Jay asked.

"Sure. It's going to cost a great deal of money actually to find the warehouse, to salvage anything worth displaying in your museum, and unless we have something to show—a collection of coins or a whale lance—we're going to have a hard time persuading anyone to underwrite serious archeology."

Jay agreed. The Historical Society could not afford to sponsor an ambitious project of this kind. The organization had trouble meeting its current obligations. Jay pointed to the Mulford House to make his point. It was clear from where we were sitting that the structure needed a new roof. An eroding foundation wall at the rear of the house required attention.

We remained silent for a long time. It was getting late. The Mulford Farm cast long shadows across the open ground. From the barn I was able to see the local library, looking in the soft light exactly as it was supposed to look, like an English building in America, a reminder of the Kentish roots of those first settlers who had migrated to the end of the island. Buell Lane leading up to David Mulford's house was filling with traffic.

It seemed a pity to end the search. We felt that we were so close.

"You know," I observed, finally breaking the silence, "I called a number of archeologists who specialize in the colonial period. There was one at Yale, another in Boston, and a couple at Williamsburg. They all said the same thing. They didn't know of a single site like the one I described at Northwest Harbor. The major warehouses were located for the most part in cities—Boston and New York, for example—and they were either totally destroyed or radically disturbed by urban development."

I did not have to convert Jay. He was as curious as I about what could be found at Northwest Harbor. But then, so were the scholars to whom I had talked. They appreciated just how little of the material culture of that earlier period survived. The truth of the matter was that somewhere beneath the sandy soils of Northwest Harbor lay what seemed to be an almost unique ruin, and early American workplace, a trading center that linked a small colonial village with an expanding Atlantic economy. And ironically, because Samuel Mulford's generation had managed to kill off most of the right whales, the land where the warehouses once stood had been allowed to return to forest and pasture. Their excesses had inadvertently helped to preserve a record of the Whale Design.

Jay and I enjoyed speculating about what we might uncover at the warehouse site. Our research suggested that late seventeenth-century commercial structures of this sort—at least, those in New England—generally combined two separate functions. They provided wharves as well as warehouse facilities. Much of the packing would have taken place within the warehouse itself. It was here that the coopers would have constructed the hogsheads—large watertight barrels—in which the whale oil was shipped to a Boston or London market. But the coopers also packed hides and meat, much of it destined probably for the West Indies, where the high temperatures destroyed the contents of any containers not carefully sealed.

Because these hogheads were so heavy, colonial merchants often located their warehouses near the water—in other words, as close as possible to where the ocean-going ships docked— and in many colonial ports this meant constructing buildings on marshy ground. A great door—much like a large barn door—would have opened onto a long wharf running directly from the warehouse to the waiting vessels. Indeed, it might have appeared to someone viewing only the building's exterior as if a boathouse of some sort had been placed on top of the wharf. This blending of different work spaces probably explains why the records of colonial East Hampton sometimes speak in confusing language of a "warehouse *or* wharf." The entire edifice would have been made of wood, pilings, planking, and siding. Even if the merchant had had a good supply of cedar posts—a wood most resistant to rot—he could not have expected his warehouse to last more than a generation. Normal maintanence must have been a constant problem, for if the building escaped winter storm damage, it would have been under constant attack from various insects and worms.

It is difficult to say how large these colonial warehouses might have been. No doubt, size varied considerably depending upon the character of the goods that the merchant actually exported. Cereal crops, for example, required different storage facilities from those for oil and bone. Moreover, the dimensions of the warehouse must in some way have reflected the owner's success as a businessman. We know that Mulford was a substantial local importer; he also rented space to other merchants such as Hemstead. It seems likely, therefore, that Mulford would have had some sort of office in his warehouse, a special room separated from the noise and confusion of packing where he could write commercial letters.

But this was all simply conjecture. As both Jay and I were fully aware, only a trained professional archeologist could discern whether Mulford's warehouse looked anything like the building we now projected onto the landscape of Northwest Harbor. We were searching in fact for postholes, slight discolorations in the soil indicating to people who could read such evidence something about the dimensions of this colonial structure.

"Postholes are not going to draw many visitors," I grumbled.

Jay nodded.

But we knew that if we were lucky there might be more. Pieces of broken ceramics thrown into an ancient trash pit. Bits of metal associated with the day-to-day activities of a colonial warehouse. There might be nails. Perhaps a knife blade or part of a discarded tool. There might be coins. Splinters of glass. The cloth and leather items would certainly have disintegrated long ago, but a gun lock or whale lance could have survived the years in the wet sand.

These artifacts were waiting to be discovered. Without our intervention, of course, they possessed no meaning. They were without context or identity, like the planes taken from old toolboxes and organized in patterns without history. We had already created an interpretive scheme in which these fantasized items could be arranged, classified, and defined. We would give them a purpose, to be sure, not the one that some seventeenth-century artisan had intended, but an apposite one nonetheless.

From this perspective, I had to admit that the actual recovery of lost artifacts would not make the story that I was telling about East Hampton any more "true" than the stories other people had told. Rather, the pieces of glass and pitted metal—nothing intrinsically beautiful about them—would help people living in the community today to tell a more dramatic story about themselves. The artifacts that we imagined somewhere at Northwest Harbor had in their very physicality the capacity to translate an abstraction into something more, an imagined past with texture, body, feel, and color.

V

*A*lmost everyone I encounter in East Hampton agrees that Tom and Cathy Lester hold vital clues to solving the mystery of the warehouse. Tom has spent most of his adult life fishing the waters of East Hampton. In fact, he is a member of that most endangered local species, the Baymen. One afternoon in late August the Lesters invited Jay and me to their house to tell us what they know about the secrets of Northwest Harbor.

As we park the car, it occurs to me that I have seen this house before. Not in East Hampton. But along country roads in other parts of America. The yard contains an astonishing collection of "things"—I can think of no better word to describe them—connected presumably with commercial fishing. I cannot begin to identify most of what I see. To the outsider the scene suggests utter confusion, a chaotic disregard for appearance, but I suspect that there is an order here that only the owner can fully appreciate. The open space around Mulford's warehouse probably once looked like this. At least, I hope it did.

Several large dogs watch our movements. A woman who I assume correctly is Cathy emerges from the modest, rectangular house. She persuades a powerful brown retriever that we intend no harm, and, though I suspect he would prefer confrontation, he silently follows the visitors into a back room where Cathy has already opened a huge map of Northwest Harbor.

Even during our initial exchange, Cathy strikes me as tough, mentally and physically, ruggedly handsome rather than pretty. There is something about her that makes me think of American Indians. Perhaps it is the strong, broad features of her face. Or perhaps the association is triggered by more subtle mannerisms. One cannot be in her presence for very long without being impressed by her self-control. It does not seem to come easy. She speaks in short, articulate bursts, never raising her voice. The effect of her extraordinary self-restraint is to

Cathy Lester

rivet attention even more forcefully upon the energy and passion that crackles just beneath the calm exterior.

There must, of course, be another side to this woman's personality. I was informed that she is a political activist that some people find threatening. Cathy's greatest offense, it seems, is getting involved in public issues that have traditionally been settled by men and women who do not share her view of the world.

I imagine that if I had known Cathy for a long time, I might have witnessed a dramatic change in her behavior. Something seems to have awakened this woman, stirred a kind of populist anger, a deep sense of injustice, and now there is no holding her back. I do not really know that she went through such a personal transformation, of course. All I know is the woman who has invited Jay and me to into her home. For us she has no past. She has probably never heard of the outspoken seventeenth-century women who refused to accept the social conventions that their socially insecure neighbors prescribed.

The room where we talk contains collections of curiosities that the Lesters have apparently carted home from the woods and the sea. To say that these items—pieces of Indian pottery, for example—are displayed would be misleading. They are just there. Their presence in this house reflects a kind of salvage mentality. The satisfaction of owning these historic fragments comes from the conviction that they could have been destroyed, indeed, probably would have been destroyed, had the Lesters not intervened. Preservation is the goal, for in themselves the objects do not seem to generate much pleasure. Their very existence symbolizes the threat of change. They remind the Lesters of all that has been lost, of sites throughout East Hampton that have been destroyed to make way for modern development.

Tom finally joins us. He has been sleeping, recovering from a full day of work that began before dawn, and, as he enters the room, it is clear that he is not yet fully awake. He seems a little disoriented. It crossed my mind that we have made a terrible mistake by coming here. Tom is one of the largest men that I have ever met, a giant in this small room, and since he has not bothered to button his shirt, his immense bulk seems almost menacing. He is too massive for this confined environment. Tom rubs his eyes, fumbles for a cigarette, and waits for Cathy to tell the strangers about the warehouse.

Together, we examine a large map of a 626-acre section of Northwest Harbor known locally as the Grace Estate. This area includes the bank where the whale was tried. Tom examines the document. Sharp lines trace the coastline; all the major roads have been marked. But for him, the map is somehow incomplete. The details are culturally out of focus. Missing here are the overgrown trails and paths that he has used since he was a boy; missing too are particular boulders scattered along the beaches, each of which for him recalls a great storn, fouled lines, or good catches. Cathy senses his frustration and translates his rambling reminiscences into precise locations. For her, the map is a battle chart.

As we take an imaginative walk along the bluffs near the Kirk place, Tom becomes much more animated. Like Cathy, he wants desperately to preserve a local past that is a powerful source of personal identity. For him, the flow of time is measured in part by the passing generations of Lesters who have lived in East Hampton. But, for Tom, genealogy involves something more than the tracing of a single surname. It conjures up a complex web of human relationships, a chronicle of intermarriages going so far back into the history of this community that he suspects that he is related one way or another to almost everyone in East Hampton. He excludes, of course, the newcomers who flooded into the town after World War II. The others, that older community, he describes as a large, though not necessarily happy, family. All these people are in some important sense Mulfords, and Edwardses, and Lesters, a vast assemblage of cousins.

Tom has great difficulty, however, abstracting these various people from the environment in which they have lived. Each person carries a story in his very name, a story or set of stories that has meaning only in the context of East Hampton.

Couples lived in certain houses that Tom can see in his imagination. Without the house, they would not be the same people. The men that he recalls are associated with particular fishing vessels, or troubles that they have endured, or women that they have married. As one goes further and further into the history of the town, the stories lose their sharpness. The details get confused. But it never seems to occur to Tom that someone who lived in 1650 or 1750 might have looked at the water or the woods any differently from the way he does today. He sees history as continuity, not change. The only justification that he can think of for studying the past is the discovery of persistence. "We should know where we came from," he says, referring not simply to Lesters, but to an entire community.

Tom informs Jay and me, in fact, that the best way to learn history is to listen to the "ol' timers" and keep your mouth shut. He is not talking about the people who run the local Historical Society or the antiquarians who spend their hours in the archives of the village library. He does not hold such people in contempt. It is just that they do not know how it "really was." Such information can only be gained by listening to old men talk about other old men that they remember having listened to as boys.

From this perspective, of course, change is a disaster. It disrupts the human links in an oral tradition. Since the local people—the "true" local people—are conservative by temperament, change is almost by definition something caused by outsiders. And as we explore the colonial history of Northwest Harbor, it becomes increasingly clear that Tom feels threatened by what he sees as the accelerating pace of change. Indeed, he suffers from a sort of historical vertigo, and I suspect that he compensates for his own uncertainty about the forward direction of the flow of time by loudly celebrating "Bonacker" culture and crusading for the survival of the local Baymen. He wants to preserve the few remaining tracts of open land in East Hampton, not only, I would guess, because he cares deeply about the endangered plants and animals, but also because these familiar spaces contain something of his own history. If they

Tom Lester

are transformed beyond recognition, he will lose his ability to tell a convincing story about himself within this community over time. When I ask him why he so doggedly resisted the development of the Grace Estate, he answers only, "There was so much history involved, we could not give it up."

Though he never says so, I conclude that Tom views me as a resource who can be appropriated for his own purposes. I am an outsider who just may legitimize an interpretation of local history in which he and his family will have a secure place. This attitude does not bother me in the least. I am willing to listen, to learn, and to record. Many people in East Hampton see Tom simply as the quintessential Bonacker, a romantic survivor from an earlier, perhaps simpler, time. The last of the Baymen. A symbol rather than a man. And though he plays the part with skill, Tom and Cathy seem to know full well when he is being patronized. They sense that the great network of old families is actually a very fragile thing on which to place their hopes for the future of East Hampton. They have seen too many local people—members of the ancient clans—auction off their own heritage.

Cathy takes a more populist view of history. For her, the old maps of East Hampton tell a story of the betrayal of public trust. She believes that the colonial roads, many of which have long ago fallen into disuse, belong to the ordinary people. It causes her an almost physical pain to see the steady privatization of the local landscape. Throughout East Hampton, she tells us, the old paths and trails are being transformed into house sites. Developers seize what she regards as the common heritage, and because history of an earlier public ownership has been effectively erased from the public memory, no one bothers to protest the fencing off of the woodland. In a letter recently published in the local newspaper she urged the community "to preserve a perpetual peace for the restless spirits wandering in dissatisfaction of past mistakes for not recognizing the future value of preservation."

If this is a radical philosophy, it is one that the American revolutionaries would have understood. It subverts economic privilege. Whereas Tom perceives the history of Northwest Harbor in highly personal terms, she sees it as a set of abstract rights and principles that must be defended. And while Tom largely relies on memory, she pores over the old records, a self-taught historian. Cathy's particular bêtes noires are the developers and those members of the local government who she is convinced have abetted the developers. It is she who gives me an apocalyptic bumper sticker announcing: NORTHWEST: THE LAST STAND.

Tom claims to know exactly where Samuel Mulford built his warehouse. He jabs a huge finger at a site on the map a few hundred feet south of the Kirk place.

"This is the way I see it," Tom begins in a gravel voice. Cathy has heard it all before, but she listens once again, providing details only when he pauses or seems at a loss for words.

Tom bases his theory about the location of the warehouse as much on personal experience and common sense as on documentary evidence.

"What would Mulford have needed?" he asks.

And before anyone at the table can answer, Tom responds, "Deep water." The bay in front of the warehouse would have had to be deep enough to accommodate a ship fully loaded with barrels of oil and bone.

It happens that the Grace Estate site qualifies. Tom came across a mysterious "hole in the water" not far from where he now locates the colonial warehouse. This discovery occurred years ago while he was harvesting scallops. But even then, the underwater depression struck him as highly unusual. It is the kind of thing, he assures us, that sticks in one's memory. Tom does not believe that Mulford and Schellinger had actually excavated this unusual "hole"—something that would have been almost impossible, in any case—but it seems to him quite likely that two such accomplished seventeenth-century seamen would have known of its existence.

Tom then invites Jay and me to "think like Indians." By that he seems to mean that he wants us to imagine ourselves to be common laborers hired to work at the Mulford warehouse.

We have got to put ourselves into the minds of the people that we are studying—a reasonable proposition, but I have trouble understanding just where Tom is leading us. Once again the correct answer is water. He assures us that these hardworking men would have demanded access to fresh drinking water. If there was not a source of water nearby, he argues, Mulford would have had to cart water to the warehouse, a tedious and difficult job. But, as Tom has discovered in his walks through the Grace Estate, a spring surfaces conveniently near to the place where he thinks the merchants built their warehouses.

Tom rejects the theory that the beach has eroded substantially over the centuries. As usual, he draws upon his own experience. For many years he has set nets and hauled lines at Northwest, and he know that the wind, even during the severest winter storms, comes out of the northeast. The uplands and low bluffs protect the beach as well as any ship anchored over the hole in the water.

The evidence—however circumstantial its character—is beginning to pile up. Jay and I listen in fascination as Tom explains the function of the bluffs that run along the beach in this section of Northwest Harbor. The workers could not easily move the heavy hogsheads of oil around. These bulky containers could have weighed as much as a ton. The elevation, however, allowed the laborers to roll the barrels down to the wharf without too much aggravation. It does not occur to me—at least not at this moment—to inquire how Mulford and his crew transported boxes of imported merchandise back up the bluff to the warehouse.

And then there were the names of the old roads. How, Tom challenges us, could we explain the fact that Merchant's Path and Whalebone Landing Road had once intersected very near to the place where he now locates the warehouse? Tom claims to be able to trace Whalebone Landing Road all the way from the center of Amagansett to the shore of Northwest Harbor, although no one else seems capable of doing so. In other words, a substantial highway built sometime during the late seventeenth century connected East Hampton's most productive whaling area directly with the local port facilities. The road is now broken up, destroyed for the most part by modern construction, but Tom and his friends have identified deep ruts on the Grace Estate that they believe must have been formed by the great wagons hauling whale products from Amagansett. Moreover, he adds, the ruts are located precisely where one would expect to find Whalebone Landing Road.

Occasionally, Tom pauses. He lights another cigarette. Cathy has been following her husband's interpretation on the map, pointing to the "hole in the water," the Indian spring, the abandoned roads.

Only a few days ago, Tom continues, he reexplored the entire area.

"What about the ticks?" I enquire.

"Picked fifty-seven off my body," he responds almost with pride. Tom does not show the slightest fear of the ticks. What he saw on this recent visit to the Grace Estate was a strange depression in the woods near Whalebone Landing Road. To be sure, it could have been nothing more than a kettle hole produced by the glaciers. But there is a tendentious glint in Tom's eye. The depression might have been caused by the compaction of the earth around an old foundation. Perhaps it was the warehouse. One could never tell. The forest near the Kirk place was poorly lit; the shifting shadows in the late afternoon played tricks on the imagination. Perhaps there was nothing there at all.

Even more curious were some wood pilings—obviously very old—that Tom had first spotted from his fishing boat. These huge logs may have once supported a wharf, but, according to Tom, no one to whom he has ever talked remembered such a structure in this area. Probably the pilings dated from the nineteenth century. Did a farmer perhaps build a wharf for his own convenience? Of course, wood exposed to these conditions would have decayed over three centuries. Still, as Tom reminds us, it seems a bit odd that these pilings should appear so close to where he thinks Samuel Mulford once loaded his vessels. Perhaps there is some peculiar connection between the posts and those early colonial entrepreneurs.

And, even more curious, he has recently dredged up from a place not far from the hole in the water a mysterious piece of metal, a fitting from a vessel by all appearances, but like nothing Tom has ever seen before. It is probably just something that a passing ship lost in a storm. There is no reason to associate the article with Mulford's time. None at all. And yet these are things to think about. Odd coincidences?

Like a native storyteller in some exotic land, Tom knows how to stimulate the imagination of two eager travelers. He is the keeper of local legend, the one who remembers the wisdom of the old men, the tribal elders. He spins a web of plausibility around an interpretation, embellishing here and there, hinting of the possibilities that await the sedulous explorer. He is no different from the other local people who have claimed over the decades to be authentic keepers of the past. He is simply telling a different, more personal, story, one that just might save his world.

"What about the bank where the whale was tried?" I ask. "Do you really think that anyone could have killed a whale at Northwest?"

About that he has no doubts. Tom informs us that even within living memory people occasionally caught whales in these waters. His own father took one here in 1955. Tom describes the whale in loving detail: seven feet high and twenty feet long. He confesses, however, that the offshore whales generally preferred the open ocean, and so it seems likely that the name on the old road maps—the bank where the whale was tried—must have commemorated a rather unusual event at Northwest Harbor.

"This is the way I see it," Tom says, tracing a small circle on the map with his finger. "The other warehouses were probably here too."

He explains that the various seventeenth-century merchant-whalers must have built their warehouses fairly close together, certainly within eyesight. The reason for this, Tom argues, is that an isolated structure in the woods could easily have been robbed; nothing too serious, to be sure, a tool perhaps, a bit of rum. It made good sense not only to consolidate the warehouse activities, but also to hire someone to keep watch for suspicious strangers. I have not seen any references to such a person in the archives, but Tom insists that security is a matter of common prudence. Mulford and Schellinger must surely have appreciated the risks and have taken measures to secure their property.

"So, what have we got?" I break in. Jay and I review the arguments that the Lesters have presented for this location. It is really nothing more than a compelling brief based on circumstance and speculation. But, at this moment, it is all that we have. We wish, of course, that a couple of seventeenth-century nails had worked themselves to the surface of the Grace Estate, something tangible. If we only had found a piece of the actual warehouse, we could raise funds for proper archeology.

The excitement of potential discovery overcomes our initial skepticism. Jay and I conclude that the site must not be disturbed until we obtain professional assistance, and we urge Tom to discourage amateur archeologists—annoying weekend diggers armed with metal detectors—from attempting to locate the treasure on their own. He agrees to do what he can.

But as Tom and Cathy well understand, the greatest danger to the warehouse will come not from curious diggers, but rather from a developer who has just purchased the entire Grace Estate for the express purpose of building scores of new houses. It is a multimillion-dollar project, one of the most ambitious ever planned for East Hampton. Almost overnight Northwest Harbor has become a battlefield. The contest pits a powerful businessman against a loosely defined alliance of Baymen and ecologists. Two and a half centuries have passed since the local merchants and whalers deserted this place for Sag Harbor. The remains of that earlier commercial community are now about to be incorporated violently into the modern capitalist culture of the Hamptons. After a long journey we have reached the temple at Philae only to discover that it will soon disappear beneath the waters of the Nile.

VI

*T*he present had ambushed the past. At least, that is how I came to view the warehouse crisis. Never before had I been in a situation quite like this. The pasts that I had studied before becoming the Resident Humanist of East Hampton had seldom conversed with the present. Indeed, like many other historians, I sometimes felt a little frustrated that nothing that I had written had made much impact upon the society in which I actually lived.

But in this case the present seemed positively intent on eradicating a local past, or perhaps I should say, an interpretation of a local past. What was at stake was not simply the survival of a colonial warehouse site. The development of Northwest Harbor threatened to expunge a new story that the town could tell itself about itself, about commercial dreams and ecological exploitation, about the political, racial, and environmental implications of the Whale Design. An elusive warehouse had come to symbolize a new imagined history.

A group of investors had just purchased the 667-acre Grace Estate. The chief architect of this deal was Ben Heller, a successful Long Island developer who for many years had been a part-time resident of East Hampton. Heller had also acquired another large parcel of land on the other side of Northwest Creek, and it was reported that he intended to build several hundred housing units on what many local people regarded as a particularly beautiful, relatively undisturbed area of the town. Although Heller apparently planned to preserve a considerable amount of open space at both locations, opposition to the project quickly surfaced, and during the summer of 1983 the town government rezoned the entire area, a change in the rules of development that meant that Heller would be able to construct only a fraction of the units that he had originally envisioned.

This made Heller very unhappy. From his perspective, the zoning change amounted to a betrayal of trust. After all, he and his partners stood to lose a great deal of money, and during the period when Jay and I were busy searching for the Mulford warehouse, Heller launched a counterattack. A long letter from Heller addressed to the East Hampton planning board reviewed the entire dispute, and, in the course of his brief, the developer vowed to defend his rights, even if that meant suing the town "to the fullest extent possible."

Although I was no position to judge the merits of Heller's case, I could appreciate the chilling effect that his words had on other members of this community. Legal actions translated into huge fees, and it was assumed that major developers have virtually limitless resources. Certainly, no one wanted to cross Heller. Even in conversations among my friends at the Historical Society, people spoke of the controversy over the Grace Estate in guarded language.

Although no one seriously thought that Heller cared one way or anther about the efforts to reinterpret local history, we proceeded with caution, weighing the evidence that we had before us very carefully. Could we approach Heller if we did not know for certain that the Mulford warehouse was really located on his property? What if his opponents heard of our research and used it in the zoning debate? If we could not demonstrate beyond reasonable doubt that the warehouse was located along Whalebone Landing Road, and if our preliminary and largely circumstantial findings obstructed Heller's multi-million-dollar project, then it seemed possible that we would find ourselves involved in a legal battle for which we had neither the will nor the resources. Moreover, the staff of the Historical Society was understandably reluctant to enter what was viewed as an essentially "political" matter. Quite literally, they could not afford to take sides on such a divisive subject.

As the public debate over the future of the Grace Estate grew more acrimonious, Jay and I continued to search for evidence that would definitely place the warehouse on the site where the Lesters had said it might be found. As we soon discovered, however, we were not alone. Heller himself, in compliance with local planning regulations, had hired a pair of local archeologists to "walk over" his land at Northwest Harbor. This exercise was not intended to be an exhaustive survey. The people who did the work dug no holes, nor in the limited time that they had available could they have profitably done so. Rather, they examined surface features, looking for ancient roadbeds, house foundations, piles of shells left by preconquest Indians. They also studied the early town records.

The report that the two consultants submitted is an interesting document. Like us, and like Tom Lester, to whom they talked, they concluded that the Mulford warehouse would be found eventually beneath the soil somewhere near the intersection of Merchant's Path and Whalebone Landing Road. The contours of these long-abandoned highways, they reported, were still clearly visible to the naked eye. Their research convinced them that the modern Grace Estate must have been the center of seventeenth-century commerce. "The gentle waters of Northwest Harbor," observed the archeologists, "became their [the early settlers'] most convenient link with the outside world. Their shallow-draft boats had little trouble loading and unloading at the Northwest beach. Year after year the merchants' carts made the round trip from East Hampton and its neighboring hamlets to Northwest Harbor. After a third of a millennium, the deep ruts made by those carts can still be seen penetrating the woods from Old Northwest road to the low cliffs of the harbor above."

But for all their good efforts, these archeologists had been no more successful than we had been in actually locating the warehouse: no coins, no nails, no pieces of glass or pottery, nothing. Just a powerful conviction that it must have been here. "Samuel Mulford is presumed," they noted in their report, ". . . to have built a warehouse and wharf on the beach at the point where Old Whalebone Landing Road ends. A search of this area yielded no trace of the warehouse. On the beach there are some spurs of water-worn wood in the sand. Several yards up the beach, also embedded in the sand, are edges of a small barrel. While any connection between these phenomena and Samuel Mulford is extremely unlikely, further study of both should be undertaken."

That, of course, was precisely what we were not prepared to do. Without substantial outside funding, the Historical Society could not afford to sponsor a proper archeological investigation of the Grace Estate. In any case, it did not have permission to trespass on land that now belonged to Ben Heller and his associates. And without definite proof of the warehouse's having existed on a certain spot, we could not very well obtain a grant. It would surely have been awkward to ask a foundation to underwrite what really amounted to no more than a fishing expedition. The days passed, each one bringing closer the inevitable breaking of ground for the massive new construction. One map of the Heller project published in the local newspaper showed the outlines of a new house on the precise location where I believed that Mulford had once built his warehouse.

The Resident Humanist hounded David Swickard. Sometimes I grumbled about the impending destruction of three centuries of East Hampton history. I tried to take the intellectual high ground, reminding David of the interpretive possibilities buried beneath the sand at Northwest. At other times I sounded a bit querulous, even to myself. How, after all the research I had done, could my friends so idly contemplate the destruction of the Mulford warehouse?

Even to suggest that David, Jay, and the others were somehow not doing their part was, of course, unfair. The problem was my standing within East Hampton. On what authority could I claim to speak for the warehouse? This was not, after all, my community. I had been brought here to conduct original research for a new interpretation of the Mulford Farm, not to lead an archeological expedition to the shores of Northwest Harbor. Moreover, I represented no local constituencies, no institutions, not even the Historical Society. Most of its members, I am sure, had not the slightest idea of what I was doing in East Hampton. We could not quite justify an approach to an embattled figure such as Heller simply on the grounds that perhaps, just maybe, he had purchased a symbol of a forgotten local past.

And yet, in the end, that is exactly what we did. David sent Heller a letter describing the work of the "Resident Humanist" and requesting an interview. A meeting was scheduled at his home, and on the appointed day, David, Jay, and I drove out to see the man at the center of the storm. We were intimidated; we joked nervously in the car about lawsuits. Our fears connected us at that moment to the earliest settlers of this community. They too must have worried about being sued by their neighbors. Then as now, residents of East Hampton appealed to legal authority to define the character of local society, to distinguish winners from losers. As we traveled along the village roads with seventeenth-century names, I decided that I represented the historical interests of Samuel Mulford. It was for him that I would be negotiating with the developer of Northwest Harbor.

Heller did not live in a starkly modern structure. To be sure, his house made a statement—there are almost none in East Hampton that do not—but instead of proclaiming radical individuality, Heller's rambling, brown-shingled home spoke of tradition, of a community that established itself here before World War II and that has become the standard of conservative good taste.

Heller ushered his guests into a brightly lit sitting room overlooking a spacious, well-tended yard. His tone was formal, but not brusque. Despite his informal dress, he was a serious businessman, and something about his manner strongly communicated a conviction that time is money. The telephone rang. Property bought or sold in another town. Polite interruptions while we tried to look like the kind of people who might have something that our entrepreneurial host might want to hear.

I suppose that Heller did not quite know what to make of us. The controversy over the Grace Estate had exposed him to a great deal of public abuse, and, within minutes of our arrival, he made it clear that he had been wronged or, at the very least, badly misunderstood. He was probably feeling us out. Were we just another group that had come here to execrate the local developers? Were we people who instinctively regard men like Heller as enemies of all that is good and beautiful?

As we discussed East Hampton's colonial history, Heller gradually relaxed. I told him of Samuel Mulford and the Whale Design. He seemed genuinely interested. I spun out an interpretation of the local past with all the passion I could muster until, as in a holograph, the warehouse stood before us, a mental construction that we imagined in such minute detail that it acquired a real presence.

Heller possessed a curious, probing mind. I suspect, however, that he had never given much thought to East Hampton's seventeenth-century origins. His sense of local history was not tied up with genealogy, and so he could not view the community's development from the same perspective as a Mulford or a Lester. To such people, he assumed, he would always remain something of an outsider. But though his own identity was not linked to a lost community at Northwest Harbor, the process of interpreting and reinterpreting the past, of inventing stories about ourselves that shape our perceptions of the future, seemed fully to engage his imagination. He confronted Samuel Mulford on an intellectual level.

What we wanted was permission to slip in between the lawyers and the bulldozers. If Heller would allow us—again, it was not clear exactly for whom we spoke—to carry out salvage archeology at the Grace Estate, we might save something of the town's commerical past. Perhaps a team of people sifting through the shallow mold near the "bank where the whale was tried" could uncover a posthole or broken tool, artifacts that we could carry back to the Mulford Farm as testimony not only of a lost colonial past, but also of an extraordinary last-minute effort that managed to preserve one of East Hampton's many pasts against the inevitable tide of modern development.

My presentation concluded, I was unabashedly pleased

with myself, though I suspect that my appeal occasionally verged on the melodramatic. Heller had probably heard it all before. Not, to be sure, about the historical significance of the warehouse. But about the trees and scallops and colonial water birds. Each petition had to be assessed within a complex financial calculus. Postponements cost money. Interest on loans had to be paid. But there was also the problem of public relations. Heller did not want to be known as the man who destroyed the colonial past.

He asked probing questions. Who would we hire to do the archeology? How much time did we need? And since we were certain that we knew exactly where the warehouse was located, we assured Heller that the salvagers could do their work quickly, perhaps taking only a few weeks. It was only a matter of finding the right people and a run of good weather.

The minutes passed slowly.

Heller finally announced that he would let us salvage whatever we could at Northwest. The details, he explained, looking at me, could be worked out by counsel. I could instruct my lawyer to draw up the appropriate papers and send them around to his lawyers for review. He foresaw no problems. Agreements of this sort do not take very long to complete.

Another pause. David and Jay were clearly anxious to leave.

"There is just one other point," I remarked.

Heller shook his head in amazement. He anticipated my audacity. He understood instantly that I wanted him to pay for the search.

I argued that salvage archeology of this sort cost a good deal of money, more than the Historical Society could provide at such short notice, and that if he helped with the finances, we would be off his land at Grace Estate a whole lot faster.

Heller was smiling. He asked us how much money we actually needed.

I stated a figure—a fairly modest sum that I now suspect would not actually have covered such an ambitious project—and with a wave of a hand, Heller indicated that he would pay half the cost of archeology.

With that settled, we thanked Heller and headed back to the Historical Society. We were excited. The meeting had gone much better than any of us had expected. We were going to find Mulford's warehouse after all.

But then, as I reviewed our conversation with Heller, I experienced second thoughts.

"What's your problem?" Jay asked.

"I don't even have a lawyer. Do you?"

VII

*S*oon after we had completed these negotiations, the pace of events affecting the future development of the Grace Estate suddenly accelerated. The threat to this last section of open space sparked an unprecedented public outcry in East Hampton, and in the scramble to defeat Heller's planned development, people of all sorts and from all backgrounds came to the defense of Northwest Harbor.

The intensity of the protest must have suprised even Heller, a man who had impressed me as being extraordinarily canny. In any case, during this period the local newspaper carried stories of possible deals that were in the works. Heller had apparently suggested that if the Town of East Hampton offered him a fair market price for the contested property, he would gladly sell it. There was talk of a major contribution from the nature conservancy.

These rumors had the effect of raising the public debate to an even higher pitch, and almost every issue of the *Star* contained letters from readers anxious to let their neighbors know where they stood on the preservation of the Grace Estate. Since a successful bid from the town government would inevitably raise local property taxes, the debaters often presented their arguments in terms of value for investment. Put simply, was the land at Northwest Harbor worth saving? Was it worth approximately ten dollars per person per year in net taxes?

Most letter writers—even those who resented the profits

that they thought that Heller stood to make—seemed willing
to pay the price. I was fascinated by the arguments that they
advanced in support of their position. Some asserted that Northwest somehow symbolized the community's "ties with the
past." By that, they apparently meant that the area was still
relatively untouched, a sanctuary for plants and animals, a place
that reminded them of what East Hampton might have been
like before they themselves had so transformed the landscape.
One editorial, for example, explained that the sale gave "East
Hamptoners the opportunity to preserve much of a tract that
was for centuries past of the common heritage, containing
woods, kettleholes edged by trailing arbutus and princess pine,
Scoy's Pond, extensive marshland, rare woodland creatures, and
Indian and Colonial sites."

From time to time, Mulford's warehouse surfaced in the
great East Hampton debate. Though the lost structure obviously
did not possess the rallying powers of the trailing arbutus and
princess pine, it was doing its part in the battle to generate
popular support for a six-million-dollar deal. The Historical
Society announced its intention to apply for a federal grant to
be used "to explore East Hampton's early involvement in international trade with which the warehouse was connected, so
shattering any myths of this town's isolation in Colonial
days."

Unfortunately, the myth-shattering warehouse refused to
appear when we needed it most. The newspaper honestly described the state of our research. "No one knows where the
remains of an early 18th-century warehouse, known as the Mulford warehouse, are," one *Star* reporter wrote. "It is believed
to be along Northwest Harbor. Some say the land has eroded
and it is in the Harbor, some say it is south of the Grace Estate,
and some that there is a chance it is on the Grace Estate." The
story even noted—a little sarcastically, I suspect—that the Historical Society had sponsored "a short-lived search for the Mulford warehouse and wharf."

There was a marvelous, obvious irony about all this. The
warehouse as a historical symbol did not fit smoothly into an

ecological discourse, one that included a nostalgic appeal to a lost way of life and a call to preserve a pristine natural environment. Mulford and his colleagues had exploited nature, developed Northwest Harbor, killed the whales, and harvested the trees. It was true that the new commercial interpretation of early East Hampton history shattered myths about isolation and self-sufficiency. But there was more to the tale than that.

The voters of East Hampton eventually accepted Heller's proposal. A referendum passed 2,488 to 1,600, authorizing the town government, in cooperation with the nature conservancy, to purchase approximately 516 acres of the original Grace Estate. This section included Whalebone Landing Road, the Kirk place, and the "bank where the whale was tried." Heller and his partners held on to the remaining land, which was now zoned for five-acre lots.

Everyone seemed to have emerged from the controversy victorious. Heller celebrated his own liberation from what had become an impossible situation. He told an interviewer, "In all my years in East Hampton I never saw anything like it. This was a major exercise in democracy, for better or worse." He insisted—as he had done when we talked with him—that he had always had the best interest of the community in mind. "I feel I've done a rather responsible job on behalf of the Town, though they didn't know it. There were people with very deep pockets who wanted to buy the property, not to sell for acquisition but to develop at any cost. There were a number of unsavory buyers, but I kept them at arm's length in order to negotiate with the Town."

The man who had represented the town in these negotiations found this interpretation self-serving. Heller, he declared in a newspaper interview, is "a man who is used to making decisions, and the right ones on investments. But in this situation I got the feeling he and his wife suffered from the perception he was abusing the virgin forest."

This may have been an overly cynical assessment of Heller's motives. I was not in a position to know. In any event, the sale of the land freed the developer from any obligation to pay for archeology. The area on which we had tentatively located the Mulford warehouse was now administered by a small committee representing joint interests of the Town of East Hampton and the nature conservancy. The group—it bore the imposing name Grace Estate Management Committee—included David Swickard and Tom Lester.

On a warm summer evening, I attended one of their meetings. The members of the committee were discussing a policy for recreational land use, and, after a tedious discussion, they decided that hikers who walked trails of the Grace Estate— some of them seventeenth-century roads—could cook food only at certain designated sites. There was a rub, however. The visitors who wanted to build fires had to provide their own wood. They were specifically prohibited from gathering dry sticks within the conservancy.

I enjoyed seeing Tom Lester again. After the meeting I joked with him about returning Northwest Harbor to a prehistorical situation. Even the Indians who once gathered shells along the bluffs would now be warned about spoiling the environment.

He laughed. We were both pleased that the warehouse had safely made it through the political wars.

VIII

*B*ut if the warehouse had somehow weathered the zoning wars, it had also migrated. Or perhaps it would be more accurate to say that the warehouse remained where it had always been. It was the interpretation that kept changing.

We had not intentionally placed the warehouse on the "bank where the whale was tried" in order to obstruct the development of the Grace Estate. Other people, men and women not ordinarily concerned with the history of early East Hampton, had imagined a warehouse on this land, very much as I suspect that they imagined rare birds and plants. Whether they existed in fact, of course, they were concepts, abstractions, symbols whose capacity to mobilize public opinion did not depend on actually having been seen. It was comforting just to know that they were out there. Few persons would have cared to walk the tick-infested woods of Northwest Harbor to find either Mulford's ruins or to observe a representative of an endangered species. History and ecology blended in a rhetorical defense of a tradition that no two people probably would have defined in precisely the same way. And in the great debate over the "last stand," the warehouse was of general significance only insomuch as it contributed to the preservation of a natural landscape.

Jay was the first to realize that Mulford had probably constructed his wharf-warehouse complex several hundred yards south of Heller's disputed land. As I came to appreciate, Jay has the attributes of a first-rate historical detective. Though he too fell under the hypnotic charm of the Lesters, he never could dispel lingering doubts. The pieces did not quite fit together. The case for a site along Whalebone Landing Road depended too much on commonsense assumptions, too much on "thinking like an Indian." And after the legal dust of the great contest over the Grace Estate had settled, Jay decided to contact a respected Boston university with a department that specializes in something called public archeology.

The people who run this organization, like almost everyone else whom we had talked to outside of East Hampton, shared our excitement about the possibility of locating a large colonial warehouse. When the director, Ricardo J. Elia, briefly visited the area, he did not rush out to Northwest Harbor with a metal detector. Until we had located the warehouse site—say within a hundred square yards—we would not find this level of technical sophistication very helpful. There was no point in searching for the archeological equivalent to the needle in the haystack.

So instead of heading for Northwest Harbor, Rick—as he insisted on being addressed—concentrated on traditional documentary evidence, especially on local records describing the construction and survey of early roads. Here, he explained, was where one might expect to find reasonably precise measurements of spatial relations. Even if we did not encounter references to the Mulford warehouse, we could at least acquire a more a detailed knowledge of the character of the early highways, and in the process, learn something more about the erosion of the beaches and the changing local topography.

Rick immediately pointed out that the mysterious ruts that we had seen on the Grace Estate were not unusual. It seemed unlikely that they had been cut into the thin soil by Mulford's heavy, oil-bearing wagons during the colonial period. What we saw in the woods was almost certainly a trail left by logging vehicles in the late nineteenth or early twentieth century. They were a reflection of intense modern usage, rather than antiquity.

Then there was the question of names. Rick could find no colonial reference to Whalebone Landing Road. It was not even entered on a detailed 1873 map of the harbor. That did not necessarily mean that Tom Lester had been incorrect or that a commercial road had not once run from Amagansett to the bluffs south of the Kirk place. But by calling a central element of the argument for the Grace Estate into question, Elia effectively broke the spell. We were prepared to rethink the evidence.

Rick urged Jay to go back to the early town records. Perhaps we had somehow overlooked an old map. This was the voice of experience. His suggestion—really a hunch that a crucial piece of evidence would soon turn up—shifted the focus of the entire warehouse search. Jay came across a reference in a WPA guide—an unpublished typescript kept in the Long Island Collection of the East Hampton Library—that mentioned a crude early nineteenth-century map of Northwest Landing Road. Since whoever prepared this WPA report had presumably viewed the map as recently as the 1930s, it seemed highly probable that this document still existed. The guide mentioned a "Book G" of the local town records. Not surprisingly, the map did not appear in the printed volumes of the town records published during the nineteenth century. It would have been difficult to reproduce material of this sort. Fortunately, as Jay had learned, the local library had a microfilm copy of the original records, and he set out to discover whether Book G contained new information about the warehouse.

The microfilm, however, offered no help. Where the map should have been located, Jay found only a handwritten page of text. That might well have been the end of the story, but, on a hunch, Jay decided to drive out to the town clerk's office to examine Book G for himself. And there—just where the WPA guide had promised—he found the map of Northwest Landing Road. Someone had carefully folded it against the back of a page, and when the modern microfilmer rushed through the volume, he apparently had not seen the survey drawing.

This 1828 diagram showed Northwest Landing Road cutting off from the highway known as Old Northwest Road just before it reached Mile Hill or Powder Hill (even in 1828 the surveyors were not certain about the correct name of this little hill). The road traced a long arc around the base of the hill, and when it reached the lower, presumably less firm, ground near the water, it took the straightest path to the so-called common landing area.

On the map, Northwest Landing Road looks like a large, rather clumsily drawn question mark. Where the dot at the base of the question mark should have appeared, there was a warehouse. It was not Mulford's warehouse, to be sure, but it was located exactly where one would have expected to find a building of this sort. It faces northward out into what appears to be the open water of Northwest Harbor. The entire road from Old Northwest Road to the place where Miller Dayton had constructed a wharf or warehouse was exactly 150 poles, about a half-mile.

The chance discovery of this little map proved to our satisfaction that the shoreline of Northwest Harbor had not changed radically over the centuries. Indeed, Northwest Landing Road looked in 1828—with one notable exception—almost exactly as it does today, and if one measures 150 poles (2,475 feet) from Old Northwest Road down toward the modern harbor, one finds oneself in the middle of a parking lot, several hundred feet east of the current mouth of Northwest Creek.

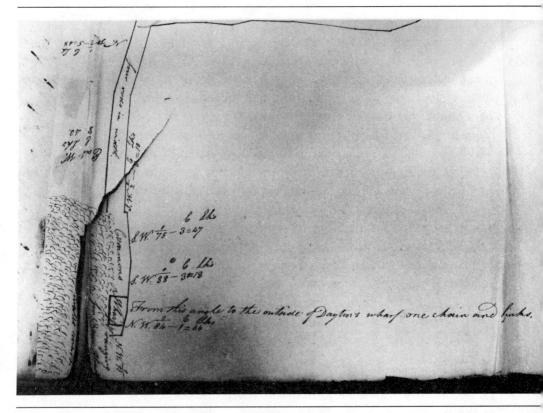

Map "G" from Old Town Records

Jay argued that Miller—a small nineteenth-century re-
tailer—would most likely have constructed his wharf on or very
near the site that Mulford or Schellinger had used. The thesis
seemed plausible. The map indicated that in 1828 the area around
Northwest Creek had been low and marshy, exactly the type
of location that Rick Elia and others had said that the colonial
merchants would have most favored. The "cycle" theory of
warehouse building was not mere speculation on Jay's part. He
discovered a deed in the East Hampton trustee records that
appears to have been written during the late 1770s. The town
allowed a certain Daniel Dayton to "have a flat *near the old
warehouse* at Northwest for four shillings and nine pence." The
curious reference to an "old warehouse" begs explanation. Is

this the building that Mulford had constructed earlier in the century or perhaps another building—Schellinger's warehouse, for example—for which we possess no genealogy? Was it perhaps positioned "near" the older warehouse, a few feet to the west?

Whatever happened during the Revolutionary era, Miller Dayton—Daniel's son—received a lease in 1823 for "a piece of land lying near the mouth of Northwest Creek for the purpose of building a wharf." This sounds as if Miller intended to put up an entirely new structure, the one that appeared in the 1828 map as a dark rectangle at the end of Northwest Landing Road.

There seemed no way short of actual digging to demonstrate whether this site—like those ancient cities uncovered in the eastern Mediterranean—contained a layered history of East Hampton. One could imagine warehouse built upon warehouse, each perhaps a little smaller, a little less impressive than the previous one, a tale of commercial continuity and decay. The important point was the Jay's lucky find provided the basis for a new working hypothesis. It forced us to reconsider much that we had come to take for granted or, more likely, that we had simply not noticed because we were looking for something else.

Rick Elia, for example, discovered in an antiquarian history of Suffolk County a reference to a 1713 document that we were unable to locate, but that appears to have been genuine. The quotation describes the laying out of a "common landing" at Northwest Creek. The highway leading to this site—in other words, Northwest Landing Road—runs to "the east side of Captain Mulford's warehouse or wharf; the said landing place to be 15 or 16 poles [248–265 feet] by the water eastward of the said warehouse or wharf." Even more suggestive was an entry in the East Hampton records for April 6, 1715:

Loose Leaf C—Captain Samuel Mulford entered the swamp that lieth on the right hand of the path that leads down to Northwest landing place, the first swamp on that side of path entered as part or all of his part of the half acre division.

Northwest Creek Harbor

Of course, there was no reason to conclude that this little piece of swampland was directly related to the warehouse. Perhaps Mulford wanted an additional source of marsh grass for his cattle. After all, as we have seen, the warehouse itself was built on town land leased to Mulford only so long as "he or his heirs shall continue said warehouse." Still, the grant definitely places Samuel on this road during the period of the Whale Design, and it seems perfectly logical that he would have wanted to acquire other property near the center of his commercial activities.

However interesting this new material was, there appeared to be an insurmountable objection to locating the Mulford warehouse on Northwest Landing Road. If one measures 150 poles from the start of the road, one finds oneself standing in the middle of a crumbling macadamized parking area. The mouth of the creek is still more than a hundred feet down the road; there is no place to moor a vessel larger than a day sailer. And yet this seems to be the place where Dayton—if not Mulford—constructed the wharf/warehouse.

The answer turned out to be a radical restructuring of Northwest Creek. Within the memory of older residents, the little creek had snaked its way along the eastern side of the landing area—in other words, a hundred feet or more to the east of its current location. Exactly why some government agency decided to alter the course of this shallow tidal stream is not clear. Tom Lester explained that its meandering character offended outside officials, who thought that creeks should take a more direct, efficient path to the sea. He told us that county workmen had taken tons of sand and gravel from Russell's Neck and used it to fill the old creek. The digging opened up a new channel. Another old resident who remembered going "gunning" at Northwest Harbor blamed a hurricane for radically changing the appearance of the town landing.

A check of various nineteenth-century maps confirmed that Northwest Creek had indeed flowed over against the eastern side. This information helped explain the location of the Dayton warehouse. In 1828 it *had* looked out onto the open water of Northwest Harbor. The road to the landing ended not in a parking area, but at the edge of the creek.

One detail remained. The present Northwest Creek is fairly shallow, not a channel that could accomodate a sailing vessel carrying a full cargo of whale oil. This problem had apparently bothered one of the town's early twentieth-century historians, for in a passage quoting the full text of Mulford's 1702 lease from the town, Harry Sleight added, "Old men have told me the channels at Northwest were much deeper years ago."

On the basis of all this evidence, Jay and Rick estimated that the Mulford warehouse must have been located fairly close to the end of the old Northwest Landing Road. As Rick stated in one report—not, I suspect, without an amused appreciation of the convoluted history of our search—"I suppose we should have taken the modern evidence at face value; that is, we knew that all the references to the warehouse mention it as being at Northwest Landing, or at the town landing. This area is still called the same thing today, and Northwest Landing Road is also still so named."

It would be no easy task, of course, to locate the actual warehouse. That kind of work is terribly time-consuming and quite expensive. After all, the laborers who carved the new channel for Northwest Creek may have buried the Mulford site under a huge quantity of sand and rock.

Still, Jay was optimistic. "The warehouse is somewhere out there," he assured me. "It is probably preserved under the parking lot, certainly in that area. The important thing is that it's safe for future generations. There is not going to be any development on county land."

EPILOGUE

The Worlds of Samuel Mulford

The decease of the sachem Poggatacut was an important event with the Indians. His remains were transported for burial from Shelter Island to Montauk. In removing the body, the bearers rested the bier by the side of the road leading from Sag harbor to Easthampton, near the three mile stone, where a small excavation was made to designate the spot. From that time to the present, more than one hundred and eighty years, this memorial has remained as fresh, seemingly as if but lately made. No leaf, nor stone, nor other thing, has been suffered to remain in it. The Montaukett [sic] tribe, though reduced to a beggarly number of some ten or fifteen drunken and degraded beings, have retained to this day the memory of this event, and no individual of them now passes the spot in his wanderings, without removing whatever may have fallen into it. The place is to them holy ground, and the exhibition of this pious act does honor to the finest feelings of the human heart. The excavation is about twelve inches in depth, and eighteen in diameter, and will probably continue undisturbed, until the active spirit for improvement which is abroad shall have reached this district, and forced its way over the present barbarous road into the secluded grounds.

David Gardiner, *Chronicles*(1840)

The Settlement at Northwest offers 21 building sites on 49.5 acres bordering the former Grace Estate. . . .

Established in the early 1700's, this portion of Northwest Harbor was occupied by a small hamlet, complete with its own schoolhouse.

Whales caught at Sagaponack and Mecox for whale oil were transported over Merchants Path to Northwest Harbor. Whale oil, whale bones [sic], firewood, tallow and hides were exported. In turn timber, rum, molasses and other goods were imported.

The Settlement at Northwest remains as unspoiled and rustic as it was when originally settled, and is one of the few beautiful and charming areas still available today.

Advertising brochure for
the Settlement at Northwest:
Cook/Pony Farm Real Estate, Inc.

Sounds of construction fill the air at Northwest Harbor. More than a year has passed since local voters authorized the purchase of most of the Grace Estate. Since that time I have not visited East Hampton, and, though my friends have tried to keep me informed about anything affecting the Mulford warehouse during this period, I am still surprised by how rapidly the area has been transformed.

The preservation of the Grace Estate seems to have had the effect of accelerating the development of other sections of Northwest Harbor. At the end of Mile Hill Road, for example, where children once attended summer camp, a sign announces the establishment of the Northwest Settlement. Survey stakes help prospective pioneers compare the merits of one expensive lot to those of the others. Some properties provide magnificent water views; others possess wooded privacy. A few prime offerings run all the way to the beach and may include the great trees where I first observed the nesting osprey.

What I find most surprising, however, is the wording of a real estate brochure. The text reveals dramatically that it is not simply the landscape that has changed. So too has the rhetoric of the past. The colonial history of this area has itself become a commodity, a marketing stimulus for what may well be the final development of Northwest Harbor.

During the crusade to conserve the Grace Estate, embattled residents had urged their neighbors to preserve a "way of life." It was a romantic view, powerfully evocative because it drew upon a mythic sense of local history. These people wanted to protect nature—however defined—and, since the existence of an ancient warehouse on the contested land seemed to promote their cause, the advocates of tradition tacked an early commercial history awkwardly onto what became in fact a rather unstable bundle of arguments. It was difficult to maintain—though some managed to do it—that Samuel Mulford was legitimately

Osprey Nest at Northwest Harbor

part of the same story that included endangered water birds.

Within the new promotional literature, I hear echoes of my own research. But in the translation, the meanings that I had attached to past events have somehow gotten scrambled. The developers of the Northwest Settlement are not imagining the same history that I imagined. In their telling, colonial commerce has been invested with charm, stripped of even the possibility of subverting the "unspoiled and rustic." The story of Samuel Mulford's world has lost its sting. Successful entrepreneurs have replaced the self-sufficent yeomen of an earlier mythology, and in this telling of history there does not seem to be a place for the "losers" of the past, for the men and women of different races and backgrounds who were systematically excluded from the profits of the Whale Design.

I

*I*t's summer and the historian returns," Tom Lester jokes when we meet again. He says I am like a migrating water bird, and when he hears that I have returned to East Hampton, he knows that it is time to renew the search for the Mulford warehouse.

He stoutly rejects the idea that the structure is located under the parking area at the town landing. If the "experts" claim that the ruin can be found in that area, then they are just mistaken. What do they know, for example, about mud? Tom points out that a seventeenth-century wagon heavily loaded with whale oil would have sunk down to the axle in the swampy ground at the end of Northwest Landing Road. Merchant's Road—its very name suggests its commercial function—bypassed the old town landing and ran north into the upland that would eventually be called the Grace Estate. These roads, Lester insists, were constructed on the firmer soils. The colonial builders knew what they were doing. Interpretation is a matter of common sense.

Moreover, assuming a confidential air, Tom informs me that two strangers from another community "down the island" had recently found a very old Dutch coin near the "bank where the whale was tried." They were using metal detectors. Before Tom could talk to them, however, the pair of treasure seekers disappeared. It is not clear to me whether anyone in East Hampton actually saw the coin, but the rumor of its existence has reinforced Tom's conviction that the Mulford warehouse had been located on the bluffs above the "hole in the water."

But, despite Tom's continuing fascination with the search, others in East Hampton have clearly lost interest. Indeed, many people who Tom thought would be staunch allies in the battle

Advertisement for the Settlement on Northwest Harbor

to save the Grace Estate never bothered to come forward. In conversation with Jay and me one evening, he complains in sorrow as much as anger that we received no help during the fight to save the Northwest from the Historical Society, or from the gun clubs, or from the politicians.

And by extension, if such people—even some who bear the surnames of the original settlers—refused to take a lead in saving an open area from the developers, it seems unlikely that they will now assume responsibility for locating the warehouse. Tom finds the whole experience discouraging. When push came to shove, the real Bonackers had proved distressingly thin on the ground.

"So nothing's happened?" I ask. "No money for archeology? No grants?"

"That's right," Tom replies.

Cathy steers the conversation in a different direction. She tells me that at a public meeting that had been called to discuss a new housing project at Northwest Harbor, she cited the research that Jay and I had done. She raised the possibility that this construction might accidentally destroy the Mulford warehouse. What would happen, she asked, if the builder encountered colonial artifacts? Were there procedures for preserving the colonial past?

The developer doubted that there was anything left in the area to disturb, but, finding himself confronted by such a knowledgeable opponent, he wisely compromised. He agreed to allow an independent "historical" observer on the building site to monitor the excavation work. If any late seventeenth-century artifacts turned up, the historian could temporarily halt the project. Cathy is obviously pleased that colonial history has finally been given—in this one case, at least—a voice in the future development of Northwest Harbor.

We return to the warehouse. What would it take, I ask the Lesters, to promote public interest in our work? To raise funds for a proper archeological investigation?

Tom is not optimistic that anything can be done. He points out that as long as people think that the Mulford site has been preserved under a town parking area, they see no reason why they should rush to dig it up. The warehouse will be there when East Hampton is ready to find it.

Cathy, however, is more enthusiastic. For her the search represents a political challenge. We must appeal to the "ordinary" people of East Hampton, she urges. These are the men and women who must be made to feel part of the effort to rescue the community's early history. She can imagine launching a massive educational effort to mobilize the local people. A populist rising! A reaffirmation of traditional culture! It will be a campaign to instill pride in those who increasingly find themselves pushed to the margins in the name of progress.

I am not sanguine about such an effort ever getting off the ground. But it could. I do not underestimate the Lesters.

II

*T*he Historical Society could not do much about the warehouse at Northwest Harbor. To be sure, David Swickard encouraged me to continue my research, and even after the money for the "Resident Humanist" had been exhausted, he and Jay welcomed me back each summer. David wrote a couple of grant proposals; Jay mounted an exhibit at the Mulford House called "The World of Samuel Mulford." But despite their continuing support, the search for the warehouse at Northwest Harbor stalled.

As David patiently explained—he had now been appointed the director—the society had established institutional "priorities" that left no excess funds for digging up the town landing. It was a familiar litany. Salaries had to be paid, a roof at Mulford Farm to be repaired, exhibitions at Clinton Academy to be mounted. There was always some more pressing activity that served to postpone serious consideration of an archeological project that could, after all, fail to yield tangible results. It was the risk of public debacle that was ultimately the most frightening factor. How could one explain to a board of directors that scarce financial resources had been squandered on a search for a phantom warehouse?

III

*I*t broke in upon Judith Hope's busy schedule. As East Hampton's town supervisor, she was in an excellent position to assess whether it would be possible to raise funds for a search for the Mulford warehouse. We talked in her offices about the colonial history of her community, and though she had not been aware of the town's commercial origins, she did not find anything objectionable about my interpretation of its early history.

Indeed, I specifically asked her whether she preferred a more pastoral history, one populated by self-sufficient agrarians, but the question struck her as badly posed. What was the use of myth if it did not conform to the facts? The town supervisor saw no reason—political or philosophical—to reject the conclusions of honest research. In any case, she had no trouble imaging East Hampton as a commercial community, as one in which market forces had from the very beginning of settlement determined the character of society.

Other business demanded attention. It was clear that Hope had given serious thought to the meaning of tradition in this community, and I would have liked to discuss with her the process of historical interpretation.

I did, however, press her on one question. Did she think that it would be possible to raise money in East Hampton for archeology at Northwest Harbor?

"Yes," she replied without the slightest hestiation.

"You can anticipate no problems?" I inquired. "After all, the warehouse may be on publicly owned property."

Hope was silent for a moment. She saw challenges rather than obstacles. The concept of a different kind of history, one in which a colonial warehouse played a major symbolic role, would have to be sold to the residents of the town. It would require education. And, of course, I could not expect the town government to foot the entire bill.

I thanked the town supervisor for her time. As I was departing, she had one last thought. "Don't call it an old warehouse," she warned.

I must have looked confused.

Warehouse, Hope counseled me, was a word that might conjure up negative images for many local people. She did not elaborate. Perhaps warehouses were associated with dirt and crime. Perhaps men and women had migrated to East Hampton to escape an urban world of warehouses. What, I wondered, was another name for warehouse? How much could one change the language of interpretation and still preserve that interpretation?

IV

I decide that Ben Heller may be able to help. At a moment of crisis, he had offered support, and now that he has divested himself of the Grace Estate, I think he may provide useful insight on how to mount a campaign to locate the lost warehouse.

I discover to my surprise that Heller speaks openly about the controversy over the Grace Estate. In the tranquillity of his own home, he seems reflective rather than bitter. It has been a good fight. And now looking back at these events, Heller admits that he made at least one major miscalculation. He failed to appreciate the deep symbolic significance that Northwest Harbor had for the residents of East Hampton, even some who had only recently migrated to the end of the island.

"It was a mistake to buy sacred property," he observes.

"Sacred?"

Heller argues that his opponents—and he speaks of them with a begrudging respect—imagined that their own identities were somehow bound up with the preservation of a particular piece of land. It was not, in other words, a battle over economic interests. Rather, the development that had been originally proposed for the Grace Estate threatened to sever local men and women from a world that they had already lost. Indeed, from one that they themselves had deserted long ago. During the controversy, they spoke of walking at Northwest Harbor as children, of gathering wildflowers, of observing rare water birds, and even of snowshoeing through the deserted woods on cold winter days.

It is not that Heller doubts the sincerity of the opposition. Perhaps one or two of these people really did trek through the deep snow. That is not the point. Behind the rhetoric, he insists, was a nostalgic vision, a view of the community that could not or would not incorporate the changes that had in fact already transformed the character of East Hampton.

I ask Heller what the concept of tradition meant in this context. After all, it seems to have become an ubiquitous term in the public discourse of East Hampton. It appears in protest letters as well as advertisements.

Heller responds that it means very different things to different people. His answer is not intentionally glib. The automobile had radically altered the character of this society. Before World War II, it might have been possible to speak of a single community, of shared values, perhaps even of a common history, but the development of a mobile culture had destroyed homogeneity. It is this change that many local residents find most difficult to accept.

But however much people attempt to disguise the transformation, they can not credibly maintain that somehow "tradition" has survived into the late twentieth century. There are traditions in East Hampton, not a single tradition. And for Heller at least, this is not a particularly upsetting turn of events. Change will occur whether anyone desires it or not. It has happened for three centuries in East Hampton. It will go on occurring. The challenge for a modern society is not to resist change, but to control it, to shape the future in ways that will best serve the welfare of the community.

Heller adds that it is distressing to witness the suffering of the local Baymen. They have played an important role in the history of East Hampton, and now that commercial fishing is no longer a viable economic activity in this area, the fishermen have been absorbed into a popular mythology. It is currently fashionable to be a Bonacker in East Hampton. A dying industry has been awarded a privileged status.

But about such matters, Heller insists, one has to be hard-headed. Like everything else, professions come and go. Social and technological change puts people out of work; it is an inevitable element of the historical process. In fact, progress of the sort that Heller represents can create new jobs for the local population.

This sort of economic realism, Heller readily admits, does not currently have much appeal in East Hampton. It is a self-consciously historic community. People like himself, newcomers to this society, are concerned to preserve appearances. They live in weather-beaten shingle houses, even when doing so often means that they must endure personal discomfort. In other words, outsiders come to East Hampton looking for tradition, and, though they are never certain exactly what it means, they resist changes that they fear will compromise what they do not fully comprehend.

Heller reminds me that he still intends to develop Barcelona, the headland located on the western side of Northwest Creek. As was the case with the Grace Estate, this project has already generated controversy. The battle of the "last stand" will be fought once again. This time, however, Heller appreciates the historical dimensions of the contest. He tells me with a touch of pride that his lawyers have immersed themselves in the local archives. They have examined the maps of the ancient roads as well as the colonial town records. Heller vows that this time around he will not be beaten by history.

We talk of Samuel Mulford. I informed Heller about the warehouse at our earlier meeting, but on this visit, we are less pressed for time. I tell him not only of a structure, but of a set of meanings that I associate with a building that disappeared from the records sometime during the 1720s. When I complete the story, I ask Heller whether it would be possible to raise money locally for archeology. Would people in East Hampton contribute to such a search even if the cost rose to as much as several hundred thousand dollars?

"It would be a snap," Heller assures me. If I make the enterprise fashionable, he says, I can expect generous support from all segments of the community.

I am momentarily taken aback by the direction that our conversation seems to be taking. It is the word *fashionable* that causes me trouble. I have the same sinking feeling that I experienced in the office of the town supervisor. Both Hope and Heller have been extremely helpful, generous with their time, but somehow in our discussion a symbol has become divorced from what I see as its proper historical context. I was not sure that Samuel Mulford was a person whom modern residents should regard as "fashionable." The point of studying that earlier past was not to celebrate commerce—although that was surely part of the interpretation—but to reveal the social and ecological consequences of unrestrained economic development.

I try to express these doubts to Heller, but I am not certain that he appreciates exactly what I am getting at. He advises me simply to be honest with my interpretation. After all, it is my history. I have to please myself.

I have clumsily exposed myself to a barrage of clichés. Perhaps he interprets my doubts as weakness. Does he think that if I were mentally tough I could ignore how other people packaged the warehouse?

In any case, Heller may sense my discomfort. As I am leaving, he warns me that once I have published a history of East Hampton, my interpretation will be used in any way that my readers please. They will pick and choose among the facts. They will transform a community that I have imagined into one that they imagine. No matter what I do they will tell themselves their own stories about themselves. At some point I will probably not even recognize my own invention.

V

"*I* have a surprise for you," Jay announces. He is grinning like a Cheshire cat. "I found it! The warehouse. And you have been in it. It's been right in front of our eyes the whole time."

I am dumbfounded. Is Jay pulling my leg? Before I can mount a protest, he drags me out of the offices of the Historical Society, down Main Street, past the colonial homes and local library. We march straight into Mulford Farm, passing his new exhibition, "The World of Samuel Mulford." He hardly pauses before the little cases containing articles of late seventeenth-century commerce. Standing in front of an uninviting door at the rear of the building, he fumbles for a key.

The little room behind the door has never been open to the public. In fact, it has served for many years as a kind of unofficial storeroom where employees placed personal belongings. When the Mulfords last lived here—the father and his son—the area apparently was a kitchen. During the 1970s the historical society installed an ugly water-heater here where the visitors would not see it. The high-peaked roof of the room has been left open, and from rafters that have not been painted for a very long time hang cobwebs.

"This is it," Jay exclaims proudly. "This is the Mulford warehouse. We just didn't know where to look."

I am unpersuaded. The room seems too small ever to have functioned as a warehouse. Moreover, there is the not insignificant matter of location. The town landing at Northwest Harbor is about six miles away.

But Jay has already anticipated such obvious objections.

"Look at the rafters," he urges. "Look carefully. See where the roof rafters join the frame."

I do not understand what he is getting at.

"That's an example of bird's mouth framing," Jay says. "It is a building technique that predated the extensive remodeling that Matthew Mulford carried out after his father's death. In other words, this room comes from an earlier period, and I suspect that someone—probably Matthew—moved it to its current location."

To be sure, the ends of the rafters look remarkably like great predatory birds about to bite into the framing beams. It was this particular anachronism that initially sparked Jay's curiosity. Previous research had revealed the kitchen was not part of the old house. It was built separately and then attached to the main structure. It was also somewhat larger and, more important, open from floor to ceiling. A present dividing wall

Bird's Mouth Framing at Mulford Farm

and loft were built after the addition was made, sometime around the mid-eighteen century. The warehouse was an obvious candidate for building materials. No one, especially an eighteenth-century farmer like Matthew Mulford, would have wasted such a convenient resource. As Jay well understands, the original warehouse may have been much larger. Matthew probably salvaged whatever he could from the "wairehouse" that he had inherited from his merchant father. This was the building that, according to an old deed, Samuel gave to his son in consideration of "love, good will and affection."

It is just a theory, of course. Jay admits that it will require a lot more research to prove that the building in which we are standing is actually Mulford's warehouse. He predicts, however, that possession of the warehouse—a real "smoking gun" at last—will make it easier to raise money for archeology at Northwest Harbor. The existence of a visible past will help persuade people of the feasibility of actually finding artifacts buried at the town landing.

These revelations do not have the emotional impact that I might have anticipated. To be sure, I am pleased that Jay has uncovered this new lead. Perhaps the dark little kitchen will in fact turn out to have been constructed from the warehouse. As I have already learned, buildings in East Hampton seem to migrate. They are part of a portable heritage. Someday in the future a historian will probably discover David Mulford's barn in a neighboring town and wonder how it had managed to survive in greatly altered form.

At the same time, there is no denying that the warehouse now seems a little like one of the carpenter tools in Jay's collection. It has been stripped of context. An imagined structure has been absorbed into an agrarian world, and, for these many years, it has been telling visitors to Mulford Farm stories about a self-sufficient community that Old Fishhook had never known.

VI

"There's one last thing I would like to know before we leave East Hampton," I tell Kelly.

"What's that?"

"I wonder what the man who invented the slogan 'Share Our Traditions' had in mind."

"Let's ask him," Kelly responds.

And that is what we did. The offices of Donald J. Clause are located about a mile outside the village of East Hampton, on the main road leading to Amagansett. Except for a large sign urging passersby to "Share Our Traditions," there is almost no external indication that this building houses a successful real estate business. Indeed, the carefully maintained, brown-shingled structure reminds the visitor of the old homes that one finds in the historic district.

The Clauses—father and son—meet us in the reception area. Though both men extend a warm welcome, I sense a certain stiffness in our initial conversation. The senior Clause seems more reserved than does his son, a young lawyer who appears to have a good sense of humor. I suspect that they cannot quite believe that I really come to talk to them about an advertising slogan. Like other developers in East Hampton, the Clauses have found themselves at the center of public controversy, and these experiences may have made them a little wary of strangers asking questions about local tradition.

The senior Clause invites us to follow him up a narrow, open-backed staircase, which as we soon discover, leads to a private office. As we trail along, he observes that while the stairs are awkward to negotiate—we have to duck our heads under a low beam—he decided not to remodel this part of the old house. He wanted to preserve as much of the building's traditional character as he could.

The office at the top of the stairs is surprisingly large. It may have functioned over the centuries as a huge bedroom for generation upon generation of children. The Clauses have covered the floor with a deep-pile carpeting. An occasional runner extends up the wall and then across the underside of the dark wooden beams that presumably support the roof. A high ceiling above these carpeted beams has been left open.

The senior Clause takes a seat behind a large desk located at the far-end of the room. He motions for us to make ourselves comfortable on one of the overstuffed chairs that he has arranged in a great semicircle around the desk. Behind Clause is a remarkable window. From a distance the panes have the appearance of stained glass, and, in the late morning light, the patriarch of the firm is silhouetted against a glowing background of red and gold.

The conversation does not proceed smoothly. It strikes me as overly formal, more like legal maneuvering than an open-ended discussion about the meaning of tradition in East Hampton. The senior Clause addresses most of his remarks to me. In this situation, Tony and his son seem like seconds whose presence only serves somehow to heighten the strain.

I explain that over the last several years I have been talking to various local people about their perceptions of the past. I have asked them how they interpret East Hampton's long history and, more, how they think they fit into the stories they tell about this town. Often, during the early moments of these interviews, I have drawn attention to the phrase that the Clauses have used in their advertising, "Share Our Traditions." The well-known slogan usually sparks a spirited discussion about the meaning of history in a society desperate to make the right decisions about its future.

Clause asks me how they respond. What do they say about his slogan?

I tell him the truth. I have encountered many different reactions. Clause gives me a searching look that I find difficult to interpret. Perhaps I strike him as intentionally evasive or strangely naïve. Perhaps the whole encounter seems a little absurd.

Whatever thoughts may cross his mind, he assures me that "Share Our Traditions" is a sincere expression of his feeling for this region. Though he was not born in East Hampton, he has come to love the town. In fact, it was the beauty of its architecture—the warm appearance of the wood-shingled houses scattered along Main Street—that persuaded him originally to move here from New Jersey over thirty years ago. He confesses that his explanation may sound corny, but the fact of the matter is that he really wanted to share with other outsiders like himself what he has discovered in East Hampton.

It is not so much a tradition as the appearance of a tradition that Clause is now selling in this community. In this, he is not alone. An empty heritage has been transformed into a commodity, and for mobile Americans cut off from a past that can provide them with a secure historical identity, the roadside invitation to share someone else's tradition no doubt stirs residual longings. And in all probability the appearance of tradition is easier to accept than is an actual tradition that raises awkward questions about historical exploitation and future development.

Clause talks of his own efforts to preserve the symbols of tradition in East Hampton. He mentions the Reverend Lyman Beecher's house on Main Street. The Clauses purchased this building for a new office, but when they petitioned the village planning committee for permission to make what they perceived as minor structural changes, they were summarily rebuffed.

The son shows Tony and me the architectural drawings that the Clauses presented to the village for consideration. In order to make a suitable office building out of this eighteenth-century house, the Clauses insisted that the entire structure must be rotated a few feet on its lot on the corner of Huntting Lane. The realtors also proposed some extra parking spaces. But that was all. The building was still the Beecher house, protected for future generations, and yet, despite all their assurance, people who had another view of tradition stubbornly resisted a creative use of history. No progress has been made. And instead of becoming a new real estate office, the home of Lyman Beecher now stands vacant.

Just as we are preparing to leave, I am seized by a kind of nervous inspiration. I speculate that if Samuel Mulford were alive today, he would probably be involved in real estate. He might even be a developer.

Clause smiles broadly. "Could you," he urges with genuine enthusiasm, "write that up? Just a paragraph? I could use that."

Clause is already imagining a new story that he can tell himself about East Hampton. I should have seen it coming.

Tire Tracks in the Sand, Northwest Harbor

Sources

Dorothy King never once complained about my requests for additional books and manuscripts. Though she is a woman of few words, she probably knows as much about the early history of East Hampton as anyone I met in that community. She is in charge of the Long Island Collection, an indispensable source for anyone studying local history. It is housed in a richly paneled room in the East Hampton Public Library. It is here that one will find the Mulford and Schellinger papers as well as miscellaneous colonial archives. With the exception of the seventeenth-century probate records located in the Suffolk County Court House in Riverhead, New York, and the back issues of the local newspaper, found in another part of the library, all the manuscripts cited in the text can be found in the Long Island Collection. For the reader who would like to learn more about the early history of East Hampton as well as the expanding Atlantic economy, I have listed some useful titles.

"Account of the Montauk Indians," 1 *Massachusetts Historical Society Collections*, 1st ser., vol. 10(1809).

Adams, James Truslow. *History of the Town of Southampton*, 1918.

Arnell, Peter, and Ted Bickford, eds. *The Houses of the Hamptons*, 1986.

Autobiography of Lyman Beecher, ed. Barbara M. Cross (vol. 1 only), 1961.

Bailyn, Bernard. *The New England Merchants in the Seventeenth Century*, 1955.

Bailyn, Bernard and Lotte. *Massachusetts Shipping 1697–1714: A Statistical Study*, 1959.

Beecher, Lyman. *A Sermon, Containing a General History of the Town of East-Hampton . . .* , 1806.

Bloch, Julius M., et al., eds. *An Account of Her Majesty's Revenue in the Province of New York, 1701–09*, 1966.

Bonomi, Patricia A. *A Factious People: Politics and Society in Colonial New York*, 1971.

Boston News-Letter, 1705–1706.

Bridenbaugh, Carl. *Fat Mutton and Liberty of Conscience: Society in Rhode Island, 1636–1690*, 1974.

Brodhead, John Romeyn. *History of the State of New York*, 1871 (volume I only).

Buell, Samuel. *A Faithful Narrative of the Work of God in East-Hampton*, 1766.

Byers, Edward. *The Nation of Nantucket: Society and Politics in an Early American Commercial Center, 1660–1820,* 1987.

Calendar of State Papers, Colonial Series, 1669–1674, 1889.

——, *August 1714–December 1715,* 1964.

——, *January 1716–July 1717,* 1964.

——, *August 1717–December 1718,* 1964.

"Col. Robert Quary Report [1708]," 2 *Proceedings,* Massachusetts Historical Society, vol. 7(1887–89).

Cronon, William. *Changes in the Land,* 1983.

Demos, John P. *Entertaining Satan: Witchcraft and the Culture of Early New England,* 1982 (an entire chapter is devoted to the founders of East Hampton).

Denton, Daniel. *A Brief Description of New-York,* 1670.

Diary of Joshua Hemstead, 1711–1758, Collections of the New London County Historical Society, I(1901).

Diary of Sameul Sewall, ed. by M. Halsey Thomas, 1973.

Dwight, Timothy. *Travels in New England and New York,* ed. by Barbara M. Solomon, 1969 (vol. 3 only).

Epstein, Jason and Elizabeth Barlow. *East Hampton: A History and Guide,* 1985.

Fernow, B., ed. *Documents Relating to the History of The Early Colonial Settlements . . . Long Island,* 1883.

Gabriel, Ralph Henry. *The Evolution of Long Island: A Story of Land and Sea,* 1921.

Gardiner, David. *Chronicles of the Town of Easthampton, County of Suffolk, New York,* 1871. (Originally published 1840.)

Gardiner, John Lyon. "Notes and Observations on the Town of East Hampton [1798]," New-York Historical Society, *Collections,* 1869 (volume 2).

Gardiner, Lion. "Leift Lion Gardiner [sic] His Relation of the Pequot Warres," *Massachusetts Historical Society Collections,* 3rd ser., vol. 3 (1833), pp. 131–160.

Generic Environmental Impact Statement (GEIS) Concerning Future Development at Northwest Harbor, Town of East Hampton, Suffolk County, New York, 1983.

Goldberger, Paul. "The Strangling of a Resort," *New York Times Magazine,* September 4, 1983.

Hart, Francis Russell. "The New England Whale-Fisheries," Colonial Society of Massachusetts, *Transactions,* 26 (1924–1926).

Hedges, Henry P. *A History of the Town of East-Hampton,* 1897.

Hedges, James B. *The Browns of Providence Plantation: Colonial Years,* 1952.

Hubbard, William. *A General History of New England,* 1848.

Hummel, Charles F. *With Hammer in Hand: The Dominy Craftsmen of East Hampton, New York,* 1968.

Innes, J. H. *New Amsterdam and Its People,* 1902.

Innes, Stephen. *Labor in a New Land: Economy and Society in Seventeenth-Century Springfield,* 1983.

Jackson, Gordon. *The British Whaling Trade,* 1978.

Jameson, J. Franklin. "Montauk and the Common Lands of Easthampton [sic]," *Magazine of American History*, 9(1883).

Kelso, William M. "Rescue Archaeology on the James: Early Virginia Country Life," *Archaeology*, 32(1979).

Kross, Jessica. *The Evolution of an American Town: Newton, New York, 1642–1775*, 1983.

Kugler, Richard C. "The Whale Oil Trade, 1750–1775," Colonial Society of Massachusetts, *Collections*, 52(1980).

McManus, Edgar J. *A History of Negro Slavery in New York*, 1966.

Matthiessen, Peter. *Men's Lives*, 1987.

Mulford, David Eugene. *Puritan Profile*, 1974.

Mulford, William Remsen. "A Genealogy of the Family of Mulford," *New England Historical and Genealogical Register*, 34(1880).

Nettels, Curtis P. *The Money Supply of the American Colonies before 1720*, University of Wisconsin Studies in the Social Sciences and History, 20(1934).

O'Callaghan, E. B., ed. *Calendar of Historical Manuscripts in the Office of the Secretary of State . . .* , 1866 (vol. 2 only). Many documents listed in this calendar were destroyed in an Albany fire.

———. *Documents of New-York*, 1850.

———. *Journal of the Voyage of the Sloop Mary*, 1866.

O'Callaghan, E. B., and B. Fernow, eds. *Documents Relative to the Colonial History of the State of New York*, 1856–1887.

Palmer, William R. "The Whaling Port of Sag Harbor." Ph.D. thesis, Columbia University, 1959.

Pelletreau, William S. *East Hampton*, no date.

Rattray, Everett T. *The South Fork: The Land and the People of Eastern Long Island*, 1979.

Rattray, Jeannette E. *East Hampton History and Genealogies*, 1953.

———. "Long Island Off-Shore Whaling," New York State Historical Society, *Proceedings*, 31(1933).

Records of the Town of East-Hampton, 1887–1905.

Salisbury, Neal. *Manitou and Providence: Indians, Europeans, and the Making of New England, 1500–1643*, 1982.

Saville, Foster H. *A Montauk Cemetary at Easthampton [sic], Long Island*, Indian Notes and Monographs, Publications, Museum of the American Indian, II, no. 3(1920).

Savitt, Todd Lee. "Samuel Mulford of East Hampton." Master's thesis, University of Virginia, 1970.

Salwen, Bert. "Indians of Southern New England and Long Island: Early Period," in Bruce Trigger, ed., *Northeast*, vol. 15., *Handbook of North American Indians*, gen. ed. William C. Sturtevant, 1976–.

Spufford, Margaret. *The Great Reclothing of Rural England: Petty Chapmen and Their Wares in the Seventeenth Century*, 1984.

Suffolk, [New York] County Court, Sessions, vol. I, 1669–1684, *Riverhead*.

Thirsk, Joan. *Economic Policy and Projects: The Development of a Consumer Society in Early Modern England*, 1978.

Trelease, Allen W. *Indian Affairs in Colonial New York: The Seventeenth Century*, 1960.

Trustee Journal 1725-1772, East Hampton, 1926.

Truex, James and Donna I. Ottusch-Kianka, "Archeological Investigation," parts I and II, 1983.

Vickers, Daniel. "The First Whalemen of Nantucket," *William and Mary Quarterly*, 3rd ser., 40(1983).

———. "Nantucket Whalemen in the Deep-Sea Fishery: The Changing Anatomy of an Early American Labor Force," *Journal of American History*, 72(1985).

Weir, Marshall Brown. "Restoration of the Parlor at the Mulford Farm, East Hampton, New York," unpublished, 1983.

White, Philip L. *The Beekmans of New York*, 1956.

Index

Adams, John Quincy, 211–212
Adventure, 166
African-American population, 58, 110, 148, 181–184
Algonquian Indians, 81, 88, 169, 171
  history of, 105–106, 110, 112
  See also Montauk Indians
Amagansett Public Library, 60–61, 64
Anderson, Benedict, 33
Andros, Edmund, 186–187

Baker, Thomas, 129
Barcelona Point, 224, 242, 288
Barnes, Charles, 125, 127
Barnes, William, 240
Baymen, 19–20, 22, 71, 202, 204, 230, 246
  crusading for survival of, 250–252
  and disappearance of striped bass, 28–29, 30
  ecologists' alliance with, 26, 257
  suffering of, 32–34, 288
Baymen's Association, 29, 32, 33, 34
Beecher, Lyman, 6–9, 30, 40, 45, 56
  house of, 295
  A Sermon, Containing a General History of the Town of East Hampton. . ., 7–8, 43–44, 48
Birdsall, Goody, 132–133, 134, 136

Bird's mouth framing, 290–291, *291*
Bishop, Goody, 131
Bonackers, 11, 28–29, 30, 32, 67
Boston News Letter, 200
Bradford, William, 79
Brooke, Lord, 80–81
Brooklyn Museum, 35
Brooks, Goody, 130
"Brown tide," 30, 227
Buell, Samuel, 203, 209
Buell Lane, 209, 211, 214, 243

Calvin, John, 77, 96, 190
Captain Bell, 42
Carpentier, Ralph, 22, 23–24
Cedar Point, marker for warehouses at, 231, 232–234, *234*
Charles II, 158, 186
Chatfield, Thomas, 153
Church of England, 90
Clause, Donald J., 292–295
  "Share Our Traditions" slogan of, 59, *60*, 61, 293, 294–295
Clinton Academy, 6, 23, 284
Conkling, Benjamin, 170
Contracts, whale, with Montauk Indians, 169–171, 174–176, 179
Cornbury, Lord, *see* Hyde, Edward
Cotton, John, 96
Cromwell, Oliver, 97

Davis, Foulk, 121–122, 136
Davis, Mrs. Foulk, 130–134, 136
Davis, John, 121–122, 123, 241
Dayton, Daniel, 272
Dayton, Miller, 271, 272, 273
Defamation cases, *see* Slander and
    defamation cases
Deforestation, 199
Denton, Daniel, 110, 156
Diament, James, 150
Diament, Thomas, 150
Dongan, Thomas, 167–168, 188
Dwight, Timothy, 44–46, 47, 63,
    203

East Hampton Historical Society,
    20–24, 58–59, 66, 67, 264–
    265
  and Grace Estate, 259, 261
  and Jay Graybeal, 215–216
  and inventory of Schellinger es-
    tate, 151–152
  and Mulford Farm, 35, 36, 58,
    242
  and Mulford warehouse, 242,
    266, 284
East Hampton Library, Long
    Island Collection of, 214,
    270–271
East Hampton Star, 6, 27, 59, 68–
    69, 71, 74
  on Grace Estate controversy,
    266
  Letter to Editor in, 207
Economy, East Hampton's early
    consumer, 149–155
Edwards, Ann, and defamation
    trials, 117–120, 124, 130, 131,
    134
Edwards, Jonathan, 40, 203
Edwards, William, 117–120
Edwards family, 91, 117–120
Elia, Ricardo J. (Rick), 269–270,
    273, 275–276
Eliot, John, 105
Endeavour, 165

Fairfield, Daniel, 121–122, 124
Fences, importance of, 95
Fires, 199
Fishermen, commercial, 19–20,
    28–29, 32, 33
  See also Baymen
Fitzgerald, F. Scott, 82
  The Great Gatsby, 75
Franklin, Benjamin, 40

Gardiner, David, 46–47, 53, 59
  *Chronicles of the Town of East-
    hampton*, 47–49, 277–278
  on Samuel Mulford, 190–191
Gardiner, David (son of Lion),
    124–125
Gardiner, John Lyon, 40, 44–45,
    46–47, 50, 53
  on African-Americans, 181
  and Lyman Beecher, 7, 40
  and Timothy Dwight, 44
  and David Gardiner, 47
  on Montauk Indians, 180
  on Samuel Mulford, 190
  "Notes and Observations on the
    Town of East Hampton," 17,
    40–43, 63, 137, 160, 203
Gardiner, Lion, 78, 86, 103, 113,
    114–115
  characterized, 80
  and defamation trials, 115, 123–
    124, 128, 132, 133
  island estate of, 82–83
  New World activities of, 80–81
  "Relation of the Pequot
    Warres," 107, 108
  his relations with Indians, 81–
    82, 107, 109, 112
  tomb of, *84*, 85
Gardiner, Mrs. Lion (Mary), 126–
    127, 129–130, 134
Gardiner, Robert, 85–87
Gardiner family, 83–85, 86
Garlick, Goodman (Goody), 114
  and defamation trials, 124, 126,
    129–137, 139

Garlick, Joshua, 114
  and defamation trials, 122, 123,
    124, 129, 132–134, 136–137
Glorious Revolution, 188, 196
Government, Colonial village, 92–
    93
Governors of New York, relations
    between East Hampton and,
    185–189, 191–198
Grace Estate, 229, 230, 253, 257,
    282
  Management Committee, 268
  map of, 249
  old road on, 255, 270
  opposition to development of,
    252, 258–268, 269, 286–287,
    288
  preservation of, 279
  spring near, 254
Graybeal, Jay, 151, 215–220, 221
  and Mulford warehouse, 222,
    231, 235–245, 254, 259–260,
    261–265, 269–276, 282, 283,
    289–292
  his visit with Lesters, 246, 248,
    250, 253–254, 257
Great Awakening, 203

Hand, John, Jr., 121–122, 129
Hand, Mrs. John, 126–127, 131–
    132
Hand, Stephen, 138
Hedges, Henry P., 49–53, 54, 55,
    59, 97
Hedges family, 65
Heller, Ben, 286–289
  opposition to his development
    of Grace Estate, 258–268,
    269, 286–287
Hemstead, Joshua, 241, 244
*Historical and Cultural Features of
    the Town of East Hampton,
    New York,* 34
Hobart, Josiah, 35, 240
"Home, Sweet Home" house, 5
Hope, Judith, 32, 284–286, 289

Hopping, Daniel, 35
Howell, Arthur, 126, 128–129,
    131
Howell, Elizabeth, 158
  and defamation trials, 128–135
Hubbard, William, *General History
    of New England,* 156
Hunter, Robert, 193–194, 195,
    197, 201–202
Huntting, Nathaniel, 183, 203
Hyde, Edward (Lord Cornbury),
    155–156, 191–193, 194

Indians, *see names of specific tribes*

James II, 186–188, 196
James, Thomas, 52, 103, 109, 114,
    167–168
  and defamation trials, 115, 122,
    137
  grave of, 5
  replacement for, 183
  salary of, as minister, 96, 104,
    125
  and whaling contracts with In-
    dians, 173
Jameson, J. Franklin, 53–54, 62,
    63

Kelly, Tony, 19–20, 22, 69, 231,
    292–295
  and dead whale, 143–147
  and tick infestation, 231, 232–
    233
Kelsall, Trevor, 71, 74, 191
  meeting with, 64–67
  treasures collected by, 67–68,
    210
Kelsey, Carleton, 67, 70, 71, 74
  meeting with, 59–64
  and warehouse markers, 233–
    235
Kidd, Captain William, 83, 241
King, Daniel, 29

Kirk, Josiah, 233, 240, 242, 255, 270
house of, 229, 249, 253, 267

Ladies Village Improvement Society (L.V.I.S.), 32–33, 71, 235
Lee, Madeline, 59
Legal procedures, establishment of early, 93–95
Leo, Arnold, 32
Lester, Cathy, 207, 246–249, 247
and Mulford warehouse, 253, 255, 257, 260, 269, 283–284
her populist view of history, 252–253
Lester, Tom, 246, 248–253, 251
and Mulford warehouse, 253–257, 260, 268, 269, 270, 281–284
on Northwest Creek, 275
Licenses, whale, 192–193, 194, 197–198
Lillie, Luke, 123
Liquori, Lisa, 143–144
Long Island Colonial Water Bird Association, 224
Loper, Elizabeth Howell, 158
Loper, James, 158, 159, 163, 174, 204
bottle, 176, 177
Lost Tribe of Accobonac, 66, 67
Lovelace, Francis, 169

Magazine of American History, 54
Margaret, Princess, 87
Marine Museum, 22–23, 218–219, 222
Mary, 241
Matthiessen, Peter, 30, 32
Men's Lives, 11
Melville, Herman, *Moby-Dick*, 98
Merchants, 164–165
Miantonomi, 108
Mohawk Indians, 171
Monegan-Pequot language, 106

Montauk Indians, 11, 32, 42–43, 44, 56
and drift whales, 98
history of, 105–112
improvements in relations between whites and, 148, 169
purchase of East Hampton from, 87–89, 105, 111
suffering of, 49
whaling done by, 169–181
Morris, Lewis, 192
Mulford, David, 209–211, 212, 213–214, 243, 292
Mulford, Goody, 122–123, 124
Mulford, John, 78, 187, 201–202, 209, 239
and defamation cases, 129–130
"Humble Address" signed by, 188
real estate interests of, 165
slave owned by, 183
Mulford, Matthew, 183, 238–239, 290–292
Mulford, Samuel, 35, 37, 38, 52, 58, 183, 204
his attack on governor of New York, 167–168
characterized, 190–191
and Lord Cornbury, 191–192
and decline of whales, 200, 201, 202, 204
mental image of, 212–213
and Mulford Farm, 166, 217–219, 222, 235
political life of, 186, 189–191, 193–198
property in Boston purchased by, 214
warehouse of, 12–14, 209, 211, 217, 222, 230–246 *passim*, 253–276 *passim*, 279, 281–292
whale company of, 163, 165–166
worlds of, 277–295 *passim*
Mulford, William, 78, 165, 209
and defamation trials, 115–116, 122–125

Mulford family, 35, 37, 89, 209–
    211
Mulford Farm (House), 24, *36*,
    58, 64, 67, 263, 292
    description of, 5
    exhibit at, 284, 290
    fund-raising event at, 235–236
    history of, 23, 34–37, 57, 215,
        217–219, 222
    Samuel Mulford's purchase of,
        166
    occupants of, 211
    repairs to, 284
    saving of, 33, 73

Naipaul, V. S., 152–153
Narragansett Indians, 81, 106,
    108–109, 112, 169, 171
Native Americans, *see names of
    specific tribes*
New York Institute for the Hu-
    manities, 23
New York Times, 26, 32, 58, 68,
    204
Northwest Creek, *99*, 224, 226,
    227, 273, 275–276
    Harbor, *274*
Northwest Harbor, 163, 165, 202,
    209
    description of, 222–230
    map of, *223*, 246, 249
    osprey nest at, *280*
    schooner off, *13*
    warehouses at, 162, 176, 217,
        222, 228, 235
Northwest Landing Road, 223,
    273, 274, 275, 276
    map of, 271–273
Northwest Settlement, 279–280
    advertising for, 278, *282*

Old South End Cemetery, 5, 67
Osborn, John, 126
Osborne, Jonathan, 214
Osborne-Jackson House, 23

Paradise Cafe, 215, 216, 219, 222
Parsons, Randall T., 28
Parsons, Samuel, 125
Payne, John Howard, 5
Penny, Larry, 230
Pepys, Samuel, 155
Pequot Indians, 81, 106, 107–108
Pilgrims, 79
Pollution, 29, 30, 226–227
Price, Benjamin, 117, 118–120
Price, Mrs. Benjamin, 118–120
Price family, 91, 117, 118–120
Princeton, 47
Puritans, 77, 79–80, 82, 89, 97, 190

Quary, Robert, 153, 163

Racial etiquette, code of, 111
Rattray, Everett, 59
Rattray, Helen, 69–74, *72*, 200
Rattray, Jeannette Edwards, 59
    *East Hampton History and Ge-
        nealogies*, 54–56, 70
Real estate developments, 26–28
Religious practices, early, 96
Robinson, John, 78–79
Rose, John, 121, 122

Sag Harbor, 202, 215, 224, 229
Sanford, Peleg, 164
Saye and Sele, Lord, 80–81
Schellinger, Abraham, 158, 195,
        198, 231, 253, 257
    inventory of estate of, 151–152, 183
    his sloop *Endeavour*, 165
    warehouse of, 217, 231, 233,
        237, 273
Schellinger, Jacobus, 165, 176
Schellinger, William, 209
Settlers, East Hampton's first, 89–
    98
    hierarchical order among, 113–
    115
Sewall, Samuel, 155

"Share Our Traditions," 59, *60*,
    61, 292, 294
Simons, Goodwife (Goody), and
    defamation trials, 120, 123,
    126–137 *passim*
Simons, William, 122–123, 124,
    136–137
Slander and defamation cases,
    115–137
Slaves, *see* African-American pop-
    ulation
Sleight, Harry D., 59, 275
Smith, Adam, 157, 163–164, 195
    Theory of Moral Sentiments, 164
Smith, John, 80, 81
Smith, Roger, 125
Smith, William, 200
Society, transformation in East
    Hampton (1670–1730), 147–155
Sporri, Felix Christian, 141
Standish, Miles, 80
Stratton, Goody, 130
Stratton, John, 182–183
Striped bass, disappearance of, 11,
    28–29, 30, 34, 200, 204
Success, 155
Swickard, David, 21–24, 58–59,
    216, 222
    and Mulford Farm, 215, 217–219
    and Mulford warehouse, 261–
    265, 268, 284
    and tick infestation, 231–232

Ticks, 255
    infestation of, 231–233
    warning about, 224, *225*

Town House, 6, 23
Town meetings, early, 95
Tyler, John, 85

Veale, Jeremiah, 133
Veale, Mrs. Jeremiah, 126, 133

Warehouse, *see* Mulford, Samuel,
    warehouse of
Waters, Anthony, 121, 122
Whale(s), 91, 100, 138–139
    code, 100–101
    companies, 159–169 *passim*
    contracts, with Montauk In-
    dians, 169–171, 174–176,
    179
    dead, 143–147, *146*
    decline of, 200–204
    drift, 98–104, 144, 155, 157,
    160–161
    impact on East Hampton of,
    155–166, 168, 185
    impact on Montauk Indians of,
    169–181
    licenses, 192–193, 194, 197
    "poison," 145–147, 232
    watches, 99, 105, 157
Whitefield, George, 40
William and Mary, 188
Williams, Roger, 105
Winthrop, John, 78, 90
Witchcraft, 116, 127–136
Wooley, John, 115, 125–127, 131,
    138
Wyandanch, 106–112